PIRATES
AN ILLUSTRATED HISTORY

Capella

CONTENTS

This edition published in 2005 by Arcturus Publishing Limited
26/27 Bickels Yard, 151–153 Bermondsey Street,
London SE1 3HA

In Canada published for Indigo Books
468 King St W,
Suite 500,
Toronto,
Ontario M5V 1L8

Copyright © 2005, Arcturus Publishing Limited

ISBN 1-84193-326-0

Printed in China

Cover design by Beatriz Waller
Layout by Mark Latter

Text previously published as *A History of Pirates*, Arcturus Publishing Limited, 2003

Pirates Picture Credits
Chris Collingwood/Cranston Fine Arts: 125
Corbis: 6, 7, 12, 55, 67, 68, 74, 107, 121, 132, 134,
Getty Images Ltd: 9, 25, 29, 35, 42, 59, 125
Mary Evans Picture Library: 18, 31, 39, 40, 47, 52, 76, 93, 111, 119, 128, 137
Nautical Archaeology Program, Texas A&M University: 49, 61, 62
Roger Hutchins: 79, 87
The Art Archive/Picture Desk: 15, 17, 19, 20, 23, 26, 37, 69, 70, 73, 80, 81,
82, 84, 85, 96, 105, 131, 141
Topfoto: 103

INTRODUCTION

'In honest service, there are commonly low wages and hard labour; in this – plenty, satiety, pleasure and ease, liberty and power. Who would not balance credit on this side, when all the hazard that is run for it, at worst, is only a sour look or two on choking? No, a merry life and a short one, that's my motto.'

BARTHOLOMEW ROBERTS, WELSH PIRATE, 1722

Piracy has existed since men first took to the seas to trade. One of its earliest strongholds was the Strait of Hormuz at the mouth of the Persian Gulf, where ships carrying gold, silver, silks, spices, copper and teak between the Middle East and India were forced to pass. In 694BC the Assyrian king Sennacherib tried to stamp it out. The Roman emperor Trajan had another go in the first century AD, as did King Shapur of Persia in the fourth century.

Meanwhile, in the Mediterranean, early pirates preyed on the ships of Phoenician merchants carrying silver, amber, tin and copper from the trading centres of Sidon and Tyre. During the flowering of classical Greece, pirates hid among the islands of the Aegean and their deeds were recorded by Thucydides and Herodotus, and the epic poets. Alexander the Great tried to stamp out Mediterranean piracy in 330BC, but it was still going strong at the height of the Roman Empire two centuries later.

The pirates of Cilicia, operating from the southern coast of Turkey, boasted a thousand ships. They defeated a Roman fleet, attacked Syracuse on Sicily and sacked hundreds of coastal towns and villages around the Empire. In 78BC, they captured the young Julius Caesar and held him on the island of Pharmacusa for six weeks until a ransom was paid. Ten years later, they held such a stranglehold on Mediterranean trade that Rome was threatened with starvation. In 67BC a bill was passed authorizing Pompey to stamp out piracy. He assembled a fleet of 270 ships and swept through the Mediterranean. Although some pirates were successfully resettled as farmers, the campaign climaxed in a major sea battle off the coast of Anatolia. Ten thousand pirates were killed, four hundred ships captured and many more destroyed. After that, military outposts and patrols by armed galleys kept the Mediterranean safe for trade until the rise of the Barbary pirates of North Africa in the sixteenth century.

Khayr ad-Din – better known as Barbarossa – united Algeria and Tunisia under the Ottoman sultanate and funded his regime by piracy. Pirate captains formed a distinct social class in Tunis and Algiers. Their ships were outfitted by wealthy backers who took 10 per cent of their booty. One of their most famous captives was the author of *Don Quixote*, Miguel de Cervantes. He was captured in 1575, along with his brother Rodrigo, and held for five years before being ransomed. With the arrival of powerful Moorish warlords in Tétouan and Rabat in 1609, Morocco became a new centre for the pirates. Again, the Alawi sultans encouraged piracy as a source of revenue.

The Barbary pirates used galleys until the seventh century, when a Flemish renegade named Simon Danser showed them the advantage of sail. This made the Tunisian and Algerian pirates an even more dangerous force. By 1650, they held more than thirty thousand captives in Algiers alone.

Piracy along the Barbary coast was the cause of several wars between the United States and Tripolitania (now part of Libya) in the nineteenth century. The British made two attempts to suppress Algerian piracy after 1815, and it was finally ended by the French in 1830 when they took over the country from the Ottomans.

However, this book is more concerned with

what was happening on the other side of the Atlantic. It focuses on the pirates of the Caribbean, though the scurvy band of cut-throats who plied the Spanish Main also pillaged the west coast of Africa and roamed as far afield as the Pacific and Indian Oceans. Caribbean piracy began after the Spanish began plundering the empires of the Inca and the Aztecs for their gold. Other European nations decided they wanted a piece of the action. However, their monarchs were reluctant to pay for expeditions to the Americas and they did not want to risk all-out war by engaging their navies. The solution was to mount private expeditions. These were backed by such luminaries as Samuel Pepys and Sir William Penn, father of the founder of Pennsylvania. These 'privateers' were given a letter of marque by the Crown: in effect, a licence to commit piracy. They would hand over part of their plunder to the Crown and, in turn, would be rewarded with lands, honours and titles.

During the reign of James I of Great Britain (1603–1625), there was a period of peace in Europe. Monarchs cut back on their navies, which meant that privateers who went to sea 'on their own account' – in other words, pirates – stood very little chance of being captured. Their numbers were also swelled with unemployed seamen. They worked from harbours

Statue of Pompey the Great, Roman emperor who spent years battling the scourge of piracy in the Mediterranean.

along Morocco's Atlantic coast, menacing shipping in the Straits of Gibraltar, and from Bantry Bay, attacking shipping in the English Channel. However, in 1614–15, the Dutch and English drove them out and they fled across the Atlantic, where piracy became inextricably mixed up with colonial wars and the slave trade.

By this time, the British, Dutch and French were establishing colonies in the West Indies. The colonists' numbers were swelled by prisoners of war from the English Civil War and criminals, vagrants, the unemployed and orphans who were transported on the orders of magistrates. Others went voluntarily, working off the price of their passage as indentured labour. However, white labourers were soon replaced by African slaves who were generally stronger than the undernourished poor of Europe's disease-ridden cities and were better able to cope with conditions in the tropics. Displaced Europeans drifted to the smaller islands and other uninhabited regions where they lived by shooting wild game. They cured the meat over wood fires by a method know in French as *boucaner* – giving them the name buccaneers.

When Jamaica came under threat from the Spanish, privateer commissions and ships were offered to the buccaneers who, though not necessarily great seaman, were good shots with a musket and handy with a cutlass, which they used to carve up carcasses. British buccaneers were joined by Huguenots – French Protestants – Dutchmen who had fought a war against the Spanish at home in The Netherlands, and Africans, largely runaway slaves. As many of the buccaneers had been indentured labourers themselves, they saw no reason to return slaves to their owners. And with truly international crews on board, they saw no reason not to attack the ships of any nation – though Spanish ships and the Spanish colonies still offered the richest spoils.

Life on board was democratic, which was revolutionary in the early eighteenth century. Meetings and votes were held on all important decisions. The captain only held on to his position if he was popular and successful, and everyone got an equal share of the spoils. Some pirates even dreamt of setting up a pirate nation.

By 1717, trade in the Caribbean was paralysed. Merchant ships could not set sail without a naval escort and piracy was seriously inhibiting the economic development of the West Indies and the British colonies in North America. In

September 1717, George I offered an amnesty to all pirates. Those who gave themselves up by 5 September 1718 would be pardoned. New courts were set up and those who did not surrender, or went back to piracy afterwards, were relentlessly tracked down by the Royal Navy and former pirates.

In 1724, a gentleman calling himself Captain Charles Johnson published *A General History of the Robberies and Murders of the Most Notorious Pirates*, though the real author is thought to be Daniel Defoe. In it he created the modern image of the cut-throats who sail under the Jolly Roger and gave almost mythical status to Blackbeard, Captain Kidd, Bartholomew Roberts, 'Calico' Jack Rackham, Mary Read and Anne Bonny. It started a craze for highly romanticized pirate stories being written by Sir Walter Scott and Lord Byron, among many others. And it was Johnson's swashbuckling villains who inspired Robert Louis Stevenson's *Treasure Island* and movies such as *Captain Blood*, which made a star out of Errol Flynn.

These books and movies are all set in a golden era of piracy that lasted a little over thirty years from 1691 to 1724, though piracy flourished much earlier on the island of Tortuga and there was another short-lived flurry in the 1820s.

Pirates' careers were rarely the swashbuckling epics of the movies. Usually they lasted no more than two or three years and often ended ignominiously at the end of a rope. Even though many pirates were brutal sadists, even during their own lifetime, they were admired as romantic heroes – men who lived life on their own terms. Ordinary low-born individuals, their rich plunder allowed them to enjoy the wealthy lifestyles of ship-board kings and lords, while their contemporaries lived in poverty and squalor.

At that time, most people lived at the beck and call of their masters. Many ordinary seamen in the Royal Navy, for example, were forced in to the service by press gangs. They were never allowed off the ship anywhere they might escape, and were frequently flogged. Pirates, on the other hand, were free from almost all constraints. They lived outside the law. Largely accepting their fate, they were determined to have an exciting life, if a short life.

Errol Flynn stars as the eponymous Captain Blood in Warner Brothers' classic 1935 tale of a sea-going Robin Hood.

CHAPTER ONE

PIRATE ATTACK

The multitude of sheltered waterways formed by the rugged coastlines of the islands and cays of the Caribbean provided the perfect lairs for the pirates from which to mount surprise attacks on their unsuspecting victims. For many a merchantman, a lookout's cry of 'Sail ho!' would be followed by the sight they dreaded most: the sinister black flag of a pirate ship.

On 14 September 1723, the *Princess Galley* was approaching the island of Barbados with a cargo of slaves brought from the West African coast when her crew saw a ship approaching with a black flag flying from her masthead. As she grew closer they could see she was a sloop armed with eight guns on her main deck. A further ten swivel guns were mounted along her rails and there were between thirty and forty pirates on board.

The *Princess Galley*'s forty-five-year-old captain John Wickstead realized that his ship was seriously outgunned by the pirates. He set more sail and tried to outrun them. But the heavily-laden merchantman was slow in the water. The sloop caught up quickly and began firing on her. By 8pm, she was alongside and Wickstead was ordered to send across a longboat. The pirates jumped in and returned to take over the *Princess Galley*. The second mate, twenty-four-year-old Goldsmith Blowers, and the ship's surgeon, twenty-five-year-old John Crawford, were held down. Lighted fuses were put between their fingers and they were forced to reveal the whereabouts of the ship's gold. The pirates soon had more than fifty-four ounces in their possession. Then they began to ransack the ship. They took the *Princess Galley*'s two quarter-deck guns and two swivel guns and sent them across to the sloop, along with gunpowder, pistols and both the bosun's and the gunner's stores. They also took eleven slaves valued at £500 each, along with the carpenter's mate James Sedgwick and the surgeon's mate William Gibbons. It was not unusual for pirates to press into service men

with the skills they needed. Two other crewmen, Henry Wynn and Robert Corp, joined the pirates of their own accord. That was not unusual either. Having stripped the *Princess Galley* of everything of value, George Lowther, the pirate captain, sailed away in his sloop *Ranger*, leaving Captain Wickstead to make his way with the rest of his crew to Barbados.

It is rare to find first-hand accounts by the victims of pirates, often because they did not survive. This one exists because the following month the *Ranger* was being refitted and careened off the Island of Blanco (Blanquilla) near the coast of Venezuela when it was spotted by HMS *Eagle*. Because the ship had to be turned on her side, so the hull could be scraped, her guns were ashore and she was defenceless. Lowther escaped, but most of the pirate crew, including Wynn and Corp, were captured. The account of the attack on the *Princess Galley* comes from Captain Wickstead's deposition to the Admiralty Court that tried Wynn and Corp on the island of St Kitts on 11 May 1724.

The Capture of the Samuel

A similar attack had taken place in the grey waters of the North Atlantic four years earlier. On 29 May 1720, the merchantman *Samuel* had left the port of London bound for Boston carrying a cargo of ironware, assorted goods in bales and trunks, and forty-five barrels of gunpowder. She had a crew of ten men under Captain Samuel Cary and three passengers. By 13 July she was forty miles east of the Grand

Banks of Newfoundland when two ships hove into view. As soon as they came within range, they opened fire and hoisted pirate flags. The smaller of the two was an eighty-ton sloop carrying ten guns and flying a Union Jack emblazoned with four blazing balls. The larger was a 220-ton three-master carrying twenty-six guns and flying a black flag with a skull and a single cutlass. With just six cannons mounted on carriages, the *Samuel* was easily outgunned. Captain Cary estimated that each of the pirate ships carried a hundred men, so his crew was outnumbered by twenty to one.

Cary was ordered to lower his boat and come aboard the pirate ship. He did was he was told and was greeted by the famous Welsh pirate Captain Bartholomew Roberts who had been leaving a trail of destruction up the eastern seaboard for the past month. In one harbour alone he had plundered and burnt no less than seventeen ships.

Roberts' men swarmed onto the *Samuel*, tore off the hatches and went about pillaging the cargo with cutlasses and boarding axes, 'with incessant cursing and swearing, more like fiends than men'. They took anything of value. The rest was hacked to pieces and thrown overboard. The pirates took the *Samuel*'s guns, along with the ship's boats, spare rigging and stores, and the anchor cables were thrown over the side. The pirates also took forty barrels of gunpowder, saying that they would never accept the King's pardon. Instead, if they were overwhelmed, they would set fire to the gunpowder with a pistol 'and go all merrily to Hell together'. The crew – with the exception of the captain and one Irishman – were forced to go aboard the pirate ship at gunpoint where they were forced into service. Meanwhile the passengers prepared themselves to die.

The pirates were discussing whether to sink the *Samuel* or set fire to her, when they spotted

A small pirate sloop, with the black flag flying at the mizzen mast, attacks a merchant ship. Pirates generally used cannon sparingly, preferring where possible to take their prizes intact.

another ship on the horizon and chased after her. In an amazing feat of seamanship, Cary and his single remaining crewman, with the assistance of the three passengers, managed to sail the *Samuel* into Boston harbour, where Cary gave an account of the attack to Joseph Hiller, a public notary.

Aaron Smith, Pirate

A more fulsome account of what it was like to be the victim of a pirate attack was given by Aaron Smith who had signed up as first mate on the merchant brig *Zephyr* in Kingston, Jamaica to work his passage back to England to get married. Her master was Mr Lumsden. That spring, the crops had failed and loading was slow. Eager to get underway, Smith purchased some coffee to be shipped on the brig. Even so, loading was not completed until the end of June. The passengers then embarked. They included a Captain Cowper, five or six children and a black woman servant. The *Zephyr* then crossed the bay to Port Royal where they picked up 'a lady of colour', with whom Mr Lumsden lodged in Jamaica, along with some more children and another unidentified passenger.

The following morning, they set sail for England. At first the weather was fine and the breeze moderate. But soon they encountered a strong wind from the northeast, accompanied by a heavy swell. It was then that Smith began to have his doubts about the abilities of Mr Lumdsen, who constantly sought his advice. Smith later discovered that Lumsden had spent most of his life at sea employed in the coastal coal trade and had little experience of transatlantic travel. He asked Smith whether he should take a windward or a leeward passage. A windward passage would take longer, Smith pointed out. But on a leeward path they would risk being attacked by pirates. Nevertheless, Lumsden took a leeward passage, heading for Grand Cayman. By this time, the winds had dropped and the journey took them four days. At Grand Cayman the locals came out in canoes to sell them parrots, turtles and shells. From there the *Zephyr* steered for Cape St Antonio, the southwesterly point of Cuba, and on their way they met a schooner from St John's, New Brunswick.

The following morning the *Zephyr* rounded

As the pirates discussed whether to sink the *Samuel* or burn her, another ship appeared and they immediately gave chase

Cape St Antonio and turned eastwards, taking advantage of a freshening breeze. The weather was fine and, ahead, they spotted two sails. At 2pm, Smith was walking on deck with Captain Cowper, when he saw a schooner making out to them from the land.

'She bore a very suspicious appearance,' said Smith, 'and I immediately went up aloft with my telescope to examine her more closely.' Smith was instantly convinced that she was a pirate. He told Cowper and they called Lumsden from below and informed him. On deck, Smith pointed out the schooner and recommended that they alter course. Lumsden obstinately refused, believing that the English flag he was flying would protect him.

Half-an-hour later they saw the deck of the schooner fill with men and she began to hoist out her boats. Lumsden finally altered his course, by two points, but it was too late: the *Zephyr* was already within range of the schooner's guns. As soon as she was within hailing distance, the schooner ordered the *Zephyr* to lower her stern boat and send her captain over. Mr Lumsden pretended not to understand the order. The schooner's response was a volley of musket shot. Lumsden then sent the message 'Aye, aye', and gave orders to lay back the main yard to slow the ship.

By this time a boat from the sloop had caught up with them and nine or ten men 'of a most ferocious aspect, armed with muskets, knives and cutlasses' boarded and immediately took charge. They ordered Mr Lumsden, Smith, Captain Cowper and the ship's carpenter to row over to the pirate ship – 'hastening our departure by repeated blows with the flat part of their cutlasses over our backs and threatening to shoot us,' said Smith. As they rowed across, Lumsden remarked that he had been very careless and had left the books, containing an account of all the money on board, open on the table in his cabin. When they reached the sloop, her captain ordered them on deck.

'He was a man of most uncouth and savage appearance,' said Smith, 'about five feet six inches in height, stout in proportion with aquiline nose, high cheek bones, a large mouth and very large full eyes. His complexion was sallow, his hair black, and he appeared to be about thirty years of age.'

At first Smith took him for an Indian. Later

he discovered that his father was a Spaniard and his mother a Yucatan squaw.

In broken English he asked Mr Lumsden what the ships ahead of him were. Lumsden said they were two French merchantmen and the pirate captain ordered all hands to make after them. He then asked Lumsden what cargo he was carrying. Sugar, rum, coffee, arrowroot and brazilwood for dyeing, Lumsden said. They were also interrogated about a schooner from New Brunswick they had met – whether she was carrying coin and whether she was armed.

Mr Lumsden was then asked if he had money on board himself. Lumsden replied that there was none.

'Do not imagine that I am a fool, sir,' said the pirate captain. 'I know that all vessels going to Europe have specie on board and if you give up what you have, you shall proceed on your voyage without further molestation.'

Lumsden repeated that he had no money. The pirate captain then said that if the money was not produced he would throw the cargo overboard and search the ship. If any money was found he would burn the ship, along with everyone on board. He also enquired if there were any candles, wine or porter – dark beer – on board. Lumsden said he had none to spare.

By then it was late evening and the breeze began to die away. The pirate ship gave up chasing the French merchantmen ahead and turned back towards the *Zephyr*. On the way, the pirates prepared for supper and began serving spirits to the *Zephyr*'s men. Lumsden, Smith and Cowper were offered some wine, but refused.

Smith was then told that he was going to be held on board the schooner as her new navigator. He protested, falsely, that he had a wife, three children and aged parents waiting for him in England, and Lumsden complained that he could not be deprived of Smith's skills.

'If I do not keep him, I shall keep you,' the pirate captain told Lumsden, to his alarm.

When they were alone, Lumsden turned to Smith and said, 'For God's sake don't importune the captain or he will certainly take me. You are a single man, but I have a large family dependent on me who will become orphans and utterly destitute.'

He promised that, the moment he was freed, he would send a man-of-war to search for

Nine or ten men 'of a most ferocious appearance, armed with muskets, knives and cutlasses' boarded the *Zephyr* and took charge

the pirate ship. He would tell the world what had happened and raise the matter with Lloyd's, so that no one would think that Smith had consented to become a pirate. Lumsden also promised, with tears streaming down his cheeks, to deliver Smith's goods to his family in England.

Soon supper was ready and the pirate captain invited them to join him, which they did for fear of giving offence.

'Our supper consisted of garlic and onions chopped fine and mixed up with bread in a bowl,' said Smith, 'for which there was a general scramble, every one helping himself as he pleased, either with his fingers or any instrument with which he happened to be supplied.'

During supper, Mr Lumsden begged to be allowed to go back on board the *Zephyr* to see the children as they would be alarmed at his absence. Smith asked to go too, but the pirate captain said that, when the two ships anchored, he would accompany the two of them on a visit.

As the pirate ship approached the *Zephyr*, the pirate captain ordered a signal shot to be fired. When this was answered, the *Zephyr* followed the pirate schooner inshore with one of the *Zephyr*'s men being told to take the lead and make soundings. When the crewman sounded fourteen fathoms, they anchored. A boat was lowered and Mr Lumsden and the pirate captain were rowed across to the *Zephyr*. Smith, Captain Cowper and the ship's carpenter had to stay on board the sloop. Soon after, some of the pirates returned to the boat with Captain Cowper's chronometer, Smiths's telescope and some of his clothes, the ship's spy-glass and a goat, which promptly had its throat cut and was flayed while still alive. The pirates told them that this is what would happen to them if no money was found on the *Zephyr*. The three men were then told to sleep in the companionway. Sleep, however, was impossible, as the carpenter told the other Smith and Cowper that Lumsden had concealed money on board the *Zephyr* and they spent the night discussing what their fate would be.

When daylight came, they could see the pirates on board the *Zephyr* beating the crew and they began to fear for their lives. Then, while the pirates on board the *Zephyr* were preparing to unload the cargo, the crew of the schooner offered them coffee and their spirits began to improve.

Aaron Smith, first mate of the **Zephyr**, *turns down the offer of a job aboard the pirate ship which captured him, in a somewhat over-dramatized contemporary illustration. Smith was eventually released unharmed by the pirates.*

had been taken. One of the crewmen returned his gold watch, sextant and some other valuables that he had asked him to hide. He packed these with his remaining clothes. He left his books, his parrot and other bits and pieces with Lumsden to give to his family should he ever reach England.

Meanwhile, the pirate ship had tied up alongside the *Zephyr* and the pirates began moving the passenger's private possessions on board. Smith managed to save Cowper's desk, claiming it as his own and saying that it contained nothing but papers. The *Zephyr*'s men were then ordered to transfer the cargo to the pirate ship. Lumsden was soon relieved of this duty, though, so that he could calm the children and stop them crying. That done, Lumsden was to show the pirate captain the manifesto. The pirate wanted only the indigo, the arrowroot and some coffee. When some brazilwood got in the way, Lumsden ordered it thrown overboard. The pirate captain ordered the men to stop, however, saying that Lumsden only wanted the wood thrown overboard so he could claim it as stolen to defraud the underwriters.

The *Zephyr*'s crew were then ordered to dismantle some of the masts, yards and spars and hand them over to the pirates. The children had their ear-rings taken and the blankets were stripped from their beds. Water and livestock were taken from the ship's store. Then Mr Lumsden and Captain Cowper were taken to the quarterdeck where they were told

At 7am, the pirate captain returned to the schooner with an armful of things, some belonging to Smith. He then brandished his cutlass over Smith's head and told him to go over to the *Zephyr* and bring back everything he needed for navigation.

'Mind and obey me then, or I will take your skin off,' he said, brandishing his cutlass again.

Back on board the *Zephyr*, Mr Lumsden again begged Smith not to resist the pirate captain. In his cabin, Smith found his chest smashed to pieces and its contents – including two diamond rings and other articles of value –

that, if they did not either produce the money or tell the pirates where it was hidden, the *Zephyr* would be burnt with them on board. Once again Lumsden protested that there was no money on board, so the children were taken onto the pirate schooner and Lumsden and Cowper were taken below decks and locked in the pump room. Flammable material was already being piled against the door when Lumsden, at last, confessed that there was money on board. When he was released he went to the round house where he produced a small box of doubloons – Spanish gold coins worth

eleven reals struck in Latin America. The pirates cheered. Lumsden insisted that was all the money there was on the ship, but the pirate captain was not convinced and Lumsden was returned to the pumps.

Cowper was then asked for money. When he said he had none, the pirate captain ordered that the flammable material around him be set alight. Cowper then produced nine doubloons, saying that was all he had and that this had been entrusted to him for safekeeping by a poor widow woman who would now be on the brink of starvation.

'Don't speak to me of poor people,' said the pirate captain. 'I am poor, and your country-men have made me so. I know there is more money and will either have it or burn you and your vessel.'

Cowper, too, was returned to the pumps and the ship was set on fire.

As the flames approached them, Lumsden and Cowper cried out for mercy and begged to be cast adrift in a boat at the mercy of the waves rather than be burnt. That way, the pirate cap-tain could keep the *Zephyr* and, if there was more money, he would surely find it.

The pirate captain became convinced that they were telling the truth. He ordered the flames to be quenched and Smith, the children and the rest of the *Zephyr*'s crew were returned to the brig. The pirates had begun eating and drinking, carousing over their booty. When they had finished, the pirate captain ordered them back to the schooner. Smith was ordered to go with them. When he hesitated, a knife was drawn and he was told that he would have his head cut off if he did not obey immediately. Smith coolly said that he had not heard the order and asked that he might have a little time to conclude his business with Mr Lumsden. He was allowed to do this and Smith persuaded Lumsden to sign a bill of lading for the coffee he had brought on board and a promissory note for £18 10 shillings to be consigned to Mr Watson, a ships' chandler in London. That done, he went aboard the pirate ship.

The pirate captain then asked Smith if he had a watch, Smith said he did. The captain took it from him and hinted that he would very much like to keep it. Smith said that it was a gift from his aged mother who he never expected to see again. He had wanted to send it to her via Mr Lumsden, but was sure that one of the pirates would take it away from him.

'Your people have a very bad opinion of us,' said the captain, 'but I will convince you that we are not so bad as we are represented to be. Come along with me and your watch will go safely home.'

The pirate took Smith back onto the *Zephyr*, gave the watch to Mr Lumsden and told his men not to take it from him on any account. Smith also used his position to recover the quadrant and clothes belonging to the son of the ship's owner who was also on board. After saying his goodbyes, Smith was forced back aboard the schooner at knife-point. The pirate captain then asked him whether he was sure that he had everything he needed to navigate as he would brook no excuses later – 'and, if I made any, he would kill me,' Smith said. Then the schooner cast loose from the *Zephyr* and Lumsden was told to proceed on his voyage – though on no account was he to head for Havana. This was where the schooner was headed and if Lumsden overtook her, the pirate captain said he would destroy Lumsden and his ship together.

As the *Zephyr* set sail, Lumsden cut loose his boats and set them adrift.

'Look at that rascal,' said the pirate captain. 'He has cut loose his old boats, and when he gets home he will say that I have taken them and get new ones from the underwriters. But I will write to Lloyd's and prevent it.'

Pirates and Women

What happened to the women on board the *Zephyr* was not recorded. Often they did not fare well in pirate hands. The notorious pirate Blackbeard frequently strangled women he cap-tured and threw them overboard. His contem-porary Stede Bonnet – the only pirate captain thought to execute his victims by making them walk the plank – also took no female prisoners. Women were neither wanted nor needed on his ship. It was thought that Bonnet became a pirate in the first place to escape a shrewish wife.

In other cases, when the male prisoners had been butchered, the women were calmly thrown overboard like so much unwanted merchandise. Indeed, many early pirates were homosexuals who had little time for women. After years in single-sex buccaneer colonies ashore or at sea in ships, they turned to shipmates, sadism or the abuse of cabin boys for sexual gratification.

Later, as pirate colonies grew up, female prostitutes were introduced. But there was little love between the sexes. Wives, where men had them, were frequently traded, sold or stolen. Alexander Selkirk, the pirate on whom the story of Robinson Crusoe is based, eloped with one woman, abandoned her and married another. The pirate William Davis married an African woman, then outraged his in-laws by swapping her for a bowl of punch when he was hot and thirsty. One unnamed pirate, on the other hand, reportedly paid a prostitute five hundred gold doubloons, just to see her naked.

Pirates also satisfied them-selves with native women who, it was said, were easier to buy than to rape. Captain William Cowley report-ed one tribe where the men had no qualms about sharing their wives with Europeans, though they became intensely jealous over advances made by other members of the tribe, while William Betagh mentions a tribe of Californian Indians where 'any man may lie with the women for a rusty knife, or a porringer of thick milk'. However, in 1719 Betagh posted a rule threatening to punish any man found drunk or performing an indecent act with a woman, black or white, on a captured ship. His men, he said, did not feel acutely the absence of women to satisfy their sexual desires.

One unnamed pirate reportedly paid a prostitute five hundred gold doubloons, just to see her naked

African women liberated from slave ships were sometimes given away as presents. Captain Woodes Rogers, a privateer who later became Governor of the Bahamas, recorded in 1709 putting his 'young Padre ashore, and gave him, as he desired, the prettiest young female Negro we had... The young Padre parted with us extremely pleased, and leering under his hood upon his black female angel, we doubt not that he will crack a commandment with her'.

However, when Captain William Ambrose Cowley took a Danish ship with sixty African slaves on board, he allowed them to freeze to death as he rounded Cape Horn. He called them 'the foulest creatures that ever I saw, they wearing nothing but sheepskins over their shoulders with wool or the women wearing a leather bag before their private parts'.

Some women captives were raped. The American pirate Charles Gibbs, personally responsible for over four hundred murders, recalled an attack on a Dutch ship bound for Holland from Curaçao, where all the passen-gers, men and women, were murdered, except for one beautiful young Dutch girl. She was taken to the west end of Cuba, kept there in a small fort for two months and, according to Gibbs, 'received such treatment, the bare recol-lection of which causes me to shudder'. Then they decided that, for their own safety, she should be put to death. They gave her poison and threw her dead body in the sea.

But pirates often treated European women with exaggerated reverence. On board the *Revenge*, commanded by Captain John Phillips, the crew adopted a regulation saying, 'If at any time we meet with a prudent woman, that man that offers to meddle with her, without her consent, shall suffer present death.' On Bartholomew Roberts's *Princess*, a pirate nicknamed Little David set himself up as the guardian and protector of captured women. This did not work out in practice though: while he protected them from the other members of the crew, he raped them himself.

Captain Henry Johnson, a blood-thirsty pirate in every other way, once prevented a woman passenger, Mrs Groves, being raped: a pair of buccaneers who killed two women dur-ing the sack of Cartagena in 1697 were sen-tenced to death. Captain Henry Morgan told his men that the women of Portobelo, which he sacked in 1668, were to be treated with gal-lantry when they raided the city. And after the capture of St Catalina, the women were locked in the church for their own protection, although he may have been keeping them safe so that they could be ransomed.

Morgan himself took a Spanish beauty at Panama but, instead of forcing himself on her, he provided her with private quarters, food from his own table and her own cook, then tried to seduce her. He failed. Later he tried to starve her, then humiliate her into submission, but still she refused him. Other pirates showed a similar delicacy, at least when it came to European women. Woodes Rogers' men spared the 'dozen handsome genteel young women' they found in a house when they captured Guiaquil, Peru in 1709, even though 'some of their largest gold chains were concealed, wound around their middles, legs and thighs etc. but the gentle-women in these hot countries being very thin clad with silk and fine linen... our men by press-

ing felt the chains etc. with their hands on the outside of the lady's apparel.'

Aaron Smith, the former mate of the *Zephyr* forced to work as a navigator on a pirate schooner, managed to escape with the help of a Cuban girl, and reached Havana, only to be arrested as a pirate. He was shipped back to England where he stood trial for his life at the Old Bailey, in a case prosecuted by the Attorney General himself. However, he was acquitted and lived to marry the fiancée who had been waiting for him, and to publish a dramatic account of his capture by pirates.

In the fighting, nine or ten of the pirates were killed – the pirate who gave evidence saw at least one slain and another thrown overboard. The captain of the *Vice-Admiral* lost a leg, another crewman an arm and others were 'shot through'.

Back on the *Philip* the pirate went below. When he came back up on deck about half-an-hour later, he saw only one French ship. He was told that the other, the *St Mary*, had sunk. He saw Frenchmen in the water, but a boat that was sent out to rescue them was recalled by the master of the *Philip*: no one was saved.

Sir Henry Morgan (1635-88) Welsh buccaneer, pirate, and governor of Jamaica. Illustration from **The Buccaneers of America** *by A.O. Exquemelin.*

Dead Men Tell No Tales

Smith was lucky, because the general consensus among pirates was that dead men tell no tales. On 22 June 1600, the crew of the English pirate ship *Philip* watched as the entire crew of a French merchantman drowned. One of the pirates told the Admiralty Court that they had come across the *St Mary* with two other ships, the *Admiral* and the *Vice-Admiral*. The *Philip* was a well-armed warship, while the other three were lightly-armed merchantmen. She hailed the *St Mary* in French and asked who they were, where they came from and where they were bound. After asking the same question of the *Admiral*, the *Philip* attacked. The *St Mary* was badly damaged and the *Philip* put three or four shots into the Admiral. The pirates were just about to board her when they discovered that one of the *Philip*'s ports was broken. As this let in the sea, the pirates broke off to make repairs. The *Admiral* and the *Vice-Admiral* hoisted more sail and made off. As soon as repairs were made, the *Philip* gave chase, firing on them with cannon and muskets. They managed to get a rope aboard the *Admiral*, but this broke. So they boarded the *Vice-Admiral* and were pulling down the flag when they were warned that the ship was sinking. They returned to the *Philip* carrying some of the *Vice-Admiral*'s guns.

S^r HEN: MORGAN

CHAPTER TWO

THE PRIVATEERS

With a letter of marque from their government – in effect, permission to attack the ships of any other country – privateers rapidly became a major source of revenue to their home governments and a menace to all others, in particular the Spanish as they sought to consolidate their hold on the New World.

It was the Caribbean, however, rather than the New World, that Christopher Columbus had discovered in 1492. Columbus had himself been a pirate, looting Venetian galleys bound for England off Lisbon in 1485, when he had sailed under the French flag. On his voyage of discovery seven years later, Columbus landed first, it is thought, on San Salvador in the Bahamas later to be renamed Walting's Island after the buccaneer who made it his headquarters. Next he landed in Cuba, which he believed to be the mainland of Cathay, or China. His fleet was then carried by adverse winds to Ayti (Haiti). Columbus renamed it La Isla Española, or Hispaniola, though he seems to have thought it was actually Cipango, or Japan. The only time he set foot on the mainland of the Americas was in 1498, when he landed on the Paria Peninsula in what is now Venezuela. He dismissed it as an island. However, his voyages had opened the door to the untold wealth that lay in the newly discovered continent.

The Conquistadores

In 1519, Hernán Cortés mounted an expedition to Mexico and in August 1521, with a few hundred men, he crushed the Aztec empire, destroying its capital Tenochtitlán and killing over 100,000 people. He sent three caravels home to Spain to tell the king, Charles V, of his triumph. To demonstrate the wealth of Spain's new territories, he packed the ships with gold and silver bars, 'wondrously wrought gold works', three hundred pounds of pearls, emeralds 'as large as a man's fist', jade statuettes, feathered masks, ceremonial robes and three live jaguars. But near the Azores the three ships were attacked by half-a-dozen French privateers under Jean Fleury of Honfleur. Two of the ships were captured so the first taste of the wealth of the New World went, not to the court in Madrid, but to Fleury's patron Jean Ango of Dieppe. Five years later people came from as far away as Paris to witness a masque Ango held at his new manor in Varengeville outside Dieppe where the players paraded the finery of the now defunct Aztec empire.

The Spanish claimed that their Aztec booty had been stolen by Fleury. The French maintained that seizing it was a legitimate act of war – Spain and France had been at war on and off since 1494. The licensing of armed private vessels – privateers – such as those sailed by Fleury was an internationally recognized practice and the king of France, Francis I, encouraged the corsairs of La Rochelle, St Malo and Dieppe to cross the Atlantic in search of Spanish treasure. 'I should like to see the clause in Adam's will that excludes me from a share in the world,' said Francis I, speaking of the Treaty of Tordesillas in which the Spanish-born Pope Alexander VI divided the New World between Spain and Portugal.

However, it was not King Francis who was putting his neck on the line, but Fleury. He had the misfortune to fall into the hands of the Spanish when he was captured by Martín Pérez de Irizar near Cadiz in October 1527. The Spanish authorities decided that, rather than exchange him as a prisoner of war, he should be summarily executed as a pirate and he was hanged publicly with 150 of his men.

This did not put off other French privateers,

who set off across the Atlantic in search of further prizes. In 1525 the explorer Sebastian Cabot ran into a French privateer off the coast of Brazil and in 1526 when Rodrigo de Acuña's galleon *San Gabriel* got separated from the rest of Garcia Jofre de Loaysa's expedition to the Strait of Magellan, she found herself attacked and taken by three French corsairs. Other squadrons of privateers were seen off Puerto Rico and Santo Domingo, as Hispaniola was commonly known during the colonial era.

In 1527, the pickings became even richer. The Spanish explorer Francisco Pizarro landed in Peru and, with a handful of men, he conquered the Inca empire, yielding more precious metal and jewels to be shipped back to Spain. Meanwhile in Mexico, the Spaniards put the remaining Aztecs to work mining more gold and silver. The Spanish were only interested in the wealth of Mexico and Peru, and colonized few of the Caribbean islands which they called the Islas Inútiles – the 'Useless Islands'. This made them havens for privateers, who went

ashore for food, water and wood to make essential repairs to their ships. The local Arawak and Carib Indians preferred them to the Spaniards, who treated them barbarously, slaughtering them, enslaving them and working them to death. One Spanish observer wrote, 'I witnessed how the residents give a better reception to Lutheran Frenchmen than to those who go forth to colonize and conquer.'

The French Privateers

In 1529, after a peace treaty was concluded between France and Spain, French ships began to visit the Americas in growing numbers – much to the resentment of the Spanish who considered the New World their exclusive property. They treated even honest merchants trading with the West Indies as if they were pirates. The presence of any products of the Americas on board a ship was taken as evidence of piracy, which was punishable by death.

In 1535, relations between France and Spain

Christopher Columbus sets sail on his epic voyage of discovery with his three caravels the **Nina,** *the* **Pinta** *and the* **Santa Maria,** *1492.*

began to deteriorate once again, leading numerous French ships to turn to privateering. They based themselves on the Bahamas where numerous cays – low-lying reefs or sandspits – allowed them to lie in wait for galleons beating their way out through the Straits of Florida or the Windward Passage between Cuba and Santo Domingo. Attacks on the Spanish ships carrying treasure from Peru brought the transatlantic trade to a standstill and, in 1536, resulted in a fresh war between France and Spain. The Spanish had to introduce a convoy system with their merchantmen guarded by men-of-war to continue their trade with the Americas. Fleets formed up at Seville and Cadiz for the outward journey and at Santo Domingo for the homeward leg. They carried silk and taffeta, wine from Andalusia and swords from Toledo out to the Spanish settlers in the New World. On the return journey, they carried gold, silver, pearls and emeralds from Peru, Chile and New Spain – Mexico – along with sugar, cocoa, tobacco and hides from the West Indies.

Although the convoy system afforded the Spanish some protection at sea, the Spanish settlements on Cuba, Santo Domingo and Puerto Rico were sparsely garrisoned, and their authorities warned Madrid that even the mainland settlements of Cartagena, Vera Cruz and

John and Sebastian Cabot prepare to board their ship Matthew *at Bristol as they set off on their first voyage of discovery, May 1497.*

Panama could easily be overrun by a hundred men and, in 1537, the French raided Honduras, capturing nine treasure ships.

The Truce of Nice of June 1538 brought peace between Spain and France, but did little to discourage the French corsairs, who were understandably reluctant to give up this easy route to riches. In 1540, they sacked the town of San Germán on Puerto Rico. And by 1542, France and Spain were at war again. The following February, French privateers staged another raid on San Germán de Puerto Rico, taking four caravels. But this time two Spanish galleons and two lateen-rigged caravels, manned by 250 volunteers, set off from Santo Domingo after them. Five days later, the fleet, under Captain Ginés de Carrion, commander of the galleon *San Cristóbal*, caught up with them. He sank one ship and captured the French flagship, along with forty men. Despite this success, the inhabitants of San Germán were too frightened to return to their homes and settled inland at Guayanilla. That June, six French ships under the Flemish Walloon Robert Waal, attacked the island of Margarita off the coast of Venezuela and burned the pearl-fishing town of Nuevo Cadiz on the neighbouring island of Cubagua. In July, Waal landed between four and five hundred men at Santa Maria in Colombia, occupying the town for seven days. They took anything valuable and destroyed the rest, before withdrawing with four bronze cannon and their booty. On the night of 24 July, 450 of his men took Cartagena, forcing its inhabitants to hand over 37,500 pesos in coin, then demanding a further 2,000 to spare the buildings.

The Treaty of Crépy in 1544 again formally halted hostilities between France and Spain, but did little to halt the corsairs. More settlements along the coast of New Spain – that is, Venezuela, Colombia and Ecuador – were burned and Havana and Santiago de Cuba were pillaged by the flamboyant Jacques Sores of La Rochelle and François le Clerc – known to the Spanish as Pie de Palo, or 'Peg Leg'. But this time the Spanish took their revenge. A small fleet under Pedro Menéndez de Aviles sailed into La Rochelle under the very muzzles of the shore batteries and recaptured five Spanish vessels that had been taken by the French corsair Jean Alphonse de Saintonge. De Aviles' men then boarded de Saintonge's flagship *Marie*, killing de Saintonge and massacring his crew. In 1552, de Saintonge's son Antoine tried to

avenge his father's death with an attack on Santa Cruz de Tenerife, but his flagship was sunk by fire from the shore batteries, which killed Antoine Alphonse de Saintonge and his crew.

The English Take a Hand

The English had their own interests in the Americas. In 1497, John Cabot, sailing from Bristol, planted the Tudor flag in Maine, laying claim to what is now the United States and Canada. However, the pickings there were poor compared to the lands conquered by the Spanish, so the English, too, turned their hand to piracy. In 1545 Robert Reneger of Southampton surprised the *San Salvador*, homeward bound from Santo Domingo with a cargo of sugar and hides, off Cape St Vincent at the southwest tip of Portugal. Initially Reneger intended to take only the value of some of his goods that had been impounded by the Spanish authorities, and to give the captain a document to that effect. However, he discovered gold on board, which the captain begged him not to mention as it was being smuggled to Spain as part of a private venture. This, Reneger decided, meant that the gold was fair game, and he promptly relieved the Spanish of it. When the

Columbus presents himself at the court of the Spanish monarchs Ferdinand and Isabella upon his return from his first expedition to the New World.

Spanish authorities found out about this there was an exchange of diplomatic notes between London and Madrid. But Reneger paid off the Lord Admiral and Henry VIII and he retired from the sea a wealthy man to take up the lucrative post of Collector of Customs in Southampton. Where Reneger led, others soon followed, disposing of their ill-gotten gains in Baltimore or Ireland. The Killigrews and Tremaynes formed powerful West Country pirate syndicates that were not even discouraged when Mary Tudor married Philip of Spain in 1554. Piracy was seen not just as business, but as a patriotic duty. It also had a religious dimension: it was, after all, every Protestant's duty to seize the goods of Catholic Spain.

French Corsairs

While the English were making small-scale raids on Spanish shipping, the French Huguenots were organizing large-scale attacks against the Spanish colonies. On 29 April 1553, eight corsairs landed eight hundred heavily-armed men on the north coast of Santo Domingo, where they sacked the towns of La Yaguana and Monte Cristi. Santiago de Cuba was attacked again the following summer. The Spanish settlers, unable

to muster anything like the firepower of their attackers, were powerless to resist.

Among the Huguenots, Jacques Sores, formerly Le Clerc's lieutenant, came to prominence when he captured the Portuguese galleon *Santiago* off Tenerife and, as a good Protestant, threw thirty-eight Jesuits he found on board into the sea. He commanded a fleet, it is said, of 'several score' corsairs. On 10 July 1555, they landed a hundred men on Cuba, a mile and a half from Havana. Sores and his men attacked Havana's twelve-gun battery from the rear. Its twenty-four defenders surrendered at dawn on the 12th. Sores' men then occupied the town and brought their ships into the harbour, where four were careened and refitted. Sores then demanded a ransom of 500 pesos for every Spanish inhabitant, 100 for every slave and a further 30,000 pesos to spare the buildings.

Instead of paying up, the Spanish governor Dr Angulo launched a surprise counter-attack with five Spaniards, eight Indians and 220 African slaves. It failed and the pirates slaughtered their captives. Sores was particularly hard on the slaves, hanging large numbers of them by their heels around the town to discourage any further attacks. His men levelled Havana

and everything within a five-mile radius. Then on 5 August, they headed back to sea taking the fort's twelve guns with them. Word got around that Havana was now unprotected and two months later another sixteen French ships turned up in the harbour and sent foraging parties inland to seize hides and other booty.

In 1559, the famous French commanders Jean Bontemps and Jean-Martin Cotes lead a squadron of seven corsairs against Santa Marta, Colombia, New Spain. In the face of token resistance from Indians armed with bows and arrows, they took a small amount of plunder before sailing along the coast to Cartagena. On 11 April, they put ashore 300 men carrying harquebuses – heavy matchlocks that had to be fired from a stand. The invaders brushed aside the port's three dozen lightly armed defenders, and pillaged the town, though they spared the buildings for a ransom of 4,000 pesos.

Meanwhile in April 1559 Henry II of France and Philip II of Spain had signed yet another peace treaty. But what the Catholic Henry II signed made little difference to the Protestant Huguenots, especially as Henry II died in July after being hit on the head with a lance at the tournament held to celebrate the peace. Three

Illustration of Fort Caroline, built by French colonists on Florida coast in 1564, from an engraving by Theodore De Bry.

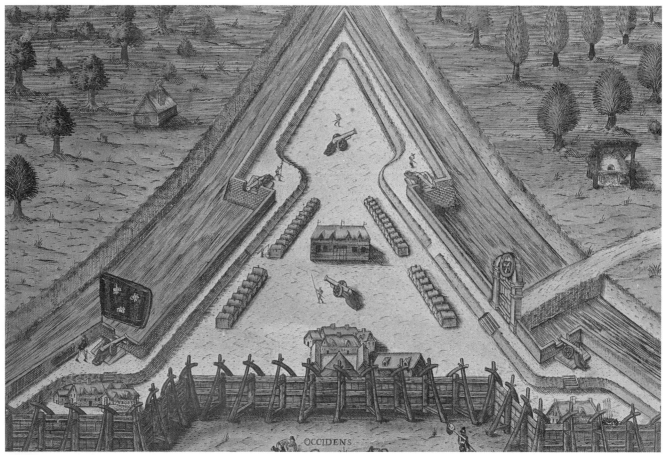

Spanish galleons, including a two-hundred-ton merchantman under Captain Bartolomé Rodriguez named the *Santa María*, were plundered later in the same year, and a Spanish ship bound for Havana chose to off-load its cargo on the coast nearby rather than risk losing it to a French corsair hove to outside the harbour. In 1561, Huguenots also sacked Puerto Cabellos and Trujillo on the north coast of Honduras, and Campeche, Mexico. But the Spanish began to fight back. In a second attack on Campeche in July 1561, a raiding party of thirty men was landed by three small corsairs. This was beaten off by the locals and a French corsair and its crew of thirty were captured off Guanaja Island, off Honduras. Three Huguenots were executed on the spot. The rest of the crew was taken to Guatemala in chains.

> **The privateer Jean Bontemps was killed by an arrow through the throat and his head was taken to Santo Domingo as a trophy**

Jean Bontemps himself was killed while trying to take over the island of Curaçao, then a Spanish possession, in 1572. He and his seventy men would normally have made short work of the defenders, but the attack took place in the pouring rain, depriving them of their firepower. Bontemps was killed by an arrow through the throat and his head was taken to Santo Domingo as a trophy.

All this, however, did little to discourage the Huguenots. They attempted to establish a permanent base on land in the Americas to harass the Spanish treasure ships. In 1562 – forty-five years before the British established their first colony at Jamestown in Virginia – two ships and a large sloop under the command of Jean Ribault of Dieppe and carrying 150 Huguenots from Le Havre sighted the coast of Florida off St Augustine. They turned north, exploring the coast up as far as what is now South Carolina and building a small fort – Charlesfort – on the southern tip of what became Parris Island. Ribault left two dozen volunteers there under Captain Albert de la Pierria, promising to return in six months with reinforcements. However, when he returned to France he found a full-scale religious war in progress. This delayed his return and the fort was abandoned after a year. In 1564 the Huguenots finally returned to Florida when Ribault's lieutenant René de Laudonnière brought three hundred Huguenot settlers on three ships. They built a large compound named Fort Caroline at the mouth of the St John's River near present-day Jacksonville. Like other early colonies in the Americas, Fort Caroline suffered starvation, disease, mutinies and Indian attacks. In a bid to escape these harsh conditions, a group of colonists seized two shallops and went back to the business they knew best – piracy.

The following year Ribault himself returned to the Americas bringing six hundred more colonists on five ships. He, too, found it hard to give up old ways and captured two small Spanish treasure ships on the way. This brought down the wrath of Pedro Menéndez de Aviles, the nemesis of Jean Alphonse de Saintonge twenty years before, now a knight of the Order of Santiago. He arrived off Fort Caroline with his flagship the *San Pelayo* and four consorts. Ribault's ships cut their anchor cables and fled out to sea. They outran de Aviles, who decided to put into harbour at St Augustine, thirty-five miles to the south. Two shallops were sent to fetch cavalry from Santo Domingo while de Aviles' men dug in. On 16 September 1565, a force of four hundred men, half of them carrying harquebuses, set off towards Fort Caroline. They were delayed by a hurricane but, four days later, they attacked.

Anticipating this, Ribault had gone back to Fort Caroline and taken off 600 men – the bulk of his forces – with the aim of taking St Augustine and attacking de Aviles from the rear. The plan failed because the hurricane that delayed de Aviles shipwrecked Ribault, scattering his men along the coast without food, water or firearms. One hundred and twelve of the defenders of Fort Caroline were slaughtered at the cost of not a single Spanish casualty. Seventy women and children were captured, while Laudonnière, Ribault's son Jacques and about sixty other survivors managed to escape and make it back to France. After taking Fort Caroline, de Aviles set about hunting down Ribault's men. On 10 October Ribault and three hundred of his men surrendered. They had their hands tied behind their backs and their throats slit at a place south of St Augustine now called Matanzas, which means 'killings' in Spanish. Only five youngsters were spared. Another 150 Huguenot survivors surrendered near Cape Canaveral on the condition that their lives would be spared. They were

herded on board the *San Pelayo* to be taken to Havana. But on the way they rebelled, took over the ship and sailed it to Denmark.

The Spanish renamed Fort Caroline Fort San Mateo, as they had taken it on St Matthew's Day, and left a small garrison there under Captain Villarroel. In 1568, the Gascon sea rover Dominque de Gourgues arrived with 280 Huguenots on board three ships and besieged the fort. Vastly outnumbered, Captain Villarroel and his men escaped under cover of darkness and tried to flee south towards St Augustine. Thirty of his men were killed and 38 captured. In revenge for the killing of Ribault and his men at Matanzas, they were put to death.

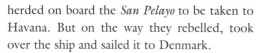

As French privateering went into decline, the English privateers, led by men such as Sir Francis Drake, began to flourish in their stead

However, by this time, the religious wars at home in France had sapped the strength of the Huguenots, and French privateering went into decline. English privateering, meanwhile, was on the ascendancy. Although England had been Spain's stoutest ally during the wars between Spain and France, they began to fall out over religion. With the death of Mary Tudor in 1558 and the accession to the throne of Elizabeth I, England became a firmly Protestant nation, while Spain was using its immense wealth from the Americas to fund the counter-Reformation. Spain had recently become even more wealthy due to a new method of smelting silver which extracted the metal from previously unusable low-grade ore. However, they would not let even friendly nations share in the wealth of the Americas, or even trade with their colonies there.

John Hawkins Puts To Sea

In 1562, Plymouth merchant John Hawkins made the first of three voyages to the Caribbean. He had three ships – the 120-ton *Solomon*, the 100-ton *Swallow*, and a captured Portuguese vessel. First they visited the Guinea coast, where they picked up three hundred African slaves. Early in 1563, they arrived off the north coast of Santo Domingo. Hawkins had already come to an understanding with a Spaniard named Lorenzo Bernáldo, commander of 120 cavalrymen deployed specifically to

stop Hawkins, so the slaves were landed without incident. Hawkins was so well-connected that some of the goods he purchased with the profits were to be taken back to England in a Spanish boat, sailing via Seville. Although this came to the attention of the Spanish authorities and the goods were impounded, Hawkins had carried more than enough home in his own ships to make him the richest man in Plymouth.

When he planned a second voyage in 1565, he attracted a horde of wealthy backers, including Queen Elizabeth herself. Along with the *Solomon*, the *Swallow* and the fifty-ton *Tiger*, he took the queen's own ship, the 700-ton *Jesus of Lübeck* which carried thirty guns. They picked up four hundred slaves from Sierre Leone and took them, via Dominica, to Margarita Island, but the Spaniards there refused to trade. So Hawkins sailed westwards along the coast to Borburata, near present-day Puerto Cabello, Venezuela. There, after a show of force, the inhabitants were happy to trade. This was standard practice in the Caribbean, as the Spanish colonists had at least to pretend not to deal with other nationals to mollify the authorities in Madrid. Hawkins used the same tactic at Ríohacha, Colombia, to dispose of the rest of his cargo and return with profits even greater than those from his first voyage.

The queen ignored the protests of the Spanish ambassador as Hawkins prepared to sail again. On this third voyage, though, things went drastically wrong. First, he had trouble procuring slaves. Then, when he sent his young relative Francis Drake ahead to securing watering at Ríochacha, he was fired on. After a short gun battle, Drake pulled back out of range and blockaded the port. When Hawkins arrived five days later, he put two hundred men ashore. They made short work of the Spanish defenders and occupied the town. Hawkins then sent a detachment led by an escaped slave into the jungle to seize the treasure the Spanish had hidden.

They went on to Santa Marta, where after a mock battle to satisfy honour, the local governor agreed to trade. The following month, Hawkins tried the same tactics at Cartagena, but this time the Spaniards meant business and Hawkins withdrew empty-handed. Heading north across the Caribbean, his little fleet ran into a hurricane, and was forced to seek shelter in the harbour of San Juan de Ulúa, opposite Veracruz in Mexico. This was where gold and silver mined in Peru and Chile arrived after

being mule-packed over land from Acapulco on the Pacific coast, along with spices, silks and jewels from the Orient.

Hawkins' flotilla arrived at nightfall, and the harbour lookout mistook it for the Spanish plate convoy that turned up every year at that time to pick up the silver. In the morning, Hawkins hoisted false colours and took on board the pilot and the entire welcoming committee. Then the English ships sailed into port under the Spanish guns. They moored and took over the entire island before the Spanish realized they were harbouring foreign intruders. Hawkins hoped to provision his ships and make essential repairs, then leave without further trouble, but two days later the real plate convoy turned up – eleven galleons in all – carrying the new viceroy of New Spain, Martín Enríquez. Hawkins sent word that he would allow them to enter harbour, provided they let the English ships refit and leave port unmolested. After crossing the Atlantic, the Spanish ships were low on food and water. At sea off a dangerous lee shore during the hurricane season, they had no choice but to agree, but Enríquez had no intention of honouring the agreement. That night Spanish troops slipped on board a hulk lying next to the English ships. Hawkins grew suspicious and opened fired on the hulk, while the English ships prepared to get underway. The Spanish then overran the English garrison and seized the shore batteries, opening fire on the English ships. The battle raged all day. Of the six English ships, only the vice-flagship *Minion* under Hawkins and the fifty-ton *Judith* under Drake managed to escape. One hundred men ashore surrendered to the Spaniards while two hundred survivors were packed on the *Minion*. Unable to resupply his ship, Hawkins set sail for England. He reached home with just fifteen of his men still alive.

Sir Francis Drake

Hawkins had tried to trade with the Indies and failed. The attitude now turned much more piratical. Between 1568 and 1572, French and Dutch Protestant privateers went into partnership with England's West Country pirates. English pirates bought commissions from the Huguenot leader Henry of Navarre and sold their plunder on the Isle of Wight, a noted haunt of pirates.

In 1570, Drake returned to the Caribbean with the small ships *Dragon* and *Swan*. Little is known about what occurred on this voyage and it is assumed that his activities were piratical. It is known that he wanted to avenge San Juan de Ulua and Drake, the son of a lay preacher, was a committed Protestant. His favourite reading was *The Book of Martyrs*, a graphic and polemic account by the Puritan John Foxe of those who had suffered for the Protestant cause. He was already well known for his exploits and it is assumed that the queen gave her approval. He also sailed under a simple prayer, 'O Lord, make us rich, for we must have gold before we see England.'

The following year he went back to the Caribbean again with the 25-ton *Swan*, this time

Rainbow portrait of Queen Elizabeth I of England (1533–1603), regal sponsor of enterprising English privateers such as Sir Francis Drake and Sir Walter Raleigh.

sailing with French consorts. A contemporary Spanish document detailing his attack on the coast of Nombre de Dios in Panama says that Drake 'did rob divers boats in the river Chagres that were transporting merchandise worth forty thousand ducats and velvets and taffetas, along with merchandise and gold and silver from other boats, and with the same came to Plymouth, where it was divided among his partners'.

In 1572, Drake returned to the Caribbean with Hawkins' backing and his 70-ton *Pascha*, besides his own tiny *Swan*. This time he carried a privateering commission from the queen, which amounted to a licence to plunder in the King of Spain's lands. He was joined by Captain James Raunce, who brought another ship and thirty men. In a hidden anchorage on the Isthmus of Darien, they assembled four barges to make a night attack on Nombre de Dios. They found the treasure depots empty and, during a brief engagement in the central square with the hastily assembled militia, Drake was wounded. This was enough for Captain Raunce who left the expedition. But Drake was made of sterner stuff. He set up a small shore base in the Gulf of

After John Hawkins had tried unsuccessfully to trade with the Spanish colonies, the English attitude became much more piratical

San Blas and harried the Spanish Main – that is the mainland of South America – as far east as Curaçao. The following year, when the plate convoy put in at Panama, his men made an overland trek into the dense jungle in an attempt to ambush the mule train bringing silver plundered from Peru across the isthmus. Although they were aided by local tribesmen and runaway African and Indian slaves, known as cimarrones, who had no love for the Spanish, the attack failed when a drunken sailor alerted the mule train guards. During the trip, standing on a high ridge, Drake saw the Pacific which until then was barred to all but Spanish ships. Half Drake's men – including his brother – died of yellow fever and jungle sores. But two weeks later, when everything seemed lost, they captured a mule train stacked with silver and gold. They drifted down the river with their plunder for six hours, up to their waists in water, eventually making their way back to their ships. Drake's

name and fortune was established by this expedition, and he returned to England rich and famous.

Circumnavigation

In 1577, Drake sailed across the Atlantic again, this time at the head of a squadron of five small ships. The aim was to sail through the Strait of Magellan in southern Chile and plunder the coast beyond. Before he left, the queen herself told him she 'would gladly be revenged on the King of Spain for divers injuries that I have received'. It took sixteen days to sail though the Strait of Magellan. In the process, Drake became separated from his second in command who, thinking that Drake's ship was lost, returned home, leaving the *Golden Hind* to sail on alone. Drake's flagship made its way up the coast of South America, which was quite unguarded as no hostile ship had ever entered these waters. Seizing provisions at Valparaíso, he attacked passing Spanish merchantmen. One, the Manila galleon *Cacafuego*, was carrying 'thirteen chests full of reals of plate, four score pound weight of gold, and six and twenty tons of silver'. The *Golden Hind* soon sank below her watermark with bars of gold and silver, minted Spanish coinage, precious stones, and pearls. Even after jettisoning half his booty to keep his ship afloat, Drake's voyage yielded a 4,700 per cent profit.

After taking more than he could carry, Drake tried to find the much talked-of Northwest Passage home, around what he named New Albion – the Pacific Northwest. Drake and his men were the first Europeans to glimpse what is now western Canada. Defeated by the cold – a complete transit of the Northwest Passage by sea was not made until 1906 – the *Golden Hind* turned westwards, sailing sixty-eight days out of sight of land until they reached a line of islands, probably the remote Palau group. From there Drake headed to the Philippines, then the Moluccas or Spice Islands, where he concluded a treaty with the local sultan giving the English the right to trade for spices, previously a Spanish monopoly.

Drake's seamanship was superb, but he was

sailing in totally uncharted waters, and perhaps inevitably, his ship struck a reef. He managed to get her off with no great damage, however, and was able to proceed to Java to resupply. After calling at Java, he sailed across the Indian Ocean to the Cape of Good Hope where, two years after entering the Strait of Magellan, the *Golden Hind* returned to Atlantic waters with just fifty-six of the crew of a hundred left aboard.

Drake's ship arrived in Plymouth harbour on 26 September 1580, laden with treasure and spices. He was now a wealthy man and renowned as the first captain ever to sail around the world, the Portuguese navigator Ferdinand Magellan having been killed fighting with natives on Mactan Island, in the Philippines, before completing his circumnavigation. He was the first Englishman to sail the Pacific and the Indian Oceans. Despite Spanish protests about his piratical conduct while in their imperial waters, Queen Elizabeth granted him an audience when he arrived in the Thames estuary. For six hours she questioned him about his

epic voyage in which she herself was a shareholder. Then, amid great public rejoicing, she knighted him on board the *Golden Hind*, which was lying at Deptford. Very publicly, the queen had given royal approval to 'the pirate', as Drake was popularly known. This gave encouragement to other English sea rovers who sent sail for the Caribbean in ever-increasing numbers.

The son of a tenant farmer, Drake was looked down on by the queen's high-born courtiers and the government. But Elizabeth liked him. The next time he set out for the Caribbean, in 1585, he had command of a fleet of twenty-five ships. He also had with him 2,300 marines on board twenty-one warships. Two of them – the 250-ton *Aid* and 600-ton *Elizabeth Bonaventure*, which served as his flagship – were on loan from the queen. They were accompanied by the 400-ton galleon *Leicester* and Sir Martin Frobisher's private merchantman, the *Primrose*. Drake's orders were to cause as much damage as possible to Spain's empire.

The fleet of Sir Francis Drake and Sir John Hawkins moored in New Spain during a trading expedition, when the Spanish attacked without warning. Only two English vessels escaped, carrying Drake and Hawkins to safety.

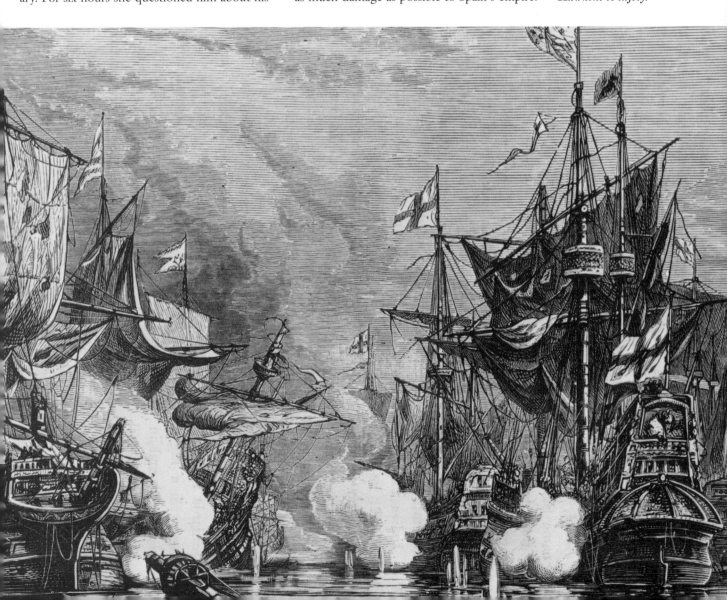

First he headed for Hispaniola, where he seized a Spanish vessel carrying a Greek pilot, who told him that the best landing place for his force was at the mouth of the Jaina River, ten miles west of the island's capital Santo Domingo. That evening, 800 English troops were landed under the command of Christopher Carleill. The following day, Drake's fleet stood off the harbour, prompting the Spanish to scuttle two of their ships to block the harbour entrance. Carleill's force attacked them from the rear at noon and the Spanish promptly surrendered. Drake occupied the city for a month, ransacking it and burning its buildings until its inhabitants, who had fled inland, handed over 25,000 ducats in ransom.

Afterwards Drake set sail for Cartagena, then the biggest Spanish city in the Caribbean. The governor Pedro Fernández knew that Drake was coming and mustered his defenders. He had 450 men armed with harquebuses, 400 Indian archers, 100 men armed with spears, 54 cavalrymen and 20 armed African slaves on land, and in the harbour he had two well-armed galleys under veteran commander Pedro Vique Manrique. This defence force, however,

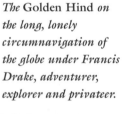

The **Golden Hind** *on the long, lonely circumnavigation of the globe under Francis Drake, adventurer, explorer and privateer.*

although formidable, had heard of Drake's fearsome reputation and knew the size of the force that was about to descend upon them. A week after leaving Santo Domingo, Drake sailed directly into the large outer harbour at Cartagena, landing Carleill and 600 men who circled around to the north. Meanwhile Frobisher kept the fort at Boquerón occupied. The following morning, Carleill attacked, overrunning the outer defences. Morale collapsed. The galleys ran ashore and their crews fled, while the galley slaves revolted. Some thirty Englishmen were killed during the fighting, as opposed to seven or eight Spaniards, but by the following day resistance was at an end. Cartagena was occupied for over a month and comprehensively plundered, until its inhabitants came up with 107,000 ducats to save it.

Drake also plundered St Augustine in Florida and captured Santiago in the Cape Verde Islands, before returning to England. The scale of this campaign was unprecedented and its effect was cataclysmic. The Bank of Spain collapsed. The Bank of Venice, whose principal debtor was Philip II of Spain, nearly foundered, and Germany's principal bank, the

Bank of Augsburg, refused to extend the Spanish monarch any further credit. Even Elizabeth I's principal minister Lord Burghley, who loathed Drake and his tactics, conceded that 'Sir Francis Drake is a fearful man to the King of Spain'. Privateering became a major force in international affairs. At a time when the English government owned only a handful of men-of-war outright, English sea rovers became its principal weapon in the undeclared war against Spain. The privateers' efforts were economically significant too: over the remaining fifteen years of Elizabeth's reign, between one hundred and two hundred expeditions set out from England every year, bringing back between £150,000 and £300,000 in booty stolen from the Spanish.

Squire Thomas Cavendish

Drake's circumnavigation of the globe inspired Suffolk squire Thomas Cavendish, who fitted out his own expedition at colossal expense. On 21 July 1586, he sailed from Plymouth with three vessels and 123 men. After passing through the Strait of Magellan, he attacked Spanish settlements along the Pacific coast. Off the coast of California, he seized the treasure galleon *Santa Ana*, setting fire to it and the five hundred tons of cargo on board. 'Along the coasts of Chile, Peru and New Spain,' he wrote in his report to his patron Lord Hunsdon, 'I made great spoils. I burnt and sunk nineteen ships, both great and small. All the villages and towns that I landed at, I burned and spoiled.'

He made his way back to England via the Philippines, the Moluccas, Java and the Cape of Good Hope. His sole remaining ship, the *Desire*, sailed up the Thames in 1588 with her bows glinting with gilt and her topmasts wrapped in cloth of gold. Her sails were hung with multi-coloured silk grass from the South Sea and Cavendish and his crew strutted on deck dressed in magnificent silk and brocade.

His second expedition in 1591 was paid for by selling and mortgaging his manors; on this occasion, however, his fleet failed to traverse the Strait of Magellan, and he died in the North Atlantic on his way back to England, cursing the 'insolent, mutinous mariners' whom he blamed for his failure.

The defeat of the Armada in 1588 left the Spanish weakened. In the three years following, English privateers brought home so much sugar and so many hides that the London market was glutted and ships were re-routed to Hamburg to reduce losses. The rich and titled, including Sir Walter Raleigh and the Earls of Cumberland and Essex, also got in on the act. Edward Glenham of Benhall in Suffolk sold his family seat to finance an expedition which aimed to capture St George's Island in the Azores. And when such colossal ventures failed, their authors quickly turned to seaborne robbery. Defending his fellow freebooters against the censure of Francis Bacon, Raleigh said, 'Did you know of any that were pirates for millions? They only that work for small things are pirates.'

> ## 'Did you know of any that were pirates for millions? They only that work for small things are pirates.'
> *SIR WALTER RALEIGH*

Pirate Democracy

However, the strongly libertarian tradition of the pirates had already begun. True, Drake had been a martinet. He was one of the few Elizabethan captains to impose iron discipline on his crew. Punishments on his ships where harsh. The penalty for pulling a knife on an officer was the loss of a hand. Assaulting a shipmate brought three duckings from the yardarm. Anyone caught stealing would have their head shaved and smeared with a mixture of feathers and boiling oil, while falling asleep on watch, blaspheming at dice or cards or 'filthy talk in the mess' incurred a flogging or marooning. But under the freebooters of the Caribbean the men were less inclined to put up with this discipline. Richard Hawkins, Sir John's son, likened ships' crews to 'a stiff-necked horse which, taking the bridle between his teeth, forceth his rider to do what him list [choose]'. By the 1590s, it was common practice for the captain to consult the crew, who often forced him to alter course or change the objective of the expedition.

Young men from coastal towns from Bristol to the Wash would quit farms, apprenticeships and life in service to run away to sea, even though they risked their lives from scurvy, dysentery, gangrene, drowning, marooning and violent death. Why should they work for forty

shillings a year, they reasoned, when they could make more than that as their share of the spoils from a single rich prize, as well as what they might earn from pillage – that is, stealing things that did not belong to the cargo, including the personal effects of the passengers and crew of a captured vessel and anything above deck?

Every man was supposed to bring what he found to the mainmast, where it was shared according to rank, but in the heat of the moment, it was easy for a bit of pillaging to turn into the wholesale sacking of the ship. The crew was supposed to get a third of the value of the booty. This meant that they were at the mercy of the promoters' arithmetic, so it was not unusual to pilfer from the spoils before they were inventoried and divided. When William Ivey, master of the privateer *Tiger*, was accused of 'making spoil of the goods', he said, 'shite on thy commissions' and, along with the quarter-master and master's mate, he stabbed the captain and threatened to throw him overboard.

Not that the captains were conscientious: many sold off part of their stolen cargoes in Tunis or Algiers, or had it smuggled ashore in Ireland or Wales. The men's pilfered items would be bought by black marketeers for a fraction of their value, then the money squandered on drink and dockside doxies.

The authorities turned a blind eye to all these practices. As George Carey, a prominent businessman, pointed out, 'Her Majesty shall not need to espy the faults of those who will venture to do her service.' Many did not even bother to take commissions, confident that they would be able to buy their way out of trouble when they returned to England.

The Venetian ambassador Giovanni Scaramelli wrote home in 1603:

How just is the hatred which all people bear the English, for they are the disturbers of the whole world...And yet not only do they take no steps to remedy the mischief, but glory that the English name should be formidable in this way. The queen's ships do not amount to more than fifteen or sixteen and her revenue cannot support a greater charge, so the whole strength and reputation of the nation rests on the vast number of small corsairs. They make the politicians partners in their profits, without the risk of fitting them out, but only a share in the prizes, which are adjudged by legal creatures appointed by the politicians themselves. This unhappy kingdom has come to such a state it has fallen from lofty religion into the abyss of infidelity.

The life of a pirate appealed to the rebellious and individualistic spirit of the English. Many a Roundhead fortune was founded on Spanish gold and some have seen in the get-rich-quick attitude of the privateers the beginnings of the social change that was shortly to sweep away the divine right of kings. But there were dangers. The son of a wealthy Devon family John Oxenham was Drake's lieutenant at Nombre de Dios. In 1574, he fitted out his own expedition and returned to the secret anchorage on the Isthmus of Darien with a 140-ton ship and seventy men. After the locals warned him that the mule trains were now too heavily guarded to raid, he beached his ship among the trees at the water's edge and camouflaged the masts with branches. Leaving four or five men behind to guard the ship, he set off with the rest on foot.

When they reached a river that flowed out into the Pacific they built a sailing barge and sailed downstream. When they reached the Pearl Islands in the Gulf of Panama, they seized two treasure ships from Lima. After plundering them, Oxenham foolishly let them go on their way to Panama, where they alerted the authorities. Oxenham then was pursued and captured. His men were shot, while Oxenham was taken to Lima and hanged in the main square.

The defeat of the Spanish Armada had also weakened Spain's position in the Netherlands and Dutch Protestants, denied access to Spanish trade, took to privateering and piracy. In 1593, ten Dutch merchantmen were captured off the coast of Nueva Andalucía (Argentina). Their captains were hanged and their crews taken as galley slaves. The Spanish were also harsh on their own subjects who traded with interlopers. In 1605, the governor of Santa Domingo marched into the town of Bayahá on the north-west coast of Hispaniola with 150 men, read a proclamation from the king condemning the 'inveterate and pernicious traffic' between the inhabitants and the pirates and ordered them to move to the southern coast of the island where their trading could be more closely monitored. The town was then burnt down. The inhabitants of nearby Monte Cristi, Puerto Plata and La Yaguana were also forcibly resettled and Admiral Luis Fajardo swept along the coast with a Spanish battle fleet the following year to evict any stragglers.

The Dutch war of independence from Spain resumed in 1621, after a twelve-year truce, giving Dutch merchantmen the excuse to turn to privateering again. In 1624 Pieter Schouten led three ships through the Caribbean to sack the towns of Sisal and Zilam on the north coast of the Yucatán Peninsula and seize a Spanish galleon trading with Honduras. The following year, Boudewijn Hendricksz led fourteen ships in an attack on Puerto Rico. He landed 800 men who invaded San Juan and besieged its citadel only to be repulsed with heavy casualties.

But the Dutch were not discouraged. In 1628, 51-year-old Pieter Pieterszoon Heyn – better known as Piet Heyn – led an expedition of thirty-one ships carrying 1,000 soldiers, 2,300 sailors and 679 cannon. They cornered and took an entire Spanish convoy laden with treasure from Mexico in the harbour at Matanzas on the north coast of Cuba. The expedition had been enormously expensive to mount: it nevertheless made a profit of seven million guilders. Back in Holland it took five days for the thousands of chests of coin and bullion to be loaded onto more than a thousand mule carts to be paraded through the streets of Amsterdam in a triumphal procession behind Heyn's coach. Spain, having misguidedly based its economy on the mineral wealth of the Americas, again found its credit weakened and Heyn's booty provided the money for the Netherlands to continue with its bitter struggle for independence against the Spanish, an independence finally won in 1648.

Francis Drake is knighted by Queen Elizabeth I on board his ship the **Golden Hind** *at Deptford, September 1580. Drake had just returned from his successful voyage around the world.*

CHAPTER THREE

THE BUCCANEERS

Originally hunters and vendors of cured meat products, the buccaneers of Tortuga were joined by runaway slaves, ex-convicts, and marooned sailors to become a force to be feared by the treasure ships which plied the trade routes between the New World and Spain.

When the Spanish residents were moved from the northeastern coast of Hispaniola in 1605, they left their livestock behind and soon huge herds of pigs and cattle were roaming the area. These attracted hunters. The few remaining Arawak Indians taught them how to cure strips of meat on a wooden grate called a *boucan*. The French called the result *viande boucanée* which the huntsmen traded for rum, brandy, provisions, clothes, tobacco and guns – preferably long-barrelled muzzle-loaders from Nantes or Bordeaux – with ships that put into harbour along the Banda del Norte. This earned the huntsmen the name *boucanier*, or buccaneer. Curiously, the name only stuck in English. The French called pirates *flibustiers*, or filibusters.

They also sold beef and pork jerky, hides and tallow – fat rendered from the meat which was used to coat the hulls of ships to protect them from the teredo worms that bored their way through the planks. Their numbers were swollen by convicts and indentured labourers who had been displaced from the plantation by African slaves, better suited to work in the tropical climate, along with runaway slaves. These fugitive Africans were known as maroons, from the Spanish cimarrone. Some of their white counterparts were also maroons, having been left on these untamed shores with nothing but a musket, shot and a jug of water as punishment, and buccaneers were also known as marooners. As they made their living by hunting, they became expert shots. They were also skilled with the cutlass, which they used to carve up the carcasses of the animals they had killed.

Typically they lived in bands of six or eight and made binding agreements to share all they had. Some lived as homosexual couples. This was known as *matelotage*, from the French for sailor. The two *matelots* would keep their property in common with the longest-lived inheriting. When women joined the buccaneers on Tortuga Island off the northern coast of Hispaniola, *matelotage* continued but, if one man married, the woman was shared by the two partners. However, in the middle of the century, when France tried to stamp its authority on Tortuga, the governor sought to introduce heterosexuality to Tortuga by importing hundreds of prostitutes.

These early buccaneers cannot have made very fragrant sexual partners, as no amount of washing could have banished the stench of guts and cooked grease that hung about them. They smeared their faces with tallow to keep insects away and their home-spun linen shirts would have been stiff with dried blood. Their trousers, belts, boots and round, brimless hats were made from untanned hides. They lived in huts roofed with palm leaves and slept next to smoking fires to keep the insects away. Each man would carry a six-foot matchlock and would have a cutlass or two stuck in his belt, along with powder horns, bullet bags and coiled mosquito nets for nights spent in the open.

A common food was warm marrow sucked from the bones of a freshly-killed animal and their favourite pastimes were gambling and sharpshooting – that is, drinking a potent mixture of rum and gunpowder which became the regular tipple of latter-day pirates. Among the buccaneers, men took nicknames, abandoned their past lives and asked – and expected – no questions.

During the rainy season when the hunting was poor, the buccaneers turned to piracy. They attacked at night because during the hours of

darkness, the wind blew towards the Atlantic carrying treasure ships through the Windward Passage between Hispaniola and Cuba. It reversed during the day, but buccaneers were less interested in incoming ships: it was out-bound vessels that carried the treasure.

The buccaneers used canoes made from hollowed out tree-trunks or single-sailed barques. These would be packed with gunmen. They worked on the principle that four muskets were as good as one cannon, and manoeuvred so that the bows of their craft always pointed towards the prize, presenting the smallest possible target. Moving in under a barrage of extremely accurate fire, they would attack from the rear, jamming the ship's rudder and swarming up the stern.

The Spanish authorities soon grew alarmed at this home-grown piracy and sought to stamp it out by slaughtering all the cattle and pigs that the buccaneers depended on for their livelihood. But instead of starving out the buccaneers, this simply forced them to take to piracy full time with Tortuga – Turtle Island – as their first headquarters. It had fresh water, fertile soil, sheltered anchorages, a defensible harbour and was ideally positioned to attack ships coming through the Windward Passage. Occasionally the Spanish tried to wipe out the pirate colony there, but the buccaneers defied their every effort and Tortuga became 'the common place of refuge of all sorts of wickedness, the seminary … of pirates and thieves,' according to an early visitor.

The first major triumph of the Tortuga pirates came when the buccaneer Pierre le Grand and twenty-eight men captured a vice-admiral's flagship from a treasure convoy. When they had spotted the galleon, they were near starvation and weak from thirst and exposure. But they voted to attack that night. They drilled holes in the bottom of their little boat to bolster their courage and made straight for their quarry. Catching the captain and his officers off guard playing cards, they seized the ship and sailed directly for the corsair port of Dieppe. Like the English, the French cared little whether their 'privateers' carried a letter of marque, just as long as they were harming the enemy and bringing wealth home to the country. Le Grand was content with this one prize and never went to sea again. However, le Grand inspired the other Tortuga buccaneers, though they were not always so lucky. The French

buccaneer Pierre François sailed south to raid the pearl fisheries off Venezuela in an open boat crewed by twenty-six men. When they came upon a dozen canoes guarded by two men-of-war, they lowered their sail and mixed in with the pearling fleet. When they came alongside the smaller of the two men-of-war – though it still carried sixty armed men and cannon – they demanded that it surrender. A fight ensued and the buccaneers won. But they were not content with the haul of pearls they found on board and attacked the larger man-of-war. This time they lost and were captured.

A typical buccaneer captain, complete with musket, flintlock pistol and stolen treasure, as seen by artist Howard Pyle. The reality was likely to be far less glamorous, however.

Seventeenth-century map of Hispaniola (modern Haiti and Dominican Republic) in the Caribbean. Tortuga, the infamous 'pirate island' of legend, is off the north-west coast.

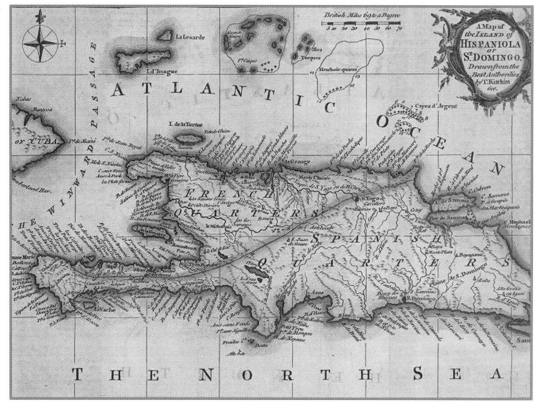

Buccaneer Ships

These early buccaneers favoured small single-masted sloops that could be rowed or sailed. They were fast, easily manoeuvrable and could operate in shallow water. Those made in Bermuda were considered the best. They carried up to fifty men and from eleven to fourteen guns. The English pirates favoured cannon, while the French preferred knives and small arms.

From about 1640, the Tortuga buccaneers began calling themselves the 'Brethren of the Coast' and pledged themselves to follow a strict code called the Custom of the Coast. They would elect their captains and agree to the articles under which they would sail. The first thing they would decide in their ship-board council meetings was where they should head for provisions – particularly meat, as buccaneers ate little else. Usually they raided Spanish pig farms, but manatees, or seacows, and turtle, fresh or salted, were also favourites.

Dividing the Booty

The next item on the agenda was the division of the booty. The general principle was 'no prey, no pay'. The captain and the owner of the ship would get an extra share. The salary of the ship-wright or carpenter who rigged, mended and careened the vessel was also fixed. They also had to decide how much should be set aside for provisions, along with the salary of the surgeon and the amount spent on medication. The first man to spot a prize also got an extra share, while the cabin boys on board only received half a share. Finally they fixed the compensation for anyone maimed or wounded on the voyage.

'For the loss of a right arm, 600 pieces of eight or six slaves; for the loss of a left arm, 500 pieces of eight or five slaves; for a right leg, 500 pieces of eight or five slaves; for the left leg, 400 pieces of eight or four slaves; for an eye, 100 pieces of eight or one slave; for a finger the same as for an eye. All is paid from common stock,' wrote Alexander Exquemelin, a surgeon who sailed with the buccaneers and author of *Bucaniers of America*. First published in Amsterdam in 1678, it was the first book about pirates and became an international best seller. When his book was published in English, pirate Sir Henry Morgan sued him for libel and won. Exquemelin had painted Morgan as a black-hearted villain. This did not bother him. What Morgan objected to was the fact that Exquemelin had said that he had first gone out to the West Indies as an indentured servant. Morgan insisted that he 'never was a servant to anybody in his life, unless to his Majesty'. The publishers were forced to pay £200 damages

and Exquemelin had to amend the English edition of the book.

Unlike among the privateers, no private pillaging was allowed. The buccaneers made a vow not to conceal any plunder, nor to steal from one another. No locks or keys were allowed on board a pirate ship. Any man caught stealing had his nose and ears sliced off. A second offence was punished by marooning.

L'Olonnais the Notorious

The most notorious of the buccaneers of Tortuga was Jean-David Nau, otherwise known as François l'Olonnais because he came from Les Sables d'Olonne in France. Originally transported to Dominica, he completed his term of service before becoming a buccaneer. His potential came to the attention of Bertrand d'Ogéron, who had murdered the previous self-styled governor of Tortuga and taken the island for the French West India Company. An energetic governor, d'Ogéron was the man who had brought hundreds of prostitutes to the island to heterosexualize the buccaneers, though when he tried to impose the Company's monopoly on foreign trade on the island, the inhabitants fired 500 rounds at his ship. D'Ogéron had more sense than to try and discourage piracy and furnished l'Olonnais with a ship.

L'Olonnais soon became legendary for his cruelty. According to Exquemelin, 'it was the custom of l'Olonnais that, having tortured any persons and they not confessing, he would instantly cut them in pieces with his hanger [cutlass] and pull out their tongues'. After 'burning with matches and such-like torments,' he was also known 'to cut a man to pieces, first some flesh, then a hand, an arm, a leg, sometimes tying a cord about his head and with a stick twisting it till his eye shoot out'. Infamously, on a raid on Nicaragua, he cut out a prisoner's still-beating heart and ate it, in an attempt to persuade the other prisoners to reveal where they had hidden their treasure. It is said that this was too much even for some of his hardened crew who left him to sail with his second-in-command Moses van Vin. However, the split may have occurred when l'Olonnais' ship was wrecked on the coast of Honduras. It took his crew six months to build a boat, then he left half his men behind who made the best of it under van Vin.

On another occasion l'Olonnais was ship-wrecked near Campeche in Mexico. All his crew were killed in an attack by Spaniards. L'Olonnais only escaped by smearing blood and sand on his face, and hiding amongst his dead crew. He then escaped with some French slaves and made his way back to Tortuga.

In 1667, l'Olonnais teamed up with Michel le Basque. At the end of April that year, they sailed from Tortuga with a flotilla of eight small ships and 660 men. They stopped at Bayahá on the north coast of Hispaniola for provisions and to pick up more men bringing their number up to over 700. Three months later, they sighted a sixteen-gun Spanish vessel in the Mona Passage between Hispaniola and Puerto Rico. It was full of cacao bound for Veracruz. L'Olonnais chased after it in his ten-gun sloop and the two ships joined battle. After an engagement lasting two or three hours, the Spanish ship was taken.

The French buccaneer L'Olonnais infamously cut out a prisoner's still-beating heart, and ate it in front of the unfortunate man

L'Olonnais and his men stood off Saona Island off the south coast of Hispaniola and waited while a prize crew took the Spanish vessel to Tortuga to unload. When it returned, he made it his flagship. In the meantime, he had stopped and plundered an eight-gun ship carrying gunpowder and the payrolls for the garrisons at Santo Domingo and Cumaná, Venezuela. His haul up to this point was a valuable cargo of cacao, numerous chests of gems and forty thousand pieces of eight – so called because these Spanish silver coins were worth eight reals and were often cut into eight pieces to make change. Now with two large vessels added to their flotilla, the buccaneers sailed into the Gulf of Venezuela to attack the Spanish Main. L'Olonnais landed a shore-party near the battery on the bar that guarded the entrance to Lake Maracaibo, which is actually a large bottle-necked inlet in Venezuela. The battery consisted of sixteen guns, protected by earthworks which were easily overrun by the pirates. By the time they had sailed through into the lagoon they found that Maracaibo itself had been evacuated and they occupied it unopposed for two weeks. Buccaneer parties went out to outlying areas to bring in prisoners, whom l'Olonnais tortured: with little result, as the riches of the city had been moved across Lake Maracaibo to the town of Gibraltar, garrisoned by hundreds of Spanish troops. The buccaneers reasoned that the presence of so many troops meant there must be something worth guarding. So they sailed across the 'lake' and attacked, L'Olonnais leading his men into battle with the cry, '*Allons, mes frères, suivez-moi, et fait point les lâches!*' (Come on my brothers, follow me, and let's have no cowards.)

The buccaneers suffered forty dead and thirty wounded. But 500 Spaniards were dead by the time Gibraltar was taken. Their bodies were loaded into old boats, which were taken out into the lagoon and sunk. L'Olonnais' men spent a month pillaging Gibraltar. They demanded and received a ransom of 10,000 pesos to leave the buildings intact.

L'Olonnais ordered that the Spaniards should be shown no quarter, believing that the more ferocious they were on the way, the less trouble they would have taking the city

The total haul was 260,000 pieces of eight, along with jewels, silk, silverware and numerous slaves. A further 20,000 pieces of eight and 500 head of cattle were extorted to leave Maracaibo standing. Three days after the pirates had weighed anchor, the terrified population of Maracaibo saw l'Olonnais standing off the city again. A boat came ashore requesting a pilot to help navigate l'Olonnais's largest treasure ship over the sand bar at the entrance to Lake Maracaibo. One was despatched at once.

The buccaneers went to Cow Island off the south coast of Hispaniola to divide up the spoils. L'Olonnais then sailed for Jamaica, where he sold an eighty-ton, twelve-gun Spanish brigantine to Rok Brasiliano and Jelles de Lecat, two Dutch seaman who then began a career in piracy of their own.

When l'Olonnais eventually returned to Tortuga, news of his booty had spread through the taverns and brothels of the island, and men were soon clamouring to sign on with him. In 1668, he set sail again, this time with an army of a thousand men. Again, they stopped a Bayahá to take 'on board salt meat for their victuals'. They sailed along the southern coast of Cuba seizing more ships. His aim was to emulate the feat of Henry Morgan, who had sailed up the San Juan River in Nicaragua three years before and sacked Granada. But he found himself becalmed off the Mosquito Coast, unable to sail round Cape Gracias a Dios, instead drifting up the coast of Honduras. Running short of provisions, he sent foraging parties up the Aguán River. Travelling westwards, he captured a Spanish merchantman armed with twenty-four cannon and sixteen swivel guns. He took Puerto Cortés and forced two terrified hostages to lead a party of three hundred buccaneers on the inland city of San Pedro Sula. Ten miles into the jungle they captured some Spaniards, who told them that ambushes lay in wait. L'Olonnais ordered that the Spaniards should be shown no quarter, believing that the more ferocious they were on the way, the less trouble they would have taking the city. He was wrong and his initial assault was fought off. He then allowed the Spanish to evacuate the city under a flag of truce. When he took San Pedro Sula, l'Olonnais burnt it to the ground, then pillaged the outlying areas.

Back at Puerto Cortés, l'Olonnais learned that a galleon was due to arrive from Spain in the Bay of Amatique, so he posted lookouts in a couple of boats along the southern shore, while he withdrew to the other side of the Gulf of Honduras to careen. Three months later, the galleon arrived. It was armed with forty-two cannon and beat off l'Olonnais' twenty-eight-gun flagship. Eventually, four boat-loads of buccaneers managed to board her, but the booty was disappointing. Most of its cargo had been unloaded at other Spanish ports and all that was left was wine, paper and iron. Some of his crew quit. These included Pierre le Picard, who went on to have a distinguished career as a pirate captain in his own right.

L'Olonnais kept the galleon, but she proved to be a heavy sailer and, the following year, she ran aground on some islands off Honduras. His remaining men used the wreckage to build long-boats. This was where he abandoned half his crew including, possibly, Moses van Vin. L'Olonnais headed for the San Juan river where they intended to steal new boats, but they were fought off by the Spanish and forced to flee. He made another attack on the Isthmus of Darien in another attempt to obtain larger sea-going vessels. This time his landing party were attacked by Indians and, according to the sole

FRANCOIS LOLONOIS.
gebooren in Olonne in Vranckrÿck
Generaal van de Franse Roovers in Tortuga

French buccaneer captain François l'Olonnais, one of the most feared and unsavoury characters of the pirate age.

survivor, 'l'Olonnais was hacked to pieces and roasted limb by limb', thus ending the career of one the most unpleasant characters of his day, even by the standards of the time.

The Buccaneers Prosper

As the privateers and buccaneers eroded the wealth and power of Spain, other nations moved into the Caribbean. The French, Dutch, Danish and English all raised flags there.

Spanish attempts to remove them only swelled the number of recruits arriving at Tortuga. The rapidly-multiplying English settlements were funded by competing joint-stock companies. The government saw no reason to discourage this as, like the privateers before them, these cost the treasury nothing and the West Indies became a convenient dumping ground for convicted criminals, religious dissidents and paupers. Hundreds of street children from England and France were kidnapped, and sold into

indentured labour for five years. The going rate was nine hundred pounds of cotton each. Their contracts were often bought and sold, and some never attained their freedom. They were treated much worse than slaves, who cost more and whose lifetime of labour was considered an investment. Slavers also brought equal numbers of male and female slaves to the Americas as it was thought that the men would not work as well without the comfort of women. It was also a powerful incentive not to run away as there were few women in the free population. European indentured labourers were not afforded such sexual privileges.

Buccaneers were not always from the lowest social classes: one of Tortuga's most successful pirates was the son of a French nobleman

After the Parliamentary victory in the English Civil War, the islands became the enforced home of Cromwell's opponents. Seven thousand Scottish prisoners of war and numerous Irish Catholics transported to Barbados and St Kitts made these islands two of the most densely populated places on earth. Some were allowed to become smallholders, but the economy of the West Indies was changing and in the 1650s sugar became the only product of importance. This was a rich man's crop and required heavy capital investment. Tobacco farmers and other smallholders were squeezed out, and many had little choice but to join the buccaneers.

As most of these men had little experience of the sea, when ships were taken the crew was encouraged to sign articles to join the 'Brethren of the Coast' – otherwise they would simply be forced into sailing for the buccaneers with no share of the booty. Slaves on slave ships were sometimes urged to sign up too. Buccaneers who had been indentured labourers saw no reason why other men should suffer a lifetime of servitude when they could be free.

An Aristocratic Villain

Buccaneers did not always come from the lowest levels of society. One of Tortuga's most successful pirates was the Chevalier de Grammont, the son of a French nobleman. After killing a man in a duel at the age of fourteen, he ran away to sea. He joined the French Royal Marines and quickly rose through the ranks but, when he was given command of a frigate, he went into business in his own right. After capturing a Dutch ship off Martinique, he took his prize to Hispaniola where he sold it for 400,000 livres – which he spent on drinking, gambling and whoring.

As he could not return to France, he joined the 'Brethren of the Coast', who flocked to sign on with him because of his reputation for courage, generosity and fairness. During France's wars with Holland and Spain in the 1670s, Grammont rose to prominence among the privateers, commanding 2,000 men aboard six large and thirteen small ships. In 1678, as leader of the Saint Domingue contingent, he sailed as an auxiliary with Vice-Admiral Comte d'Estrées' expedition against Curaçao, Holland's major stronghold in the Caribbean. But when d'Estrées' fleet hit a coral reef off the Isle d'Aves and returned to Martinique with the survivors, Grammont and his men continued alone. They bypassed Curaçao and headed straight for a bigger prize – Maracaibo.

A new fort now guarded the approaches but, as its guns pointed out to sea, Grammont landed a thousand men who marched along the San Carlos peninsular to attack it from the rear. The Spaniards managed to hold off the buccaneers with muskets, so Grammont landed some of his cannon and, after a brief bombardment, the Spaniards surrendered.

Grammont left his six large ships outside the sand bar at the entrance to Lake Maracaibo and sailed the rest of his fleet over it. The inhabitants of Maracaibo, once again, fled. Among them was the governor Jorge Madureira Ferreira who had only been in office for a week. Grammont occupied Maracaibo unopposed and plundered the city. After two weeks, they headed on to Gibraltar which, this time, had been evacuated. The garrison of twenty-two men gave up after a short bombardment. The buccaneers then trudged fifty miles inland, taking the town of Trujillo in the face of 350 troops with four artillery pieces. After stripping Gibraltar, Grammont sailed away, arriving back at Haiti on Christmas Eve to a hero's welcome.

Eighteen months later he staged a daring attack on La Guaira, the port of Caracas, which he took one night with just forty-seven men. When news reached Caracas, the mule trains taking treasure to the coast were ordered to

return inland. A large force under governor Francisco de Alberró then set off to relieve the port but, by this time, the situation in La Guaira had dramatically reversed. In the daylight Captain Juan de Laya Mujica, commanding a contingent that had escaped capture, spotted how few buccaneers there were and staged a counter-attack. Grammont's men were forced to make a fighting retreat back to the beach. Nine were killed and Grammont himself was slashed across the throat with a machete. However, they had managed to get away with a fair amount of plunder and a number of important hostages. Grammont's reputation soared, even though his captives and much of his booty was lost in a hurricane off Haiti.

In the summer of 1682, he led a flotilla of eight pirate ships along the northern coast of Cuba. After two months standing off Hicacos Point at the eastern end of Matanzas Bay, waiting for an outward-bound galleon, Grammont returned to Hispaniola, leaving the rest of his flotilla to continue patrolling. Early in 1683, the *Diligente* and the *Cagone* under Pierre Bot and Jan Willems were in the Windward Passage where Bot captured a Spanish merchantman. He put the survivors ashore at Guantanamo, then the whole flotilla headed back to Haiti. Meanwhile, a Dutch rover named Nikolas van Hoorn had had a cargo of slaves seized by the

Spanish authorities at Santo Domingo, in retaliation for the loss of a Spanish ship, the *Francesa*, to the Dutch pirate Laurens de Graaf. Van Hoorn fled to western end of the island now under the control of the French with his twenty crewmen on board the *Saint Nicholas*. The governor there, Jacques Nepveu, sieur de Pouançy, gave him a letter of marque so that he could revenge himself on the Spanish and he joined forces with Grammont. Together they headed for Roatan Island off Honduras to muster reinforcements for a daring raid. The English pirate Captain John Coxon reported that Grammont and van Hoorn were 'trying to unite all the privateers for an attack on Veracruz', which had not been attacked within living memory.

De Graaf At Large

In the Bay of Honduras, they spotted two Spanish merchantmen, *Nuestra Señora de Consolación* and *Nuestra Señora de Regla*, at anchor which they seized, though the plunder was disappointing. They did not realize that the legendary de Graaf was careening his flagship, the *Francesa*, in a bay nearby, while he waited for the merchantmen to be laden with goods brought from a fair in Guatemala.

It was thought that de Graaf first came to the Caribbean as a gunner in the Spanish navy and

Map from 1552 of the Gulf of Venezuela, showing the Spanish port of Maracaibo, a favourite target of buccaneers such as François l'Olonnais, and Henry Morgan.

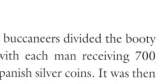
rose to become a commander before being captured by buccaneers and becoming one of them. His first recorded act of piracy was an attack on the Mexican port of Campeche on the night of 31 March 1672. His men slipped ashore and set fire to a pile of timber that had been stockpiled to build a coastguard frigate. While the landing party infiltrated the city, de Graaf's ships used light from the blaze to sail into the harbour. The defenders fled and, next morning, a merchantman, carrying a rich cargo and 120,000 pesos in silver sailed into the harbour – and into de Graaf's arms.

Soon the mere mention of his name made Spanish colonists offer up prayers to be spared his savagery. However, he carried violins and trumpets on board his vessels to entertain himself and amuse others, and it was said that he was 'further distinguished among filibusters by his courtesy and good tastes'. He was tall, blonde and handsome, with a spiked Spanish-style moustache that 'suited him very well', and he was married to a Spanish woman on the Canary Islands called Petronila de Guzmán.

In 1679 de Graaf captured the *Tigre*, a Spanish navy ship from the Windward Islands fleet carrying twenty-four to twenty-eight guns. This made him a danger to English shipping. Sir Henry Morgan, then acting governor of Jamaica, described him as 'a great and mischievous pirate'. He warned Captain Peter Heywood of the Royal Navy frigate HMS *Norwich* to be on the lookout for 'one Laurence… who commands a ship of twenty-eight guns and two hundred men' and he gave Heywood forty soldiers from the Port Royal garrison when he went out on patrol.

In 1682, de Graaf seized another ship from the Windward Islands Fleet in the Mona Passage. This was the *Francesa*, formerly the French ship *Dauphine*. She was carrying 120,000 pesos in Peruvian silver as payrolls for the garrisons of Santo Domingo and Puerto Rico. Fifty of her 250-man crew were killed. The rest were sent back to Cuba on a pink – a twenty-ton two-masted vessel rigged like a schooner. The *Francesa* then became de Graaf's flagship and, at Samaná Bay on the north coast

of Hispaniola, the buccaneers divided the booty into 140 shares with each man receiving 700 pieces of eight – Spanish silver coins. It was then that he returned to the Bay of Honduras to careen his vessel while sitting in wait for the *Nuestra Señora de Consolación* and *Nuestra Señora de Regla*.

De Graaf was furious that Grammont and van Hoorn had ruined his plans by seizing the two Spanish ships while they were still unladen. However, he agreed to join Grammont and van Hoorn in their attack on Veracruz. Seven captains in all joined the expedition.

At Roatan, Grammont rallied the buccaneers with a rousing speech at a huge meeting on the beach. Hearing that Veracruz was expecting two treasure ships from Caracas, the pirates crammed 800 men onto two of their ships and set sail. On the late afternoon of 17 May 1683, Grammont, van Hoorn and de Graaf sailed into the harbour at Veracruz flying the Spanish flag. Mistaken for the Venezuelan treasure ships, they were welcomed by bonfires and beacons. De Graaf quickly reconnoitred the port and landed an advanced force of 200 men, who would attack from the landward side. Then Grammont and van Hoorn landed the main body of 600 men at Punta Gorda. That night the two landing parties crossed the dunes and climbed over Veracruz's low stockade. In the darkened streets, the buccaneers spread out, while Grammont, at the head of a column of eighty men, headed for the governor's palace to crush any resistance there. At four o'clock, he overwhelmed the startled garrison.

Van Hoorn led the plunder while de Graaf and Grammont organized the defences against any counter-attack. Anticipating that the Spanish would send cavalry against them, Grammont raided the stables and organized a company of mounted buccaneers. At dawn the following morning, when a large body of Spanish cavalry formed up west of the city, they were amazed to see a column of a hundred heavily-armed pirates on horseback bearing down on them and they fled without a fight.

After the city was plundered, Grammont demanded that money be sent from the interior

> ## The mere mention of De Graaf's name would soon be enough to make Spanish colonists offer up prayers to be spared his savagery

as a ransom to spare the city. To emphasize his threat, he herded the inhabitants into the principal church, surrounded it with firewood and threatened to burn every man, woman and child if the money was not forthcoming. A ransom of 150,000 pesos was agreed.

The buccaneers now had a massive amount of booty to transport a mile to the shore, so Grammont rode into the church and herded the inhabitants out to use them as bearers. When their task was done, he took them out to Sacrificios Island, just offshore, where he held them until the final tranche of the ransom was paid. Some 1,500 Africans and mulattos were taken aboard as slaves, then the buccaneer fleet weighed anchor. As they made their escape, they ran into the annual plate fleet that was standing offshore, but Admiral Diego Fernández de Zaldívar had no intention of tackling Grammont, van Hoorn and de Graaf and let them escape. However, the governor of Veracruz was beheaded for letting the pirates take the city with such ease. The raid also forced the cancellation of the annual Veracruz Fair and the plate fleet carried less than half its normal haul back to Cadiz.

The Chevalier de Grammont, French nobleman turned buccaneer as portrayed by Debelle in Christian's Histoire des Pirates, *1685*

The buccaneers stopped down the coast at Coatzacoalcos to take on water, then sailed around the Yucatán to Isla Mujeres where they divided the spoils. Each man received 800 pieces of eight. However, van Hoorn and de Graaf fell out over the divisions and got into a fight. Another version of the story is that van Hoorn grew impatient before the ransom was paid and decided to send a dozen of the captives' heads ashore as a warning. De Graaf drew his cutlass and wounded van Hoorn, who was taken on board the *Francesa* in chains. Either way, van Hoorn received a cut on the wrist. The wound turned septic and he died two weeks later of gangrene.

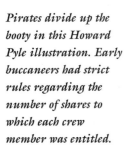

Pirates divide up the booty in this Howard Pyle illustration. Early buccaneers had strict rules regarding the number of shares to which each crew member was entitled.

To emphasize his threat, Grammont herded the people into the church, surrounded it with firewood and threatened to burn them all if more money was not forthcoming

Grammont set sail for Tortuga but his progress was dogged by adverse winds and his crew were near to starvation when they seized *Nuestra Señora de la Candelaria* out of Havana. Fortunately, it was carrying a cargo of flour. Although his men were now fed, the winds still prevented them reaching Tortuga. Instead Grammont made for Petit Goâve on Haiti, where he released the *Candeleria*. After impressing five of its crewmen and taking most of its sails, he gave the captain Luis Bernal a pass 'so that no other corsair would harm him'.

De Graaf prided himself on never taking a commission from anyone, and would put into the port of any nation. However, on 3 September 1683, while at anchor off Haiti, he sent a letter to Sir Thomas Lynch,

governor of Jamaica, offering his services to the British. Lynch was authorized to grant de Graaf a pardon. Meanwhile de Graaf and his cohorts Michiel Andrieszoon, Jan Willems and François le Sage had embarked on a new plan – an attack on Cartagena. When they appeared before Cartagena at Christmas 1683, the Governor Juan de Pando Estrada sent out the forty-gun *San Francisco*, the thirty-four-gun *Paz* and a twenty-eight-gun galliot to see them off. But the pirate vessels, though smaller, were not to be chased away. Instead, they attacked. They boarded the *San Francisco*, which promptly ran aground. After four hours, the *Paz* surrendered and the galliot was taken. De Graaf refloated the *San Francisco*, making her his new flagship and renaming her *Fortune*, later *Neptune*. They sent their captives ashore with a message thanking the governor for his Christmas present. Then they settled down to blockade the port.

In the middle of January 1684, English slave ships arrived under the protection of the forty-eight gun HMS *Ruby*. As de Graaf was now friendly with the English, he let them pass, even entertaining the English officers on board his new flagship. One of the visitors, a trader named Diego Maquet, brought a letter from de Graaf's wife. She said the King of Spain had promised him a pardon if he gave up piracy and sailed once more for Spain. Instead of taking up the offer, de Graaf ordered meat and wine from Maquet, to be shipped from Port Royal to Roatan, and then broke off the blockade.

On his way to Honduras, de Graaf spotted two ships. He followed from a distance until nightfall, then closed on one of them. It was a Spanish ship armed with fourteen guns. That night, the buccaneers crept on board and took the vessel with just two shots being fired. They found it laden with 'quinine and forty-seven pounds of gold'. In the morning, they took the other ship as well. This was an English ship laden with sugar captured by the Spanish who were taking it to Havana. De Graaf gave the ship back to her English crew and set her free with a letter addressed to Governor Lynch, again offering his services. In reply, the English promised him a pardon if he naturalized as an Englishman, swore an oath of allegiance and bought a plantation on Jamaica. They also pledged to have the English ambassador secure a pardon from the King of Spain and obtain the necessary documents for his wife to come from the Canaries, provide he pay for her passage.

But de Graaf found it difficult to give up his old ways. He intercepted a Spanish vessel off Cuba, carrying despatches saying that France and Spain were again at war – not least because of the Tortuga buccaneers' raid on Veracruz. De Graaf sailed his fourteen-gun Spanish prize to Petit Goâve to unload her cargo while Andrieszoon, Willems and the *Neptune* blockaded Cuba. Andrieszoon and Willems plundered the Dutch West Indian ships *Elisabeth* and the *Stad Rotterdam* as they approached Havana, and took the Jamaican sloop *James* which had been trading the with Spanish. But the Spanish soon took revenge on de Graaf. A privateering *piragua* spotted the *Neptune* anchored off Pinos Island to the south of Cuba. They attacked a party that had gone ashore to cut wood, killing or capturing them. The remainder of the crew cut the cables of De Graaf's flagship and fled.

Picking up the rest of his flotilla off Havana, de Graaf, still aboard his Spanish prize, sailed through the Windward Passage and headed for the Spanish Main. On the night of 17 January 1685, de Graaf's ship was fired on by a small vessel. He came about and cleared the decks ready for action. In the distance he spotted two large ships and three other smaller vessels, and feared that he had run into a Spanish fleet. Approaching cautiously, he had two powder kegs broken open so that he could blow up his own ship if needs be. This would be preferable 'to falling into the hands of men who gave no quarter and would inflict on us hideous tortures, beginning with the captain,' according to Ravenau de Lussan, who was on board. It was then that two of the more distant ships signalled. One was the *Neptune*; the other the *Mutine*, or 'Rascal', as Andrieszoon had renamed the *Paz*. The smaller ship that had fired on him turned out to be another of his flotilla, an English trader captained by Jean Rose, who had not recognized his ship in the dark.

De Graaf then ordered his fleet to sail for Curaçao. Off Bonaire, they sighted a Flemish ship out of La Guaira, which they chased and captured that evening. De Graaf dispatched a

De Graaf came about and cleared the decks ready for action. In the distance he spotted two large ships and three other smaller vessels, and feared that he had run into a Spanish fleet

ship to Curaçao to buy masts for the ship, replacing those lost in a storm off St Thomas. These were refused, but a large party of pirates enjoyed themselves ashore until they were driven out at gunpoint.

The Attack on Campeche

De Graaf then decided that what was needed was another mass attack, like that on Veracruz, and turned north again, returning to his flagship *Neptune*. In April 1685, there was another great meeting of pirates, this time at Isla de Pinos off the southern coast of Cuba. Twenty-two ships gathered there. Most of the buccaneers favoured attacking Veracruz again, but de Graaf argued that the Spanish were not going to be caught napping twice and, when they refused to pick another objective, he sailed off. Grammont followed, catching up with the Dutchman off the Mosquito Coast. Together

they hatched a plan to return to the smaller port of Campeche and headed to Isla Mujeres to prepare. They stayed there for more than a month, stopping other freebooters rounding Cape Catoche and inviting them to join them. Word of the pirates' plans soon came to the ears of the Spaniards, however, and the deputy governor of Campeche, Felipe de la Barrera y Villegas, sent a lookout boat to give warning of any attack. In late June, news came that a fleet of unidentified vessels was on its way. On the afternoon of 6 July, a pirate fleet of six large ships, four small ships, six sloops and seventeen *piragua* – two-masted flat-bottomed vessels – appeared six miles off Campeche.

A landing party of 700 men took to the boats and headed towards a beach a little way from the town. The garrison of 200 came out and took up positions along the beach. But instead of landing the pirates stood out to sea until the following morning, when they began

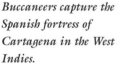

Buccaneers capture the Spanish fortress of Cartagena in the West Indies.

heading back towards their ships. This was just a feint. Before the Spanish soldiers could get back to town, the pirates turned their boats and headed into the port itself. They landed unopposed, quickly formed up into four columns and marched on the city centre.

In the harbour, Captain Cristóbal Martínez de Acevedo had been given instructions to scuttle his coast guard frigate *Nuestra Señora de la Soledad* in the event of an attack. He was supposed to drill holes through the planks and sink her, but the attack came so swiftly that he ordered the bosun to lay a trail of gunpowder to the magazine and lit the fuse. The resulting explosion destroyed the ship and demoralized the defenders, who withdrew to the citadel, where they held out for nearly a week.

On 12 July 1685, the pirates had begun bombarding the citadel when two relief columns of the Spanish militia from the provincial capital of Mérida de Yucatán came marching down the beach. Normally such a large force would send buccaneers racing for their boats, but Grammont's pirates took up defensive positions behind Campeche's ramparts. The first rank of Spaniards fell to well-aimed volleys, then Grammont circled around behind the relief columns. Caught in a crossfire, the militia withdrew in confusion. That night the garrison mutinied and fled. At 11pm two English prisoners called out to the pirates that the citadel was now deserted.

Grammont organized another troop of mounted buccaneers to pursue the Spaniards. They ravaged the countryside up to 25 miles inland. The pirates held the town for two months but, having had advance warning of the attack, most of Campeche's wealth had been taken out of the city and they found little plunder. This merely drove Grammont to terrible acts of cruelty.

On 25 August, Grammont's men celebrated Louis XIV's saint's day with fireworks and the pirates prepared to leave. But first they sent a note to Governor Juan Bruno Téllez de Guzmân demanding a ransom of 80,000 pesos and 400 head of cattle for Campeche. A few days later a reply was received. It was addressed to Deputy Governor de la Barrera, one of Grammont's captives, who was forced to read it out. The pirates, the reply said, 'would be given nothing and could burn down the town, as Spain had ample funds to rebuild it and enough people to repopulate it'.

Grammont was furious. He burned down the town and sent a message threatening to kill the inhabitants. He received another sneering response, so he paraded his captives in the main square and began hanging them. After half-a-dozen had been killed, de la Barreda and a number of prominent citizens approached de Graaf 'who they knew to be more humane than the Frenchman'. They offered 'to serve him for the rest of their lives as slaves if he saved the rest of the inhabitants of Campeche'. Lengthy discussions then took place between de Graaf and Grammont. Eventually Grammont was persuaded to halt the executions and the remaining captives were taken out to the ships.

Grammont Disappears

Early in September they left Campeche and went to the Isla Mujeres to divide the spoils. Then Grammont, now sailing van Hoorn's *Saint Nicholas* – which he had renamed *Hardi*, meaning Audacious – headed to Roatan to careen, along with Nicolas Brigaut in a captured Spanish galliot and a sloop. Grammont then planned an attack on St Augustine, now in Spanish hands, perhaps in collusion with the English settlers in the Carolinas. The three ships made their way up the Atlantic coast of Florida. Grammont and the sloop stood off, while Brigaut went inshore at Matanzas flying Spanish colours to gather intelligence. But his galliot sank in heavy weather. After three days, Grammont went inshore to discover why the scout ship had not reappeared, but was driven northwards by the same storm. He was never seen again, lost at sea with 180 hands.

De Graaf and the Spanish Navy

From Isla Mujeres, de Graaf set sail with his *Neptune* heavily laden with treasure. He was accompanied by Pierre Bot in the *Nuestra Señora de Regla* and three other freebooters. On 11 September 1685, they were sighted by a squadron of the Spanish Windward Islands Fleet under Admiral Andrés de Ochoa y Zárate, who set off after them. After four hours, Bot's *Regla* and a pirate sloop fell behind and came within range of the Spanish guns. In a desperate attempt to escape the bombardment, Bot began throwing his booty overboard to lighten his ships. But still the *Nuestra Señora de la*

Concepión under Vice-Admiral Antonio de Astina closed on him. Bot eventually agreed to strike his colours, if he was granted quarter.

The Spaniards found 130 French buccaneers on board, along with twenty Spaniards, thirteen Indians and several African slaves all taken captive at Campeche. The ship was armed with twenty-two cannon and ten swivel guns. More than 200 firearms were collected – and those did not include those thrown overboard during the chase, or those looted by the Spanish sailors who were worse than the privateers when it came to pillaging. The *veendor*, or purser, Juan Nieto, had to beat back one group of 'scoundrels, drunks and thieves' with a cutlass, and a band of light-fingered sailors was set upon by the prize-master Ensign Pedro de Iriate. The situation was scarcely under control when more sailors from the flagship *Santo Cristo de Burgo*s boarded. By the time they had taken everything they could lay their hands on, the official take was just thirty pounds of church ornaments, a little money and some dry goods in the hold.

Admiral Ochoa had been so confident of victory that he had begun the day sitting in a canvas chair on his quarterdeck. By the evening, he was frail and delirious

Four days later the *Santo Cristo de Burgos* and the *Nuestra Señora de la Concepción*, with Bot and his men prisoner on board, caught up with the *Neptune*. De Graaf, too, was forced to lighten his ship by heaving treasure overboard. The following morning, the two Spanish vessels moved in for the kill. During the day, the Spanish flagship loosed off fourteen broadsides and numerous other shots, while the *Concepción* fired off 1,600 rounds. It is a testimony to de Graaf's seamanship that he escaped with only a couple of spars shot away, even though, on occasions, he was being attacked from both sides within musket range.

Admiral Ochoa, confident of victory, had begun the day sitting in a canvas chair on his quarterdeck. By the evening, he was frail and delirious. The last rites were administered and Admiral Astina took over.

During the night, de Graaf jettisoned his guns. In the morning, the Spaniards found themselves to the leeward of de Graaf who was making his way towards the Yucatán Channel between Cuba and Cape Catoche. Astina set off after him, but in the rising wind *Santo Cristo's* weakened superstructure fell overboard and *Concepción* heaved to, to assist her damaged consort. The Spanish squadron then limped back to Veracruz, where Bot, his lieutenants and half-a-dozen Spaniards sailing under his flag were executed.

Ochoa died a few days after reaching port, sparing him the humiliation of a court martial. De Graaf, on the other hand, was far from done. He resumed his activities, stopping and seizing ships. In December 1685, he went ashore on Cuba to careen five vessels and rustle cattle. The following February he sailed into Ascensión Bay – now Emiliano Zapata Bay – on the eastern shore of the Yucatán with seven ships. Five hundred pirates went ashore and marched 60 miles inland to attack the town of Tihosuco. The inhabitants fled, leaving the pirates to ransack and burn the city. They then marched on Valladolid, 40 miles away. Again, the inhabitants fled, leaving just thirty-six men to defend the town. But the pirates did not attack. De Graaf suddenly gave orders for his men to return to their ships. It is said that a clever mulatto named Núñez had placed fake orders among the piles of valuables dropped by the fleeing Spaniards indicating that an ambush was planned up ahead. De Graaf took his spoils and headed back to Tortuga.

In French Service

But the political situation was changing. After the raid on Veracruz, both Governor Lynch of Jamaica and the French governor of Haiti invited de Graaf to make his headquarter in their ports. But by 1685, the French had given up on indiscriminate raids on Spanish colonies. Louis XIV ordered buccaneering from French islands to stop. One governor of Haiti, de Franquesnay, cracked down on the buccaneers until they threatened an armed revolt. He was replaced by Pierre-Paul Tarin de Cussy who dispensed commissions freely until the king once again ordered a ban on buccaneering.

De Graaf continued to ply the sea and in the autumn of 1686, while pursuing a small fourteen-gun barque called *Santa Rosa* off the Spanish Main, was shipwrecked. However, he managed to capture the barque in his boat, at

the cost of two killed and eight wounded, and took her back to Haiti. By this time, the Spanish were getting tired of Laurens de Graaf, or *Lorencillo* – 'Little Lawrence' – as they called him. They commissioned a squadron of privateers of their own from the Bay of Biscay to take on the pirates of the Caribbean. Before leaving San Sebastián in the Basque Country, their commander Francisco García Galán swore 'to go in search of *Lorencillo* before anything else'. However, when a lone Biscayan privateer's frigate under Fermín de Salaberría caught up with de Graaf off Júcaro on the south side of Cuba in May 1687 she was driven into the shallows and was only saved from capture by number of small Cuban coast guard vessels who came out to rescue her. De Graaf turned on them, sinking a *piragua*, taking a schooner, killing a number of Cubans and carrying others off as captives. Blas Miguel, the brother of one of the slain Cubans, swore revenge. He sailed into Petit Goâve on 10 August 1687 – St Lawrence's Day – in the hope of catching de Graaf celebrating. He had with him 85 men on a brigantine and a *piragua*. They stormed ashore but were quickly surrounded and captured. De Graaf then waded out to kill the man left guarding Miguel's boat, before breaking the Cuban on a wheel – a hideous torture where the victim is tied to a wheel and his limbs broken, before he is beaten to death.

Soon after, de Graaf was ordered by Governor de Cussy of Haiti to sail with 250 buccaneers on two small vessels to enforce the French claim to Cow Island, off the southern coast of Haiti. The French also warned Governor Molesworth of Jamaica that if British ships were sent to fish or hunt there it would be considered a breach of the truce currently in force between the two countries. In fact, de Cussy sent the buccaneers to scare treasure hunters off the wreck of a Spanish ship recently found near Cape Carcass.

The following year, de Graaf was sent out after another wreck on the Serranilla Bank, 180 miles south-southwest of Jamaica, after de Cussy learnt about it from a captured Spanish captain. He found himself in competition with a British salvor, but raised several guns before discovering that France was, once again, at war with Britain.

De Graaf immediately headed back to Haiti, stopping off on the way at Montego Bay in Jamaica. He did no harm while there, merely warning the inhabitants that he intended to obtain a commission in Petit Goâve and return to plunder the entire north side of the island. The frightened inhabitants fled to Port Royal in the south. De Graaf did return a month later with some French vessels and seized eight or ten Jamaican sloops off the north coast. Then he landed a raiding party who plundered a plantation and spread panic throughout the island, while his ships controlled the surrounding waters.

As the British had not received an official declaration of war from London, this was regarded as an act of piracy. Merchant ships were confined to port while Captain Edward Spragge of HMS *Drake* led a flotilla against the pirates. They were repulsed. A second attempt was made early the following year, but it was not until March 1690 that de Graaf's blockade of Jamaica was lifted.

However, de Graaf stayed in the offing, seizing a Jamaican sloop that had been sent to guard the turtling fleet off the Cayman Islands. From its crew, he learnt that the British aimed to make an alliance with the Spanish and to move against the French colony on Hispaniola. De Cussy ordered de Graaf to move his headquarters from Cow Island south of Hispaniola to Cap François on the north. He took with him a small army headed by de Cussy. They marched inland and attacked the town of Santiago de los Cabelleros. The Spanish responded by landing an army of 2,600 near Cap Francisco, while another 700 under the command of Francisco de Segura Sandoval marched across the island from Santo Domingo.

Despite being outnumbered three to one, the buccaneers had shown in the initial skirmishes that they were more than a match for Spanish soldiers. However, de Cussy grew overconfident and decided to stand and fight on a plain called Sabane de Limonade. It was a mistake. This time the buccaneers were not surprising a garrison in the middle of the night, and

> **Despite being outnumbered by three to one, the buccaneers had shown in the initial skirmishes that they were more than a match for Spanish soldiers**

nor were they taking on a militia torn between fighting and protecting their homes and loved ones. On 21 January 1691, in a set-piece battle, the Spanish won what they called the 'Victory of Sabane Real'. Some 500 of the French, including de Cussy, were killed. De Graaf fled into the hills, while the Spaniards, by way of a change, plundered the French settlements in the area.

A new governor named Jean-Bapiste Ducasse took over in Haiti and de Graaf became one of his leading officers. In the French records of 1692, he is described as 'sieur de Gaffe, the king's lieutenant for the government of Ile la Tortue and the coast of Sante Domingue'. De Graaf organized the defences around Cap François against further Spanish attacks. Then he led another attack on Jamaica.

In June 1694, 3,000 buccaneers landed from twenty-two ships on the eastern tip of Jamaica. They ravaged the countryside before making a feint towards Port Royal. When the English marched out to meet them, they quickly fled back to their ships. De Graaf then sailed to Carlisle Bay, west of Port Royal, and landed 1,500 men there on the night of 28 July 1694. Next day they advanced on Port Royal, where just 250 men and twelve artillery pieces were left guarding the town. Holding their fire until they were right on top of the defenders, the buccaneers loosed off a volley and cleared the English from their defensive trenches on the west side of the river. The soldiers who had marched out to the east dashed back and managed to hold the eastern bank, but de Graaf's men found themselves free to pillage the surround countryside. However, the English plantations were defended by miniature fortresses that were impossible to take without artillery, so the buccaneers had to be content with what little they could carry. On 3 August, de Graaf gave the order to withdraw, taking over 1,600 slaves with him.

The British were not about to put up with this and an expedition was sent under Colonel Luke Lillington and Commodore Robert Wilmot. They teamed up with the Spanish under General Gil Correoso and Admiral Francisco Cortés. On 24 May 1695, the combined Anglo-Spanish force attacked the French on the north coast of Hispaniola. De Graaf was in command of the defenders, but in the face of an overwhelming enemy he withdrew, leaving French farms and homes to burn. When the Anglo-Spanish army closed in on his headquarters in Cap François, he fled without a fight, leaving his new French wife, a widow named Le Long, and two daughters in Spanish hands.

De Graaf was arrested by the French, accused of signing an agreement with the Spanish as Holland was aligned with the Anglo-Spanish alliance against France. He was taken to France to stand trial and was exonerated. He returned to Saint Domingue, but his reputation was now much diminished. He waited there until his wife known as – Marie Anne Dieu-le-Veut, or 'Marianne God-wills-it', to the Spanish – and his daughters were released in a prisoner exchange in October 1698.

The End of De Graaf

Soon after the French Canadian explorer Pierre Le Moyne d'Iberville arrived at Saint Domingue on his way to colonize Louisiana and de Graaf agreed to join his expedition. On a foggy morning in January 1699, five French ships stood off the tiny Spanish settlement of Pensacola, Florida, calling for a pilot. A Spanish officer went on board the fifty-eight-gun flagship *François* and was confronted by d'Iberville's enormous interpreter who he recognized as *Lorencillo*. The visitors asked permission to enter harbour. This was denied. De Graaf was then seen to take soundings in the channel. The Spanish garrison commander protested and the ships withdrew. They stood away to the west, eventually moving on to establish their new French colony at what is now Biloxi in Mississippi. In 1700, de Graaf was listed as a king's clerk there, his last mention. He seems to have died at some time in 1704, though some say that he was one of the original settlers of Mobile, Alabama.

Ochoa died a few days before reaching port, sparing him the humiliation of a court martial. De Graaf, on the other hand, was far from done

Group of buccaneers in an open boat mount a sneak attack on a large merchantman.

CHAPTER FOUR

'THE RICHEST & WICKEDEST CITY IN THE NEW WORLD'

When Oliver Cromwell sent a fleet under command of Admiral William Penn to carry Puritanism to the New World, he could have scarcely imagined that it would be members of these crews who would found Port Royal on Jamiaca, the 'richest and wickedest city in the world'.

As the French tried to suppress piracy after gaining permanent possession of Tortuga in 1665, Port Royal in Jamaica took over as the chief haunt of the Caribbean pirates. Lying on a natural harbour at the end of a ten-mile sand spit between the Caribbean Sea and the modern Kingston Harbour, it was famous for its debauchery and rose to become 'the richest and wickedest city in the New World'.

Jamaica had originally been colonized by the Spanish in 1509, but, disappointed by the island's lack of gold, they neglected their colony there. In 1642, Captain William Jackson, backed by the Admiral of the Fleet, the Earl of Warwick – over the protests of the Spanish ambassador Alonso de Cárdenas – picked up a royal commission to plunder Spanish possessions in the New World. He sailed with 300 men, picking up another 700 or so volunteers on Barbados and St Kitts. They sacked several ports on the Spanish Main and Central America, including Maracaibo and Trujillo in Honduras. They also seized Santiago de la Vega – now Spanish Town – in Jamaica in a skirmish that cost forty English lives. The booty was disappointing, just 7,000 silver pesos, 10,000 pounds of manioc-flour bread and 200 head of cattle. However, the natural beauty of the island impressed the raiders and twenty-three of them voluntarily marooned themselves there. After winning the English Civil War, Oliver Cromwell believed it was his religious duty to export Puritanism, especially to the New World, in what he called his Western Design, urged on by his Latin Secretary, the poet John Milton. The Dominican Thomas Gage, widely travelled in the West Indies, Mexico and Central America, told Cromwell that it would be easy to eject the Catholic Spanish from the Caribbean by force of arms. In December 1654, while negotiating an alliance with Spain, he sent a force of 2,500 men under General Robert Venables on a fleet commanded by Admiral William Penn. Reaching Barbados in January 1655, they picked up more ships and another 4,000 volunteers. At St Kitts a further 1,200 joined. With this huge force, they tried to invade Santo Domingo. The first attempt was repulsed with the heavy loss of slaves and black cowhands. The port was then blockaded, but a fifty-gun ship from Spain raised the blockade at a cost of 3,000 English lives.

Reluctant to return to England empty-handed, they sailed for Jamaica, which lay at the centre of the Spanish Caribbean.

WELCOME TO PORT ROYAL

Once called 'the Richest and wickedest city in the world.' Port Royal was also the virtual capital of Jamaica. To it came men of all races, treasures of silks, doubloons and gold from Spanish ships, looted on the high seas by the notorious "Brethren of the Coast" as the pirates were called. From here sailed the fleets of Henry Morgan, later lieutenant-governor of Jamaica, for the sacking of Camaguey, Maracaibo, and Panama, and died here, despite the ministrations of his Jamaican folk-doctor. Admirals Lord Nelson and Benbow, the chilling Edward Blackbeard Teach, were among its inhabitants. The town flourished for 37 years until at 20 minutes to noon, June 7, 1692, it was partially buried in the sea by an earthquake.

Jamaica National Heritage Trust

Pre-1692 coastline

Site of
archaeological dig

North

Montego Bay
Jamaica
Kingston
Port
Royal
Caribbean Sea

Kingston
Kingston Harbour
Port
Royal
Caribbean Sea

0   3 Miles

They seized Santiago de la Vega again. Its Spanish inhabitants were given ten days to leave and were to forfeit all their property. This may seem harsh, but it was same as the conditions imposed on the English settlers when the Spanish ejected them from Providencia Island, now the Colombian island of Santa Catalina. While appearing to agree to these conditions, most of the Spaniards fled into the interior, where they formed a guerrilla army.

Although the island was now in English hands, when Penn and Venables returned to England, they were thrown into the Tower of London, briefly, for dereliction of duty. Few doubted the Spaniards' ability to retake it. And they probably would have, had it not been for an outbreak of plague on Cuba. The Spanish were unable to mount an expedition until 1657, when the Spanish-Jamaican guerrillas under Cristóbal Arnoldo Ysassi occupied the northern shore.

Establishing a Foothold

The plague had also hit Jamaica, killing 4,500 officers and men from the original 7,000 stationed there, within the first year, while the colony's naval defences shrank from thirty warships to just ten by 1656. However the English had established themselves on the south, around Port Royal and present-day Kingston Harbour. They raised a force of 500 men under the acting governor Colonel Edward D'Oyley, who drove the Spanish out. At a second encounter at Río Nuevo on the north coast, 300 Spanish were killed and 100 wounded, while the English suffered just sixty casualties. A third Spanish expedition was repulsed in 1660 and the home-grown guerrillas suppressed.

Although Catholic Spain had not been antagonistic towards the new Puritan regime in Britain, they now feared English expansionism and there was great rejoicing in Mexico City when Cromwell died in 1658. However,

Aerial photograph of present-day Port Royal, Jamaica, showing the extent of the damage caused by the 1692 earthquake.

D'Oyley was determined to keep hold of Jamaica. English buccaneers, driven from Tortuga by the French, soon found Port Royal the ideal base from which to attack Spanish treasure ships. D'Oyley also welcomed French, Portuguese and Dutch buccaneers and issued them with letters of marque, provided they attacked the Spanish, in the hope that this would keep the enemy off balance.

Port Royal harbour, which could accommodate 500 ships, was soon full. Its southern side which faced towards the sea was protected by Fort Cromwell, renamed Fort Charles after the Restoration. Colonists were recruited from Ireland and Scotland, the other English settlements in the West Indies and the jails and back alleys of London itself. By 1658, 4,500 Europeans were living on Jamaica, along with

around 1,500 African slaves. In no time, Port Royal became a boom town, full of brothels, gambling dens and taverns – forty new licenses were granted in July 1661 alone – which served a popular rum punch called 'kill devil'. The governor Sir Thomas Modyford wrote that, 'the Spaniards wondered much about the sickness of our people, until they knew the strength of their drinks, but then wondered more that they were not all dead'. There were also a couple of churches, but one clergyman who arrived from England left Port Royal on the same ship saying 'since the majority of its population consists of pirates, cutthroats, whores and some of the vilest persons in the whole world, I felt my permanence there was of no use'.

Some of Venables and Penn's officers had staged early raids on the Spanish Main with

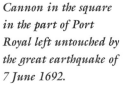

Cannon in the square in the part of Port Royal left untouched by the great earthquake of 7 June 1692.

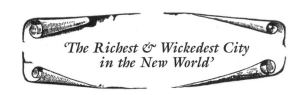
attacks on Riohacha and Santa Marta in Colombia, though the short-lived governor Robert Sedgwick condemned these actions as dishonourable. But D'Oyley sponsored and possibly even participated in a number of raids on Panama and Cartagena before he was replaced in 1661. In the six years following the English occupation of Jamaica, eighteen cities, four towns and three dozen smaller settlements were raided by Port Royal pirates – some repeatedly. Spanish colonists fled at the sight of an unidentified sail over the horizon, though settlements inland were not safe from plunder either.

Under D'Olyey's sponsorship, Captain Christopher Myngs looted Cumaná and Puerto Cabello on the coast of Venezuela in 1659, then seized treasure worth between £200,000 and £300,000 from the small town of Coro. Fleeing Spaniards left behind twenty-two chests each containing 400 pounds of silver, assorted worked silver pieces, jewels and cacao beans.

> ## In no time, Port Royal became a boom town, full of brothels, gambling dens and taverns, all of which served a popular rum punch named, appropriately, 'kill devil'

The return of this booty to Port Royal on 23 April 1659 was the cause of public rejoicing. Then it was discovered that Myngs had helped himself to the treasure before its official inspection. He was arrested and sent to England for trial. While the papers were being drawn up, he discovered that D'Oyley and other Port Royal officials had also had their hands in the till and sued. In the meantime, in 1660, the monarchy had been restored. When Charles II took the throne, he immediately proclaimed peace with Spain, so the belligerent roundhead D'Oyley was replaced by the royalist Lord Windsor. When he arrived in Port Royal in August 1662, he was barely civil to his predecessor and denied D'Oyley's petition to settle in Jamaica and sent him back to England.

Beyond the Line

However, despite the political changes, Lord Windsor was not about to end the colony's lucrative trade in piracy. He merely called in all existing commissions and issued his own. And he set up an Admiralty Court to ensure he got his share of the booty. Although England was officially at peace with Spain, this was soon undermined by Charles's marriage to Catherine of Braganza, a Portuguese princess, in 1661. Apart from this, the Caribbean was also generally considered as lying 'beyond the line' of the law, and peace treaties counted for little, especially when treasure was at stake. Plundered gold and silver soon became so plentiful in Port Royal that, as early as 1662, the government proposed establishing a mint.

In 1662, Myngs returned to Jamaica and led 1,300 men on a raid on Santiago de Cuba. Despite storms, adverse winds and a night-march over rocky terrain, he took the town. Two months later, Jamaica's island council gave Myngs permission to mount a raid on Campeche. At dawn on 9 February 1663, he landed 1,000 men. Myngs led the charge and was seriously wounded in the face and thigh. Edward Mansfield took over command and by ten o'clock, they had taken the port, seizing an estimated 300 tons of merchandise, but little silver. The raid became known as 'Mansfield's Assault' to Spanish historians.

These attacks were seriously damaging to Anglo-Spanish relations. They were also costing the Spanish exchequer dear at a time when the fabulous silver deposits at Potosi in Bolvia, then part of the Viceroyalty of Peru, were running out and Philip IV found that he could not afford to refit his Gulf of Mexico and Windward Islands fleets. So again he sued for peace. Charles II obliged with a new treaty and there was an exchange of prisoners. To the pirates of Port Royal this meant that the semi-official expeditions organized by Myngs were replaced by alehouse ventures. Myngs himself left for England, where he was knighted. As vice-admiral, he commanded HMS *Victory* during the Second Anglo-Dutch War and died of his wounds after being shot twice through the throat during the 'Four Day Fight' in June 1666.

In June 1663, Captain Barnard left Port Royal to sack San Tomé on the Orinoco and

returned with his plunder. In October 1664, Captain Cooper sailed into port on a frigate armed with ten guns, a crew of eighty and two Spanish prize ships. The larger of the two was the *María*, carrying a cargo of olives, oil, wine and several friars bound for Veracruz, along with 1,000 quintales, or 46,000 kilograms, of mercury which was used for smelting low-grade silver ore in New Spain. The Spanish ambassador, Don Patricio Moledi, complained, but Jamaica's deputy governor Sir Charles Lyttleton claimed that the latest peace treaty only banned attacks on Spanish possessions on land – ships at sea were still fair game.

One of the most notorious of the Port Royal pirates was Rok Brasiliano. Born in Groningen in the Netherlands, he emigrated to the Dutch colony in what is now Bahía, Brazil. When this was lost to the Spanish and Portuguese in 1654, he found his way to Jamaica, where he became known as 'Rock the Brazilian' to the Englishmen there. He sailed as a common seaman on privateers, rising to command his own

small barque. Recruiting a crew of buccaneers from the waterfront taverns, he seized a treasure galleon from New Spain. After each expedition, they returned to Port Royal and 'wasted in a few days… all they had gained, by giving themselves over to every manner of debauchery,' according to Exquemelin, 'and in the end [he] became so audacious that he made all Jamaica tremble.'

However, on one of his early expeditions, he was captured at Campeche and taken to Spain, where he managed to regain his freedom and return to Jamaica. In 1668, he bought an eighty-ton, twelve-gun brigantine from François l'Olonnais, installing Jelles de Lecat as his first mate. They sailed for the Mosquito Coast, where they joined Henry Morgan's attack on Portobelo in Panama in July. They then attacked Cumaná in Venezuela, returning to Port Royal with a second Spanish brigantine. This became Brasiliano's flagship, crewed by six Englishmen and thirty-four Dutchmen, while de Lecat took command of the old one.

In the spring of 1669, Brasiliano's two ships accompanied the eighty-man frigate of Joseph Bradley, a veteran of Morgan's attack on Portobelo, into the Gulf of Mexico to attack the Spanish settlements around Laguna de Términos in Campeche Bay. The three ships stood off Campeche for three weeks without taking any prizes. Brasiliano lost two men in a raid on the port of Lerma, just down the coast from Campeche, before Bradley captured a Cuban vessel which was laden with flour. They returned to Laguna de Términos, where Brasiliano careened his ship and de Lecat logged valuable dyewood. After two months' rest, Bradley and Brasiliano returned to blockade Campeche. Bradley's frigate stood off the entrance to the port, while Brasiliano scouted to the southwest. Off Las Bocas, he captured three fishermen. Under torture one revealed that a ship was expected from Veracruz, which he thought was carrying the new governor – in fact, it was carrying the official auditor. But before the ship arrived, three armed Spanish ships chased the pirates away. Brasiliano escaped northeastwards, but as he tried to claw his way around the Yucatán, a strong northerly wind shipwrecked him on Chicxulub beach, a thin sand bar just east of the present-day town of Progreso. One of the captured fishermen escaped and informed the authorities in the provincial capital of Mérida de Yucatán that the

Henry Morgan outside the city of Panama, which, the caption informs readers, he 'took from the Spaniards' in 1671.

pirates were ashore. A detachment of cavalry were sent. They found Brasiliano burying their cannon and other heavy items saved from the wreck. As they bore down on them, Brasiliano and his men took to their boats. But two were left behind. They surrendered to the Spanish, who then dug up Brasiliano's booty. It consisted of sixty cannon balls, two bronze swivel guns and a bronze cannon bearing the arms of Philip II of Spain.

Brasiliano and his men were rescued by de Lecat and taken back to Port Royal by Bradley. Soon after de Lecat and his mate Jan Erasmus Reyning seized a Spanish merchantman. Renaming it *Seviliaen*, they scuttled their brigantine and sailed their prize back to Port Royal

At that time, the Spanish were getting their own back and the Spanish privateer Manoel Rivero Pardal began raiding the coastline of Jamaica, so Henry Morgan planned to retaliate by attacking Panama. On that expedition, both Brasiliano and Bradley were wounded during the attack on San Lorenzo castle at the mouth of the Chagres river. Bradley died, but it is thought Brasiliano recovered sufficiently to join Morgan's epic march across the isthmus. He was still thought to be active as late as 1673. According to Exquemelin, he fell into Spanish hands and was tortured by the Inquisition at Campeche. When he confessed that he had hidden treasure on the Isla de Pinos, Spanish soldiers were sent and dug up more than 100,000 pieces of eight.

The Pirate Governor

Henry Morgan was perhaps Port Royal's most famous pirate. Born in Wales in 1635, he came from a military family. His uncles Thomas and Edward were both soldiers of fortune on the Continent, working their way up through the ranks in the Thirty Years War. When the English Civil War started, Thomas joined the parliamentary side, while Edward became a royalist. After the execution of Charles I, Edward went into exile, while Thomas stayed on as a major-general in the New Model Army and was second-in-command of the expedition into Flanders. How much Henry was involved in the war is not known, but he once said, 'I left school too young to be a great proficient in Admiralty or other laws, and have been more used to the pike than the book.'

At the age of nineteen, he signed up for Cromwell's Western Design as a subaltern and sailed with Penn and Venables. After their failure to take Hispaniola, Morgan ended up in Jamaica, where he survived the plague, the fighting and the generally poor conditions. When Lord Windsor became governor and reorganized the militia, Morgan became a captain in the Port Royal Regiment. He was also given a ship and a privateering commission, and sailed with Christopher Myngs on his raid on Santiago de Cuba and Campeche.

Afterwards, Morgan claimed to have remained at sea, roving for the next twenty-two months. He joined a new expedition into the Gulf of Mexico under the Port Royal veterans David Martien and John Morris. This venture was, strictly, illegal as England and Spain were now at peace and the new governor of Jamaica, Sir Thomas Modyford, ordered that 'all acts of hostility against the Spanish should cease'. This was all the more difficult for Morgan as his uncle Edward had returned to England after the Restoration

'I left school too young to be a great proficient in Admiralty or other laws, and have been more used to the pike than the book'

HENRY MORGAN

and had been appointed deputy governor of Jamaica. On his way to take up his post, he had stopped at Santo Domingo and passed an official message to the Spanish governor, proposing that they 'forebear all acts of hostility, but allow each other the free use of our respective harbours and the civility of foot, water and provisions for money'. But Henry Morgan, like the other pirate captains, claimed to know nothing of the cessation of hostilities and continued operating under his two-year-old commission from Lord Windsor.

Rounding the Yucatán in February 1665, Martien, Morris and Morgan seized an eight-gun Spanish frigate at anchor outside Campeche. On the 19th, they moored off the small town of Santa María de la Frontera at the mouth of the Grijalva River. Then a landing party of 120 pirates travelled 50 miles up the river and to the provincial capital Villahermosa de Tabasco. They attacked at four o'clock in the morning, catching the inhabitants in their beds. After sacking the city they loaded their booty and their captives on a coaster. But when they

got back to the mouth of the river, they found that their ships had been captured by three Spanish frigates sent out from Campeche.

Their retreat cut off, the pirates released their hostages and set off in the hope of finding another river channel out to sea to make their escape. But when they reached the coast once more, they found themselves confronted by their own ten-gun flagship and their eight-gun prize, crewed by 300 volunteer militiamen from Campeche. The Spanish commander José Aldana sent a message, asking them to surrender. The pirates pretended they did not understand. And when an interpreter was sent, they said that they would not give up without a fight. Instead of staying on board ship and starving the pirates out, the Spaniards then disembarked their militia. They found themselves faced a palisade reinforced with sandbags and bristling with seven small cannon, with the pirates well entrenched behind it. The Spanish force was largely armed civilians. They had little stomach for attacking such defences and were seen off without the loss of a single pirate. Next day, the pirates found their ships aground on the beach and made their escape unmolested.

They headed back up the coast, foraging and capturing small boats as they went. Off Sisal they robbed a vessel of its cargo of corn and released it with a message to the governor of Yucatán, saying that they intended to return and lay the province waste. Taking on water at Roatan, they attacked Trujillo, overrunning the port and stealing a fresh ship. On the Mosquito Coast, they hired some native guides, then hid their ship at Monkey Point, Nicaragua, before making their way up the San Juan River into Lake Nicaragua in lighter boats. They crossed the lake at night and sneaked up on Granada. On the morning of 29 June 1665, they marched into the centre of the city, fired a volley and overturned the eighteen great guns in the Plaza de Armas. Then they took over the garrison commander's house, seizing all the arms and ammunition stored there. They locked 300 men in the church while they plundered the city for sixteen hours. Then they released their prisoners, sunk their boats and made off. On their way back across the lake, they took a 100-ton vessel and plundered the island of Solentiname. They returned down the San Juan river to their ships and sailed for Port Royal that August. Although everything they had done was illegal, no one could ignore the

amount of booty they had returned with and no charges were pressed.

At the end of the year, Morgan married his first cousin, Elizabeth, who had come out to Jamaica with her father, the lieutenant governor. By this time, Edward Morgan was dead. In February 1665, news that England was once again at war with the Netherlands had reached Jamaica and Modyford sent a fleet of privateers against the Dutch islands of Curaçao, Bonaire, St Eustatius and Sabá under the command of Lieutenant Governor Edward Morgan. After writing his will, Edward Morgan left Port Royal on 28 April 1665 aboard his flagship *Speaker*. He had under his command nine privateers and over 500 men. Slowed by adverse winds, they put in at Santo Domingo for water and provisions, but were refused them. Eventually, when the privateer fleet appeared of St Eustatius, Morgan led a charge of 350 buccaneers ashore. The island was easily taken. However, in the words of his second-in-command Colonel Theodore Cary, 'The good old Colonel, leaping out of the boat and being a corpulent man, got a strain, and his spirit being great he pursued over-earnestly the enemy on a hot day, so that he surfeited and suddenly died.'

After Edward Morgan's successful raid on St Eustatius, the buccaneers refused to follow his second-in-command Cary, being 'a man of too easy disposition'. Instead, they turned on their traditional enemy Spain again, through the Spanish were neutral in the Second Anglo-Dutch War. However, Modyford needed their help and called on the buccaneers once more. Many were reluctant to put into Port Royal and put themselves under the jurisdiction of the crown, so he convened a meeting at Bluefields Bay off the southwest shore of Jamaica. Six hundred buccaneers turned up and they agreed to sail on Curaçao under the command of Mansfield.

First, they set a course for Cuba, ostensibly to take on provisions. On the way, they intercepted a Spanish barque and murdered its crew of twenty-two. Putting into the small port of Júcaro, Cuba, around Christmas, they asked to buy provisions. Permission was refused. This gave them an excellent excuse to ransack the town. Two or three hundred pirates then marched 42 miles inland, seized the town of Sancti Spíritus and set fire to it. They rounded up the inhabitants and marched them back to the coast, where they ransomed them for 300

beef cattle. Although they had no authority from Governor Modyford to plunder Cuba in this manner, some argued they had the right to do it under the old Portuguese commission issued by the French governor of Tortuga.

An emissary from Modyford turned up. The pirates assured him that they would now head for Curaçao with Edward Mansfield as their admiral, but soon changed their minds. Even Mansfield's crew refused to beat up wind for the Dutch West Indies 'averring publicly that there was more profit with less hazard to be gotten against the Spaniard, which was their only interest'. Instead, they turned to sail with the wind for the Bocas del Toro – the 'Bull's Mouths' – on the Isthmus of Panama. The pirate fleet then split in two. Mansfield led seven ships northwestwards up the coast to Cosa Rica, while the other eight sailed southeastwards down the coast against the town of Natá in the Panamanian province of Veragua.

Mansfield arrived at Portete on 8 April 1666 and seized the lookout before the alarm could be raised. He anchored his ships off Punto del Toro and the buccaneers disembarked. Their plan was to march 50 miles inland and take the provincial capital of Cartago. But first they took the town of Matina, 6 miles up the estuary. However, an Indian named Esteban Yaperi fled from the nearby village of Teotique and warned the governor Juan López de Flor, who mustered men in the mountain stronghold of Turrialba. They were lightly armed, but they did have the great benefit of protection from the jungle. Mansfield's men were soon tired by their jungle travails, and so hungry that when they came across an Indian carrying some wheat they fought among themselves for these meagre rations. Hearing of this, Governor López advanced. Mansfield and his men fled back to their ships, exhausted and near to starvation. Two of his ships promptly deserted. So, in an effort to restore his reputation, Mansfield sailed his two remaining frigates and three sloops against Providencia Island, or Santa Catalina. Twenty years before this had belonged to the English, but was now occupied by a small Spanish garrison.

The ruins of Panama Viejo, the first city on the site of what is today Panama City. Panama Viejo was burned down by the pirate Henry Morgan and his crew in 1671.

They arrived at noon on 25 May 1666. At midnight 200 buccaneers rowed ashore. According to Exquemelin, Henry Morgan was among 100 Englishmen on the raid. There were also eighty French buccaneers from Tortuga. The rest were Portuguese and Dutch. They marched across the island, rounding up Spaniards from the isolated settlements. A dawn the following day, they stormed the citadel. There were just eight soldiers asleep inside. The other sixty-two men of the garrison were scattered around their billets. The island fell without a single loss. There was little to take and the French buccaneers prevented the English sacking the church.

Morgan's pirates quickly took over the town, 'firing off their guns at everything alive – whites, blacks, even dogs – in order to spread terror'

Ten days later Mansfield sailed with 170 Spanish captives on board, leaving Captain Hatsell with thirty-five buccaneers and fifty African slaves to hold the island. He dumped his prisoners on Witches Point on the isthmus of Panama, then sailed for Port Royal, arriving there on 22 June. He was in luck. Three months earlier Modyford and the island's council had decided 'that it is in the interest of the island of Jamaica to have letters of marque granted against the Spaniard'. Nevertheless Modyford reprimanded Mansfield for taking Providencia Island without orders though, as he wrote to the Secretary of State Lord Arlington, it 'would have been an acceptable service had he received orders for it'. No more commissions were forthcoming from Port Royal, however, so Mansfield sailed for Tortuga. According to a Spanish account, he died there in 1667, poisoned. But a contemporary English account says he was captured by the Spaniards and summarily executed in Havana.

After Mansfield's death, Modyford found himself the unofficial leader of Port Royal's buccaneers. He had also inherited his uncle's mantle as commander of the privateers. In late 1667, fearing a Spanish invasion, Modyford ordered Morgan to 'draw together the English privateers and take prisoners of the Spanish nation'. He set sail with Edward Collier and John Morris, a veteran of Myngs' attacks on Cuba and Campeche

and Morgan's raids on Mexico and Panama, along with a number of French buccaneers, who at least had the excuse that France, unlike England, was at war with Spain. They rendezvoused off the South Cays of Cuba, then Morgan led a dozen ships into the Gulf of Ana María on 28 May 1668. A shore party of 700 men landed and marched on Puerto Príncipe, present-day Camagüey.

The Spanish attacked with cavalry and native lancers, but the superior firepower of the buccaneers inflicted nearly a hundred casualties on them and Morgan's men took the town by storm. The plunder went on for fifteen days, but they only managed to collect 50,000 pieces of eight. This would not go far when shared out among so many men. However, the Spanish handed over several hundred head of cattle in return for their hostages. Well provisioned, the pirates headed towards Cape Gracias a Dios on the Mosquito Coast. Morgan then proposed an attack on Portobelo. But the French buccaneers, already unhappy with the slim pickings Morgan's raid on Cuba had yielded, refused to join the attack, complaining that it was too dangerous and difficult. So with just four frigates, eight sloops and less than 500 men, Morgan sailed on Panama.

Portobelo was so heavily fortified that his only hope was to take it completely by surprise. Anchoring in the Bocas del Toro, he transferred his men into canoes which they rowed 150 miles eastwards across Mosquito Gulf. They arrived in the vicinity of Portobelo on the afternoon of 10 July 1668. That night, they landed. After a swift overland march, they approached the city before dawn. When they reached the first of the city's four forts, they captured a sentry and made him call on his comrades to surrender or die. Their answer was a fusillade of musket fire. The buccaneers then jumped over the walls and overwhelmed the fort's defenders, who were still half asleep. True to his word, Morgan locked the Spanish soldiers in the fort and blew it up.

Morgan's pirates quickly took over the town, 'firing off their guns at everything alive – whites, blacks, even dogs, in order to spread terror'. The second fort fell with ease. But a third, defended by eighty men under the command of the governor, held out. The battle raged until noon and the inhabitants of Portobelo seized the opportunity to flee to the woods with their valuables. This spurred Morgan to redouble his efforts. He ordered his men to build scaling lad-

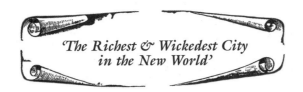
ders, which he moved up to the walls of the fort using monks and nuns as human shields. They took the fort, killing forty-five of the Spanish defenders and wounding the rest. The following morning Morgan led 200 buccaneers across the bay and forced the fifty soldiers holding the harbour castle to surrender, after some token resistance. Morgan then sent for his ships from Bocas del Toro, which were now able to moor safely in Portobelo harbour. The city had been taken at a cost of just eighteen buccaneers.

Now the butchery began. Morgan's pirates began a drunken orgy of rape and murder. Exquemelin, who was on the expedition, said that Morgan had wealthy citizens tortured until they revealed the whereabouts of their valuables. A stream of gold, silver, plate and jewels poured into Morgan's headquarters from hiding places in cisterns, garden and caves. Valuable cargoes were looted from the waterfront warehouses and, on 14 July 1668, Morgan wrote to the governor of Panama, saying, 'Tomorrow we plan to burn this city to the ground and then set sail with the guns and munitions from the castle. We will take with us our prisoners... and we will show them the same kindness that the English have received in this place.'

However, Morgan offered to spare the city if a ransom of 350,000 pesos was paid. But the acting governor, Agustín de Bracamonte, was already marching to the relief of the city at the head of 800 militiamen and replied, 'I take you to be a corsair and my response is that the vassals of the King of Spain do not make treaties with inferior persons.'

Morgan wrote back:

Although your letter does not deserve a reply since you call me a corsair, I nevertheless write you these few lines to ask you to come quickly. We are waiting for you with great pleasure and we have powder and ball with which to receive you. If you do not come very soon, we will, with the favour of God and our arms, come and visit you in Panama City. Now it is our intention to garrison the castles and keep them for the King of England, my master, who since he had a mind to seize them, has a mind to keep them. And since I do not believe that you have sufficient men to fight with me tomorrow, I will order all the poor prisoners to be freed so that they may go and help you.

When Bracamonte arrived the following day, he found that Morgan was right. He did not have enough men to storm the fortifications of Portobelo that were now manned by Morgan's bloodthirsty cut-throats. After a week sitting outside the city in the jungle, Bracamonte ordered his army to retreat, leaving a lieutenant to negotiate the ransom. This was set at 100,000 pesos. On 27 July, Morgan pulled out and returned to Port Royal with 500,000 pieces of eight, 300 slaves and a mountain of other booty. For a month, he and his men celebrated in the inns and whorehouses of Port Royal where, it was said, there was 'such a crew of vile strumpets and common prostitutes that 'tis almost impossible to civilize'.

In Port Royal, it was said, there was such a 'crew of vile strumpets and common prostitutes it was almost impossible to civilize'

In October 1668, Morgan set out again, calling for other buccaneers to meet him off Cow Island for another sortie against the Spaniards. Soon after he left, the thirty-four-gun Royal Navy frigate HMS *Oxford* arrived at Port Royal. Its mission was to suppress piracy and it was to be maintained at Jamaica's expense. But Modyford thought it might make a suitable reinforcement for Morgan and sent it after him with instructions to take Cartagena. However, the ship's captain had an argument with the sailing master and, when they put into Port Morant at the eastern end of Jamaica, he killed the man and fled. So Modyford appointed Edward Collier captain and loaded the ship with 160 buccaneers.

When the *Oxford* sailed once more on 20 December, she had new orders. She was to detain the fourteen-gun French corsair *Cerf Volant* under Capitaine Vivien out of La Rochelle, who had recently plundered a Virginia merchantman. Collier sailed straight for Cow Island, where he found the *Cerf Volant* among Morgan's fleet. He invited Capitaine Vivien on board. The master of the Virginian, whom Collier had brought along, identified Vivien, who was arrested along with his forty-five-man crew. They were taken back to Port Royal in the *Cerf Volant*, which was then renamed *Satisfaction* and returned to Morgan's flotilla.

Back at Cow Island, the thousand buccaneers gathered there decided, with the *Oxford* on their side, they had the strength to take Cartagena. That night they had a feast to celebrate the New Year and their forthcoming expedition. Morgan invited captains Aylett, Bigford, Collier, Morris and Thornbury – all well known among the pirate fraternity – to dine on the quarterdeck of the *Oxford*. Meanwhile the ordinary seamen were carousing on the forecastle 'drinking the health of the King, toasting their success and firing off salvoes' when a sudden spark ignited the *Oxford*'s magazine, blowing up the ship. Ship's surgeon Richard Browne who was at Morgan's table wrote 'I was eating my dinner with the rest, when the mainmasts blew out and fell upon captains Aylett, Bigford and others and knocked them on the head.'

Admiral Campos demanded that Morgan surrender immediately, or 'I have orders to destroy you utterly and put every man to the sword'

Only six men – including Morgan and pirate captain John Morris – survived out of a company of more than 200. Sadly, John Morris's son perished in the blast. As the sea turned red with blood, pirates from the other ships rowed out among the corpses to strip them of valuables and hack gold rings off lifeless fingers.

The loss of the *Oxford* put paid to any plan to take Cartagena and Collier headed off on the *Satisfaction* to make an independent raid on Campeche. On the fourteen-gun frigate *Lilly* Morgan led the rest of his fleet eastwards, with the intention of raiding Trinidad, then still a Spanish possession, and Margarita Island off Venezuela. But these were small beer and by the time they reached Saona Island at the eastern end of Santo Domingo, three more of Morgan's best ships had deserted him. John Morris, his loyal lieutenant, remained with him though, and he could still muster eight ships and 500 men.

At their meeting they decided to repeat François l'Olonnais' feat of two years earlier, and attack Maracaibo. They provisioned at Aruba, the Dutch island at the mouth of the Gulf of Venezuela. As they neared the bar that marked the entrance of the lagoon on 9 March 1669, they saw that it had been fortified since l'Olonnais's raid. Now a castle bristling with eleven guns guarded the channel, so Morgan's men landed and besieged it. The defenders put up stout opposition. But there were only nine of them – one officer and eight men. That night, they abandoned the fort, leaving a slow fuse burning in the magazine. Morgan and his men inched forward in the darkness and were amazed to find there were no defenders. A quick search of the fort revealed the fuse, which was extinguished 'about an inch away from the powder'.

Morgan's men then spiked the fort's guns and sailed through the shoals into the lagoon. Maracaibo had already been abandoned. The garrison's commander had ordered that all militiamen report for duty but, when only twelve of them did so, he too took to his heels. The buccaneers sacked the town and sent out parties into the surrounding countryside, where they met no resistance. Rich captives were again tortured until they revealed where they had hidden their valuables. After three weeks of this, Morgan headed across the lagoon to Gibraltar, where he did the same. He returned to Maracaibo on 17 April with a Cuban merchant ship and five piraguas, then prepared his fleet to set back out to sea.

However, while Morgan's men had been busy plundering, Spain's Windward Islands Fleet had turned up outside the lagoon, blocking the buccaneers' escape. Admiral Alonso de Campos y Espinosa had formidable fire power under his command. His squadron comprised the fifty-ton *Nuestra Señora de la Soledad* – known as the *Marquesa* for short – with fourteen guns, the 218-ton *San Luis* with twenty-six guns and his flagship the 412-ton *Magdalena* with thirty-eight guns. On board were 500 fighting men. When he found the fort at the entrance of the lagoon deserted, he knew something was amiss. He quickly re-occupied it with forty men carrying heavy muskets and managed to repair six of the guns. Then he sent inland for reinforcement, lightened his ships to enable them to cross the sandbar, and sailed into the lagoon. Admiral Campos now had Morgan bottled up, and sent him a note demanding his surrender. Otherwise, he said, he had 'orders to destroy you utterly and put every man to the sword'. He continued:

This is my final resolution: take heed, and be not ungrateful for my kindness. I have

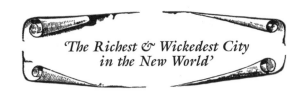
*with me valiant soldiers, yearning to be
allowed to revenge the unrighteous acts you
have committed against the Spanish
nation in America.*

Morgan read Campos's letter aloud to his
followers in the market place of the otherwise
deserted city of Maracaibo. In the uproar that
followed, the pirates made it plain that they
would rather fight to the death than give up
their booty. They had risked their lives for it
once and were quite prepared to do so again.

As the Spanish were in no hurry to come
after Morgan, he took a week to devise a plan.
On 25 April 1669, his fleet, which now comprised thirteen vessels, sailed to within sight of
the Spanish squadron and anchored there.
Suddenly, two days later, they sailed at full speed
into the blockade, led by the Cuban merchant
ship flying an admiral's colours. She headed
straight for Campos's flagship. Coming alongside, she grappled the *Magdalena* and made as
if to board her. But no buccaneers swarmed
over her rail. When the Spaniards finally leapt
over onto her decks, they found that the crew of

just twelve men had leapt overboard on the
other side. The Cuban merchantman was now
manned only by rows of dummies. At that
moment, the Cuban ship burst into flame, completely engulfing the *Magdalena*, forcing
Admiral Campos to leap into the water with his
panic-stricken men to avoid being burnt alive.

Seeing the flagship sinking fast, the
Marquesa and the *San Luis* cut their cables and
ran for the protection of the fort's guns, pursued by the buccaneers. Both ran aground and
their crews set fire to them in an attempt to prevent them being captured by the pirates.
However, Morgan's men managed to put the
fire out on board the *Marquesa* and refloated
her. For all his efforts, Admiral Campos had
simply given the pirates another prize.

The fort still blocked Morgan's escape. It
was now reinforced with seventy militiamen
from the interior and the survivors of Campos's
armada. After another assault by land the next
day was beaten off easily, Morgan sailed back to
Maracaibo and sent a message to Campos, proposing that he swap the Spanish hostages he
held for free passage. This was refused.

*Contemporary engraving
of the great earthquake
which destroyed Port
Royal on 7 June 1692,
an act, many believed,
of divine retribution
for the city's wickedness.*

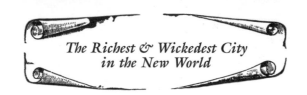

It was then that Morgan discovered from captured sailors that the fort was not as well armed as he thought. Only six of its eleven guns were in working order. So Morgan devised a new plan. A few days later, his fleet returned to the bar and moored just out of range of the guns. Throughout the day, his boats plied back and forth, seemingly landing large amounts of men. In fact, the men simply lay in the bottom of the boats on the return trip and no one was landed at all. However, this fooled the Spaniards into thinking that Morgan was planning another land assault that night and they turned their guns landward. But once it was dark, Morgan's ships simply weighed anchor and sailed out of the lagoon, dropping their captives off on the way.

Morgan returned in triumph to Port Royal again on 27 May 1669. But now it seemed that his career as a privateer was over. The Secretary of State Lord Arlington had reiterated the Crown's directive that all attacks on the Spanish must cease and, on 24 June, Modyford proclaimed that 'the subjects of His Catholic Majesty be from now until further order treated and used as good neighbours and friends'. However, by now the Spanish had grown tired of the repeated attacks of the Port Royal pirates and were determined to have some sort of revenge. On 20 April 1669, in response to Morgan's raid on Portobelo, Queen Mariana, regent of Spain, authorized Spanish officials in the Americas to issue commissions of their own. The Portuguese privateer Manoel Rivero Pardal received a commission from Pedro de Ulloa, governor of Cartagena, and sailed on 3 January 1670 with seventy men on board the *San Pedro*, which was more commonly known as the *Fama*, meaning 'fame' or 'rumour' and colloquially, 'butcher'. Rivero headed for Port Morant, where he had hoped to take slaves, but an unfavourable wind blew him past Jamaica and on to the Cayman Islands. There he burnt down half the fishermen's huts, then headed to Cuba with a canoe, a ketch and four children he had captured. He then learnt that an English privateer was lying off Manzanillo at the southeast end of the island. This was the *Mary and Jane* commanded by Bernard Claesen Speirdyke, Captain Bernard or Captain Bart to the English.

A well-known privateer, Speirdyke had sailed from Port Royal on 19 June 1663 and taken St Thomas, returning on 16 March the following year with plunder he had taken from the Spanish town of Santo Tomás. However, Speirdyke was visiting Cuba on a peace mission. He was returning some Spanish captives and carrying a letter from Governor Modyford to the Cuban authorities 'signifying peace between the two nations'. But, being a privateer, Speirdyke also took the opportunity to sell some smuggled goods clandestinely to the locals. He was just putting out to sea when he was stopped by Rivero, whose ship was flying English colours, and asked where he sailed from.

'Jamaica,' Speirdyke replied.

'Defend yourself, dog,' roared Rivero, striking his colours. 'I come as a punishment for heretics.'

The *Fama* then opened fire and the two ships exchanged fire until dark. The *Mary and Jane* made a run for it that night, but the *Fama* closed and Rivero's men boarded her. But Speirdyke would not surrender even though his eighteen men were outnumbered by more than four to one. Speirdyke – 'an obstinate, mad heretic,' according to Rivero – lay dead along with four of his men before the *Mary and Jane* was safely in Spanish hands.

Rivero sent nine of this captives back to Port Royal with a message saying that he had 'letters of reprisal from the King of Spain for five years throughout the whole West Indies, for satisfaction of the Jamaicans taking Portobelo'. Meanwhile he sailed his prize back to Cartagena, where his triumph was celebrated with a fiesta. Others joined him. Willem Beck, the governor of Dutch Curaçao, sent Modyford a copy of a commission issued to a Francisco Galesio at Santiago de Cuba on 5 February 1670, authorizing the privateer to 'proceed against the English in the Indies with every sort of hostility'. In May, Rivero was at sea again. This time the *Fama* was accompanied by the *Gallardina*, a former French corsair captured by the Spanish two years before. On 11 June they appeared off Jamaica, again flying English colours. They came upon the sloop belonging to William Harris, who was trading along the north side of the island, and pursued him, getting close enough to shout that the English were 'rogues and dogs'. Harris beached his sloop and fired on Rivero's men when they landed. But they managed to refloat her and take her to Cuba, along with a canoe they had captured.

The following week, the *Fama* and the *Gallardina* landed thirty men in Montego Bay who burnt the settlements there before escaping back to Cuba. On 3 July, Rivero returned again,

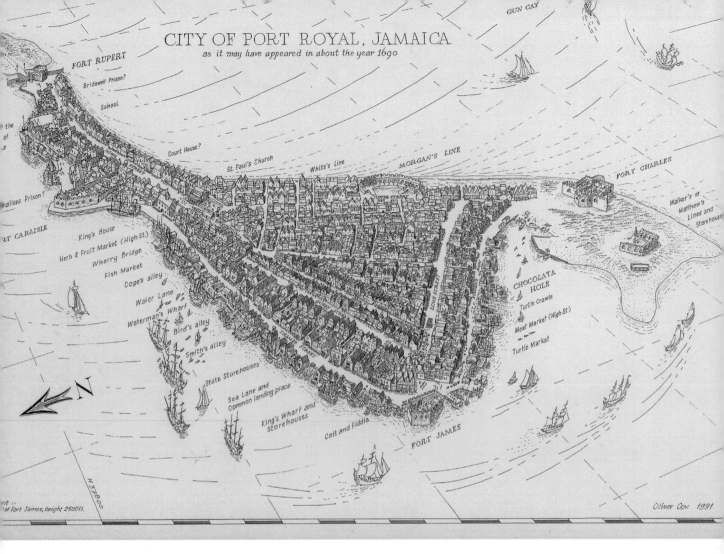

this time with the captured sloop full of new recruits. A troop of mounted militiamen watched them as they stood off, but the following night they landed 50 miles away and burnt a couple of houses. The next night they did the same. This time they left a note issuing a direct challenge to Morgan.

'I come to seek General Morgan with two ships carrying twenty guns,' it read, 'and, having seen this, I crave he will come out upon the coast to seek me, that he might see the valour of the Spaniards.'

Morgan and the Jamaican council did not rise to the challenge. Instead they decided to use it as a pretext for a full-scale attack on the Spanish – even though the Secretary of State was still calling for peace with Spain. Lord Arlington had dismissed the death of Speirdyke in a letter to Modyford as 'not at all to be wondered at after such hostilities as your men have acted on their territories'.

Despite the instructions of the government in London, on 9 July 1670, the island council passed a unanimous motion to commission Morgan 'admiral and commander-in-chief of all the ships of war belonging to this harbour'. He was to drawn them together into one fleet and 'attack, seize and destroy all the enemy's vessels that shall come with his reach'. Morgan set sail on 11 August with eleven ships and 600 men. His flagship was the 120-ton *Satisfaction* now armed with twenty-two guns. But his goal was not Spanish shipping. It was a far greater prize – Panama City, the gold warehouse of the Indies that lay, it was thought safely, on the Pacific side of the isthmus.

Morgan's Assault on Panama

Morgan headed to Tortuga, then to Cow Island, where he would be joined by another twenty-six corsairs carrying 1,400 men. While this huge fleet was assembling, foraging parties were sent out. On 16 September, Collier was sent with six vessels to gather provisions and intelligence from the Spanish Main. At daybreak on 24 October 1670, his flotilla appeared off Ríohacha, Colombia. He landed a shore party which attacked the tiny four-gun fort with such military precision that the garrison assumed they were under attack by regular troops. Among the fort's defenders were the crew of the *Gallardina*, which was lying off shore. Terrified of what would become of them if they fell into English hands, they held out for a day and a night before finally surrendering. Then Collier summarily executed a couple of the inhabitants and tortured the rest for their valu-

The way it was: Port Royal before the earthquake of 1692.

ables. 'In cold blood they did a thousand cursed things,' said a Spanish eyewitness. This process took four weeks, then Collier returned to Cow Island with the *Gallardina*, another captured ship, thirty-eight prisoners and meat and maize.

Meanwhile Captain John Morris and the *Dolphin* were out looking for supplies when a storm forced them to put into a small bay at the eastern end of Cuba. Two hours later, just before dark, Rivero sailed into the bay for shelter. Delighted to see the smaller Jamaican vessel at anchor there, he kept her bottled up for the night and planned to attack just before dawn. But Morris made the first move. He bore down on the *Fama* and boarded her. Rivero was shot in the neck and died. The rest of his crew jumped overboard. Some were killed by Morris's men; others drowned. Only five were taken alive.

There was jubilation at Cow Island when Morris sailed in with the *Fama*. She was quick-

ly renamed the *Lamb* and joined Morgan's fleet. The English privateers were even more thrilled when they learnt that Rivero was dead. One said, 'This is that same vapouring captain that so much amazed Jamaica in burning houses, robbing some people upon the shore, and sent that insolent challenge to Admiral Morgan.'

Even though, with the death of Rivero, the *casus belli* was gone, Morgan saw no reason to alter his plans. By now he had forty ships under his command, carrying over 2,000 English, French and Dutch buccaneers – among them Exquemelin. It was the largest pirate expedition ever mounted. His fleet set sail on 18 December 1670. Though the prize was the riches of Panama City, Morgan stopped off at Providencia Island on the way, which was, once again, in Spanish hands. The Spanish garrison surrendered on Christmas Day without a fight.

Morgan then sent three ships and 470 men – under the command of Joseph Bradley, Rok

Diving on the ruins of Port Royal.

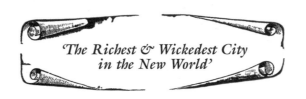
Brasiliano and Erasmus Reyning – ahead to take Fort San Lorenzo at the mouth of the Chagres River. The son of a sailor from Copenhagen, Reyning first went to sea with his father at the age of ten. He saw action against both the French and the English in the North Sea. His father was killed during the First Anglo-Dutch War (1652–1654). Reyning himself was captured during the Second Anglo-Dutch War (1665–1667) and was imprisoned in Ireland for eighteen months. After a brief reunion with his wife and child, he sailed for Surinam. With six other men, he was supposed to re-establish the Dutch colony there, which had been overrun by the French who had, in turn, been ousted by the English. When the French returned, they took Reyning to Martinique as a prisoner. He served briefly as boatman to the retiring governor, Robert Le Frichot des Friches, and accompanied him as far as Tortuga on his passage home. There he deserted, first working as a farm hand on a plantation on Saint Domingue. Then he was sold as an indentured servant to a buccaneer, but quickly regained his freedom. He went to sea again and, at the Cayman Islands, he met one Captain Casten of Amsterdam who was careening his ship. Casten carried commissions from Port Royal and Reyning signed up. They sailed for Aruba but, taking a Spanish prize, went to Port Royal to dispose of it. There Reyning joined Brasiliano and de Lecat when they bought a brigantine from l'Olonnais.

Reyning landed with Bradley and Brasiliano within sight of the fortifications at San Lorenzo at noon on 6 January 1671. Four hundred men disembarked and approached the fort 'with flags and trumpets'. San Lorenzo was defended by 360 men, under Pedro de Elizalde, who had told his men 'Even if the English were to come, they would not capture this castle.'

Reyning was in the first charge on the castle that afternoon. His company met such a withering hail of fire that Brasiliano reported that they had all been killed. Miraculously Reyning survived. The second wave was also cut down. But as the sun was setting Bradley led his men down some gullies. They crept close enough to the fortifications to toss grenades and firepots inside, setting the wooden stockade ablaze. Throughout the night the fire spread, destroying the defences and detonating the magazines. In the darkness, some 150 Spanish soldiers deserted. Even so, there were enough left to beat off Bradley's first assault the following morning. But eventually some French buccaneers from Tortuga fought their way inside with cutlasses. By this time Bradley lay fatally wounded, but he could hear the cries of 'Victoire, Victoire.' Elizalde and the remaining defenders fought on to the last man. Thirty buccaneers were dead and another seventy-six wounded – including Brasiliano and Bradley, who had been shot through both legs. He died five days later as Morgan and his main force hove into view on 12 January.

Morgan was a great tactician and a brave fighter, but he was no great seaman. As the *Satisfaction* led the rest of the fleet into San Lorenzo, she struck a reef and sank, along with the next four ships behind her. Ten men were drowned, however, the wreckage was used to help rebuild the fort, where Morgan stationed 300 men under Captain Richard Norman. Morgan then organized the construction of thirty-six canoes, which carried 1,400 of his best men up the Chagres River. They took with them as many provisions as they could carry, hoping to purchase or plunder more from the villages upstream. But the inhabitants shrank away in front of this invading army. Morgan's men marched through the jungle for seven days without any food. Some were reduced to boiling and eating their leather satchels and shoes. They were ravaged by fever and dysentery and, in their weakened state, fell prey to ambushes. Two hundred men perished on the journey. But eventually at nine o'clock on the morning of 27 January they reached the top of a hill and saw 'that desired place, the South Sea'. Below them they could see Panama City. The men were greatly heartened by the sight of a great treasure ship in the distance with smaller ships alongside. Only later did they learn that it was carrying away nearly five million pieces of eight. Its consorts were also transporting gold and jewels to safety.

Around noon, Morgan and his men came upon a great plain filled with cattle. They stopped to slaughter and eat them. Making camp within sight of the tiled roofs of Panama City, they slept well with full stomachs. At dawn on 28 January, they awoke to make their final march on the city, but found 2,000 Spanish infantrymen flanked by two cavalry companies of 300 men apiece under the command of the governor of Panama Juan Pérez de Guzmán drawn up in front of them. Though Morgan's

pirates were vastly outnumbered, they were undaunted. They advanced on the enemy behind 'red and green banners and flags, clearly visible to the Spaniards'. Morgan figured that having the rising sun behind them would work to their great advantage.

Guzmán sent in the cavalry, who charged on the buccaneers in a fast but undisciplined gallop. The first fusillade brought down a hundred of them. Then the Spanish infantry advanced, while Indians stampeded the remaining cattle at the buccaneers' rear. But still the pirates held their nerve and their accurate musket fire blunted both charges. When the Spanish infantrymen got within range of the buccaneers, they fired one volley, then threw down the muskets and ran, leaving four or five hundred dead on the battlefield. The buccaneers had lost just fifteen.

Rather than let the city of Panama fall into the hands of Morgan's buccaneers, the Spanish set fire to it, killing anyone left behind, then fled

Rather than let the city fall into the buccaneers' hands, the Spaniards set fire to it – in such a hurry to blow up the fort, they killed the forty soldiers who were still inside – then fled. The populace had already taken to the woods. Morgan's men entered the city unopposed and extinguished the fires, but three-quarters of the city had already been levelled, including the houses of its wealthiest citizens and its richly-stocked warehouses.

Morgan stayed in Panama City for four weeks, sending parties out to find those who had fled. They were cruelly tortured, but rendered little, as most of the city's wealth had been removed on the ships the pirates had seen. Ironically, Morgan missed the greatest prize that the city had to offer, and which remained in place in their midst throughout the occupation. A cunning friar had slapped a coat of whitewash over the altar in the cathedral. It was made of solid gold.

However, the Spanish did pay a ransom for the captives Morgan had taken and the booty amounted to 750,000 pieces of eight, some doubloons, ingots of gold and silver, gems, pearls, silks and spices. This was loaded onto 175 mules and carried back across the isthmus to San Lorenzo. There it was divided up. Each man's share amounted to 200 pieces of eight – around £18 a head – which few considered suf-

ficient reward for all they had suffered. There was also friction between the French, who were largely Catholic, and the English, who were Protestant. One faction had secretly provisioned a ship for an independent expedition into the South Seas. Morgan scuttled it. There followed an outright rebellion, with the buccaneers claiming that Morgan had kept the lion's share of the booty for himself.

Morgan sailed off on Bradley's boat, the *Mayflower*, with no goodbyes. The rest of his pirate army split up. Exquemelin headed off on a ship that plundered the coasts of Costa Rica and Cuba, before returning to Jamaica. Reyning had a couple of brushes with the Spanish, before coming upon a Dutch merchantman, *Witte Lam* (White Lamb), in Montego Bay. On board was his brother-in-law who had a letter for him. Reyning arranged passage back to Holland to see his family, but his farewell party grew so boisterous that the master of the *Witte Lam* slipped quietly away without him. Reyning continued his career in piracy in the Caribbean for the next twenty-seven years. When the English authorities turned against piracy, he simply marooned the Englishmen in his crew on the tiny island of Tris, where they were eventually rescued by the former privateer Lilly. With de Lecat, Reyning went to work for the Spanish, even converting to Catholicism to clinch the deal. He died when his ship ran aground in dirty weather in the Bay of Biscay in 1697. Although he has long since been forgotten in his native Holland, he is still remembered in Curaçao where local legend maintains that he left buried treasure in caves along the coast.

When Morgan returned to Port Royal at the sacking of Panama in April 1671, there was official jubilation and the island's council passed a vote of thanks. However, Charles II was not pleased. He had signed a new treaty with Madrid. Spain threatened war if the pirates who had attacked Panama were not punished immediately and HMS *Assistance* and *Welcome* were despatched to the Caribbean. They arrived in Port Royal in July 1671 carrying a new gover-

nor for the island, Sir Thomas Lynch, who was an advocate of peaceful trade with the Spanish. Morgan and Modyford were transported back to London in chains. Modyford was assured that 'his life and estate were not in danger', though he was imprisoned in the Tower. For the first year, he was kept in a cell, then he was given the liberty of the grounds. He was never brought to trial and released in 1674. Returning to Jamaica as chief justice in 1675, he died there in 1679 and is buried in the Cathedral in Spanish Town.

A Rehabilitated Pirate

Morgan was not imprisoned at all on the grounds that he was 'very sickly'. Instead, he lived in London in grand style at his own expense. He was lionized by the public and got the young Duke of Albemarle to intercede with the king on his behalf. In the summer of 1672, the Third Anglo-Dutch War (1672–1674) broke out. Hostilities with the Spanish resumed and Morgan was asked to write a report on Jamaica's security.

In January 1674, Lynch was replaced as governor by John Vaughan, Earl of Carlisle (said to have been 'one of the lewdest fellows of the age' – no mean feat in Restoration England) with Morgan as his deputy. Morgan needed a fitting title to take up his new post, so he was knighted.

Back in Jamaica, Morgan sat as a judge on the Admiralty Court, which was supposed to try pirates, boasting, 'I have put to death, imprisoned and transported to the Spaniard for execution all English and Spanish pirates I could get.'

Few people believed him. Although Morgan was now, ostensibly, a respectable plantation owner, Vaughan suspected that he was clandestinely arranging private commissions with his old friend Governor d'Ogeron of Saint Domingue and taking ten per cent of the profits. At that time, English pirates were carrying out so many commissions from the French that Charles II condemned Jamaica as a 'Christian Algiers'.

The rough-edged Morgan did not get on with the aristocratic Governor Vaughan, who brought him up before the Jamaican council on a number of charges. But Morgan was repeatedly exonerated due to his popularity, while Vaughan's haughty manner continually rubbed the buccaneers and council up the wrong way. However, Morgan spent more and more of his time in Port Royal's taverns and was eventually suspended from office for being a drunk.

As a young man Sir Hans Sloane, later the founder of the British Museum, was a doctor in Port Royal. In his West Indian journals, which with his other books formed the basis of the British Library, Sloane described Morgan as 'lean, sallow coloured, his eyes a little yellowish and belly jutting out or prominent'. He was certainly not the dashing pirate of old. 'Not being able to abstain from company, he was much given to drinking and sitting up late,' Sloane said. The result – dropsy. Sloane prescribed a series of purges and diuretics, including scorpion oil, but Morgan continued his mammoth drinking bouts. 'Falling after into his old course of life and not taking any advice to the contrary, his belly swelled so as not to be contained by his coat.' He preferred to be treated by a black obeah [African voodoo] man who plied him with 'clysters of urine, and plastered him all over with clay and water, and by it did augment his cough'. Morgan died soon after on 25 August 1688, leaving his wife of twenty years a sugar plantation of several thousand acres and over £5,000. By this time Vaughan had been replaced by Morgan's patron, the Duke of Albermarle, who ordered a state funeral. Morgan's body was paraded through the streets of Port Royal on a gun carriage. He was buried in the churchyard of St Peters, whose construction several years earlier had been funded by Morgan. This was not entirely a selfless act of Christian charity as the church had a tall tower that provided an excellent look-out point over the approaches to the harbour. As Morgan was laid to rest, Captain Wright on board HMS *Assistance* in the harbour ordered the firing of a twenty-two-gun salute. HMS *Drake* followed suit, as did all the merchantmen in the harbour.

The death of Henry Morgan marked the end of an era. Just four years later, on 7 June 1692, Port Royal was devastated by an earthquake. Much of the city, which by then had 8,000 inhabitants, sank into the sea, which finally claimed the bones of the great buccaneer. The pirate port that had brought him fame was no more and the few survivors built on the site of present-day Kingston, across the Bay.

CHAPTER FIVE

THE WEAPONS

A terrified victim was an easy victim, and inspiring terror was easier for a pirate armed to the teeth. This chapter examines what the well-armed pirate of the seventeenth and eighteenth century would have sported in his belt.

To fight for a prize ship, or better yet to scare the crew into surrendering without much of a fight, it was essential to be well-armed. Most weapons used by pirates were the same as those in common use among the other seafarers of the times – indeed, they were stolen from them. But pirates loved to festoon themselves with stolen weapons to put the fear of God into their victims.

The Cutlass

The cutlass was a rough, heavy, broad-bladed singled-edged sword usually about two feet long. It was thought to have derived from the long knives the original buccaneers used to butcher meat. Although originally developed for use on land – indeed, many employed in agriculture and forestry in the Caribbean or Central America still carry one – the cutlass became perfectly adapted to life at sea. The blade was usually slightly curved and sharpened on the outer side. It resembled a sabre, only the blade was slightly heavier and shorter – nothing like the elegantly curved, silver-basketted, shark-skin-gripped, dress sword that was fashionable among officers in the Royal Navy.

The short blade was not a disadvantage when fighting aboard a ship. With all the rigging and clutter on board deck, there was usually little room to swing a longer sword. The shorter blade allowed the cutlass to be sturdier without adding to the overall weight. A single blow with a heavy cutlass would snap an officer's fancy sword in two. It was so successful that navies around the world copied the design.

When fighting, the cutlass was used like a sabre to slash or hack at the opponent. Hacking meant that you could just as easily put your opponent out of action by chopping off his hand rather than running him through. The curving blade also made the cutlass easier to control while hacking. It kept more of the sharp edge of the blade in contact, helping it to slice through the flesh, and the thickness allowed it cleave through muscle and bone. Of course the curving blade made the cutlass slightly less effective as a thrusting or stabbing weapon like a rapier or sword. But a hacking blow can be performed more quickly than a thrust, and with a thrust there was always the danger of getting your blade stuck, leaving you defenceless.

With its short, heavy blade, the cutlass also functioned as a tool, which could be used to cut through heavy marlin lines, hack down heavy ship's hatches, and slaughter and chop up livestock. A man could fell a tree with a cutlass. They were also used to open coconuts, strike a spark to start a fire, skin a cow, split an anchor cable or slice an opponent in two.

Knives

There were a wide variety of knives on board ships. They were used to cut rope and sail, as well as cutlery. Any knife could be used as a last line of defence, though pirates usually carried dirks, mains gauche, stilettos, poignards and other types of dagger specifically designed for fighting. These had sharp points and were designed to be thrust at an opponent. They were not very effective for slashing, although typically both sides of the blade had an edge.

Daggers have hilts and cross bars like a sword. These prevent the hand from slipping forward on to the blade and prevent another blade sliding down the dagger's blade in a knife or sword fight, protecting the hand. The design

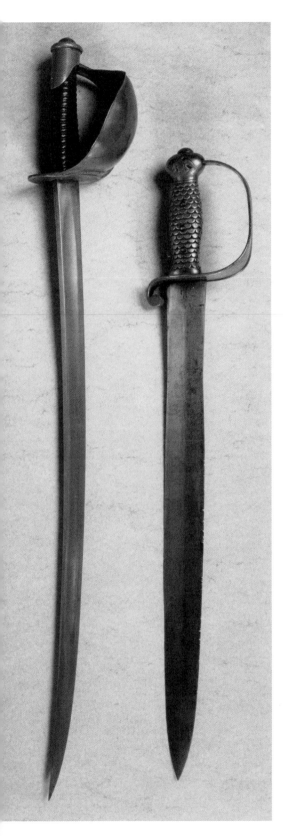

of some daggers borrows from the dainty art of fencing where knives were used to parry an attack and keep the opponent off guard. Many daggers were specially designed to break the blade of an opponent's sword. These were called parrying daggers or blade-breakers.

In sword fights, the sword was often used to make an opening or to push an opponent off balance. Then with the opponent in an exposed position, the dagger was thrust in for the kill. But pirates usually worked the other way around. A sword would be parried or blocked with the dagger, keeping the cutlass free for the counter blow.

Seamen often carried a big knife called a gully which was not specifically a fighting knife but could be used as such in a pinch. They were similar to the knives found in kitchens today, though some folded like modern pocket knives. The gully was better suited for hacking than stabbing. Typically only one side of the blade had an edge, though sometimes part of the other side of the blade was also sharpened. Gullies had numerous legitimate uses on board a ship, everything from cutting fouled rigging to being the sailor's eating utensil. As they were in day-to-day use among sailors they were quite often used in mutinies.

Other knives of a more offensive nature were common among sailing vessels in the Caribbean. The most common of these was a 'boucan' knife used by the original buccaneers to cut up the wild pig and oxen killed on the islands around Santa Domingo and Jamaica. They came in all sizes and shapes and looked like cut-down cutlasses. Although these knives were still primarily utilitarian, they could be used very effectively in combat. They were primarily designed to hack or slash an opponent as opposed to stabbing.

The Marlinespike

Another favoured weapon of mutineers was the marlinespike, or marlingspike. It had a round blade with a sharp point. Mounted in a round wooden handle it was quite similar to an ice pick used when preparing cocktails. More a tool than a weapon, it was designed to be used to separate strands in marlines – that is, the two lines of tarred rope loosely coiled around each other in a left hand turn used on board ship. They were also used to anchor lines to the ship's wooden superstructure.

Short sword of the type known as a hanger (right), compared with the more elegant but more delicate naval sabre (left).

Most captains locked weapons away for fear of mutinies. But marlinespikes had to be available to the crew for the ship to function, and they could provide a dangerous stabbing weapon.

The Pike

Hand-pikes or halberd disappeared from land warfare with the introduction of the bayonet in the seventeenth century, but they were used by the Spanish in the New World long after. They were also retained as a naval boarding weapon into the nineteenth century and were racked along the bulwarks of fighting ships.

Pikes were metal-pointed spears with a heavy wooden shaft ten to twenty feet long. They could be thrown at a target or used as a stabbing weapon in close combat. Their length made them an effective weapon against swords and knives while boarding. They were then discarded as they were too cumbersome for hand-to-hand fighting on deck. Eventually they were replaced as accurate firearms were introduced.

Axe of the type commonly used by sailors as a weapon when boarding enemy ships.

The Axe

Boarding axes were used by the pirates to help climb the sides of a ship and cut through the rigging lines. They were also handy in opening closed doors and hatches. And they could be used as a deadly weapon in close combat.

They were also employed in a defensive role. When being boarded, grappling hooks with lines would be ·tossed from ship to ship in order to pull them together. An axe was the most effective way to cut these lines and repel boarders.

Typically a boarding axe was pretty much a standard long-handled axe with a wooden handle around two to three feet long and a two pound iron – later steel – head. This was sharpened on one side and flattened on the other so that it could be used as a sledge hammer. They were not designed to be thrown. However, some American pirates used tomahawks or throwing hatchets. The term 'tomahawk' was a derivation of the Virginia Algonquian word 'tomahack'. Originally these Native North American hand axes had a stone head, but Colonial Americans traders, trappers and explorers replaced this with a metal one and came to rely on the tomahawk as standard equipment.

Tomahawks are smaller and lighter than boarding axes and could be thrown or used instead of a dagger as a parrying weapon. While not as good at cutting rigging or breaking down doors as boarding axes, they were easier to wield in close quarter combat.

The Musket

Among the 'Brethren of the Coast', the musket was a prized possession and the Spaniards believed the 'boucans' to be the best musket shots in the world.

A musket was a good sniping weapon in the right hands and could be used to clear the decks of a prize ship before an attempt was made at boarding. Fired together in a volley, heavy muskets were as effective as a cannon shot. They were also valuable in repelling boarders. Pirates also used them to hunt game when they journeyed on land and they were effective weapons in sacking towns, ambushing Spanish gold trains or facing Spanish militiamen.

In the sixteenth and seventeenth centuries, huge numbers of muskets were made for the European armies. Many found their way to the Caribbean where they could be bought or stolen by pirates. However, storing and issuing numerous different sizes of ball was an unnecessary complication if each man on board ship carried his own musket. It was best that all the muskets come from the same source, so that they had the same calibre. When a prize ship was taken, great efforts were made to standardize, or at least rationalize the pirates' armoury.

Muskets are loaded through the muzzle, rather than through the breech as in a modern rifle, and the charge and ball would be loaded separately. Pirate marksmen were skilled at knowing how much powder their weapon required and how heavily it should be tamped. Often they made up a dozen charges consisting of powder, wad and shot before a battle. They were known as 'apostles' – either for their number or the prayer that accompanied each of them – and were kept in small woollen or leather purses strung on a cross-belt. During the seventeenth century more reliable wheel-lock firing mechanisms were taking over from the flintlock. Rifling – a spiral groove cut inside the barrel that gave spin to the bullet – was also being introduced, which made muskets more accurate. However, rifled muskets took longer to reload than those that were smooth-bored.

On board ship, one of the biggest drawback of a musket was its size, usually around 5 feet long. They were usually fired at close quarters when the pirate ship was moving in on its prey, then discarded as the pirates boarded. This was because two hands were needed to fire a musket, while a pistol could be fired one-handed. Muskets were also more difficult and time-consuming to reload, and it was only possible to carry one musket, while pirates often carried a belt full of pistols.

A musketoon was a shorter version of the musket. This was less accurate but was easier to use when fighting at close quarters where accu-

Trade musket from the eighteenth century, showing flintlock firing mechanism.

racy was not a priority. However, musketoons were not very reliable as they had the standard flintlock firing mechanism of the day and, because of their size, only one could be carried into battle. Again, in hand-to-hand fighting, the cutlass and the dagger had the advantage as they never ran out of ammunition.

The Blunderbuss

Like the musketoon, the blunderbuss was a close range weapon. It was a large calibre gun with a bore of around 1 ½ to 2 inches. Some fired a very large ball while others fired several small ones or a large number of shotgun pellets. On the crowded deck of a ship it could kill and maim several people with a single blast, in effect more like a hand-held cannon than a rifle.

The purpose of the blunderbuss was to deliver a large amount of fire power over a large area, so the end of the barrel was funnel-shaped to help spread the shot. In fact, this was ineffective and did little to improve the scatter of the shot, but it did make the blunderbuss look a fearsome weapon. They were in use from as early as 1530 until at least 1840 when the Royal Mail coach service placed an order for several flintlock blunderbusses.

Pair of eighteenth-century blunderbusses. Although ineffective at long range, the blunderbuss was a terrifying weapon at close quarters.

Blunderbusses ranged in length from 14 to about 30 inches. Some were actually large bore pistols, but most had at least a small stock. However, they were not designed to be fired from the shoulder like a musket. Instead the stock was braced against the hip or held firmly between the forearm and side of the body to absorb the enormous kick of the gun. The weapon usually had no sights, so there would have been no point in attempting to shoulder fire the gun.

At close range the blunderbuss would have been quite deadly. The spread from the gun could quite easily be as much as 1 or 2 feet at a distance of 10 to 20 feet from the muzzle, and perhaps as much as 6 to 10 feet at a range of 30 or 40 feet. It would have been ineffective at any greater range, but on a sloop or a man-of-war, this would have been more than enough.

Like the musket and other firearms of the time, the blunderbuss was difficult and slow to reload. In hand-to-hand fighting it would not have been possible to fire more than one shot. After that it was little more than a cumbersome club and it would have been difficult to wield a cutlass in the right hand while holding a blunderbuss in the left. Some blunderbusses were fitted with a folding bayonet which ran along

the top of the barrel. This too was ineffective, since the barrel was too short to make it a useful thrusting or stabbing weapon.

A man leading a boarding party might have started with a mighty blast from a blunderbuss before attacking with his cutlass, not least because of the psychological effect of its huge roar and shot spraying all over the deck. However, the blunderbuss excelled in repelling boarders. It was also an effective weapon against mutineers, though there is no record of any pirate captain that favoured using one in normal combat.

Blunderbusses were never made in large numbers. This was probably because, no matter how effective they were on board ship, such a small, compact weapon had no real place on the battlefields of Europe.

Pistols

Pirates prized the pistol above all other weapons. They came in a wide variety of shapes and sizes, and were not of equal value. There were run-of-the-mill pistols, mass-produced for cavalry troops and some naval personnel. However, at the time, pistol-making was an art form and gunsmiths would make them to order. A ship's captain, for example, would often have a pair pistol commissioned as a mark of rank.

As well as paying special attention to the workmanship of the barrel and firing mechanism, the gunsmith would decorate the stock with silver and gold or ornate carvings. The dog-head, or hammer, would be carved in some ornate fashion or perhaps be shaped like a lion or a unicorn or some animal from the ancestral crest of the owner. French cavalry officers' pistols were much prized among pirates.

Captains used them as an incentive in forming boarding parties. The first man on board a prize would get first choice of any weapon they plundered, over and above his share of the booty. Volunteering to be the first man in a boarding party was almost suicidal. Typically the defenders would prepare several ranks to fire a fusillade which would cut down the first wave of a boarding party. Even if you survived that, you would be left to fight outnumbered until the second wave arrived.

Pistols were also muzzle-loaders, but they were relatively easy to reload as the barrel was short. And again a pistol with a rifled barrel was harder to reload than a smooth bore. Many people

tried to find ways of making breech-loaders but, until the development of a self-contained cartridge, most breech-loading weapons were unreliable at best.

Firing Mechanisms

During the time pirates were active in the Caribbean, the firing mechanisms of muskets and pistols underwent a transition. They started with the matchlock, which was largely confined to larger, shoulder-fired weapons, though a few pistols were made using this mechanism. A slow-burning fuse, or match, was attached to a serpentine, the equivalent of the cock or hammer. This was cocked back and small pan was filled with priming powder. When the trigger was released, the serpentine dropped the fuse into the priming pan, setting off the priming powder. The flash travelled through the touch hole in the side of the barrel, igniting the main charge and the weapon fired. This worked poorly, if at all, in the rain and was clearly unsuitable for use at sea.

Next came the wheel-lock which eliminated the use of a fuse. A small wheel of pyrites or flint was attached to a spring that was wound up like the spring of a clock. In this case, the serpentine carried a small piece of metal instead of a fuse. When you pulled the trigger, the spring was released and the wheel spun around. As the serpentine descended, the metal made contact producing sparks which fell into the priming pan and set off the charge.

Next came the snaphance, or snaphaunce. This basically put the pyrites in the serpentine, by now referred to as a dog-head or hammer. As the dog-head descended, the pyrites struck a steel plate or frizzen, which caused sparks to fall in the priming tray, firing the weapon.

Next came the flintlock, used on most of the pistols seen in the Caribbean during the golden age of piracy. Here flint struck against the frizzen in the same way as the snaphance, but there were a number of refinements. The frizzen was combined with a pan cover, which protected the powder in the priming pan before the gun was fired. They formed one spring-loaded unit. The gun could also be half-cocked, which provided a sort of safety catch.

Before firing a flintlock, the pistoleer would pull the dog-head back until it made a noticeable click. This was the half-cocked position. Priming powder would be poured down the

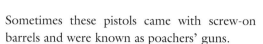

barrel. This was ground smaller and smoother than regular gunpowder. Quite often it contained more saltpetre, or sodium nitrate, making it easier to ignite. It was carried in a powder horn. Next, regular black power – gunpowder – was poured in. This was made from saltpetre, charcoal and sulphur. There were many ways that it was made giving different strengths, but all of it was weak by today's standards. If the high-quality powder used in today's small arms had been used in a flintlock of the 1700s it would probably have blown up.

Wadding was forced down the barrel, followed by the shot, or ball. The powder, wadding and ball were compacted using a small rammer or ramrod. In some cases the rammer, an integral part of the gun without which it could not be used, was attached to the pistol with a swivel so it could not be lost.

The 'Saturday Night Special' of the eighteenth century was the pocket pistol: small, easily-concealed, and deadly at close range

To speed loading, charges were often prepared ahead of time and wrapped in paper waddings and carried in a special cartridge pouch. The paper was torn open at the powder end and the powder poured down the barrel.

Once the pistol was loaded, a small amount of priming powder would be added to the priming pan, insuring that the touch hole that connected the pan to the barrel was filled. Because the frizzen and priming pan were now one spring loaded unit, it was now possible to load a flintlock beforehand.

By pulling the dog-head back another click, the pistol would be armed and ready to fire. A pull of the trigger would release the dog-head and fire the gun.

The barrel of a pistol was usually between 4 and 10 inches long and flintlocks of the time had a metal cap on the bottom of a pistol's grip as a counter balance. So once a pistol had been fired this could be used as a club. On more expensive weapons, this cap would often carry engraved designs or was inlaid with precious metal or jewels.

Long-barrelled pistols with shoulder stocks added were called pistol carbines, but in every other respect they were standard pistols. They were popular among poachers and highwaymen because they could be concealed easily.

Sometimes these pistols came with screw-on barrels and were known as poachers' guns.

One early form of breech-loading flintlock was called a 'turn-out pistol'. The barrel of the pistol unscrewed, allowing the powder and shot to be loaded into the firing chamber. Once the shot was loaded the barrel was screwed back on. This was easier and safer to load because the shot and powder did not have to be pushed all the way down the barrel. The wadding could also be discarded and no rammer was needed. In every other respect the turnout pistol worked in the same manner as a regular flintlock pistol but the barrel could be rifled to improve accuracy.

Some pistols were made with the lock on the left side of the gun instead of the right. These were known as left-handed pistols, though the design did not to make it safer or easier to fire the pistol with the left hand. Virtually any pistol could be fired just as easily with either hand. However, the left-handed lock made it easier to draw the pistol with the left hand. Most people tended to wield their sword or cutlass with the right hand, which meant that often the left hand became the pistol hand. When you tuck a flint-lock pistol into a belt it is safer and more comfortable to have the lock facing out. It also helps prevent the lock snagging on clothing as the pistol is drawn. And if you tuck a right-handed lock into a belt in a position suitable for drawing it with the left hand, the jagged lock is pressed against your belly. Putting the lock on the opposite side solved that problem, which made left-handed pistols popular among pirates.

The 'Saturday Night Special' of the seventeenth and eighteenth century was the pocket pistol. This was smaller and easily concealed. A larger version was the overcoat pistol, but it too was designed to be concealed. The common feature of these pistols was that the dog-head was centred on the pistol like the hammer on modern-day pistols instead of to one side and the priming pan and frizzen mounted internally. This type of design is known as the box lock. The box lock was more difficult and expensive to produce than a typical side-mounted flintlock. It also prevented aiming straight down the barrel of a pistol or rifle, so could only be used at extremely close range. Box locks were loaded in the same manner as any other muzzle-loading pistol. However, in the pocket pistol, the ramrod was not attached to the gun and was concealed separately.

Flintlocks were usually single-shot pistols,

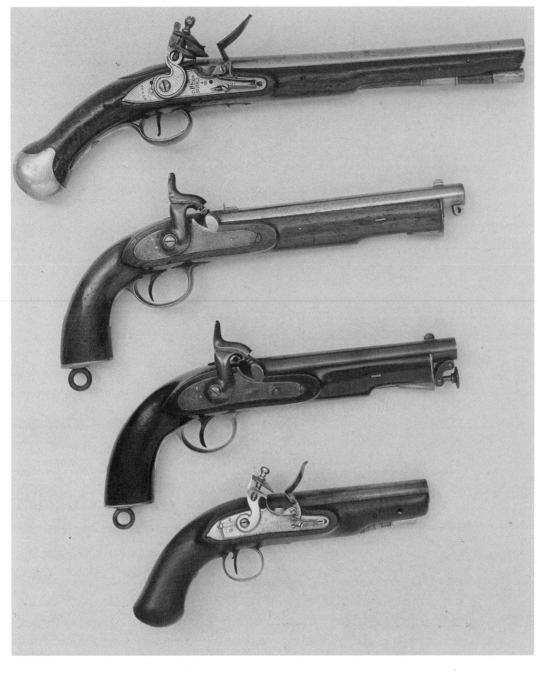

Various pistols of the eighteenth and nineteenth century: Flintlock sea service pistol; Rifled percussion pistol Percussion pistol for Indian service; Flintlock pistol.

but there were also multi-barrelled versions. In most cases double-barrelled pistols employed two separate locks, one for each barrel. The locks were arranged on one side of the gun where the barrels were arranged vertically or on either side where they were arranged horizontally. If one trigger was used, a slight pull would fire the first barrel and a second heavier pull would fire the other barrel. In some cases only one dog-head would be cocked at a time and the trigger would be pulled normally. Sometimes two triggers were employed. Multi-shot pistols were popular but also heavy and expensive to produce and sometimes unreliable.

Another way to get a multi-shot gun employed one lock and two or more rotating barrels. This was known as a turnover pistol. In this case each barrel had one lock but they were fired using a single dog-head. The barrels were loaded, the dog-head cocked and the first barrel was discharged. Then the barrel was turned over. The dog-head was cocked again and the second barrel was now ready for firing. Other methods used rotating taps. A tap was turned, exposing a different barrel's touch hole to the same priming pan.

While the multi-barrelled pistol was designed to fire one shot at a time, the volley pistol was designed to fire several barrels at once, so they were all attached to the same lock.

The barrels would fan out at different angles spreading the shot. When the trigger was pulled all the barrels would fire at once. Volley pistols often had four or five barrels. They were only effective at very close range and were difficult to load and fire.

While volley pistols were rare, volley rifles were more common and were a forerunner of the machine gun. However, they only became really practical when breech-loading and metal cartridges were introduced, long after the golden age of piracy was over.

Armed and Dangerous

The fully armed pirate would have been an awesome sight. His cutlass or 'hanger' would be hung constantly at his side. He would have worn broad leather cross-belts, usually over a dirty velvet coat, on which he hung his 'apostles'. Swinging at his sides would be a number of pistols, each hung on a silken sash and a number of knives would be shoved in his belt. Initially he would carry a musket, but this would be tossed aside when boarding ships.

He would wear a sweatband or kerchief tied

Three gun decks of a 100-gun first-rate warship, (see Chapter 6) HMS Victory, *bristle with cannon. The total weight of a broadside would have been over a ton – enough to sink all but the largest of ships.*

around his forehead to keep sweat out of his eyes. Over it, he would wear a tricorn hat, if he had one. His face would be blackened with the powder from his musket or the ship's great guns. He would certainly be unwashed. If he had been at sea for any length of time, his teeth would have dropped out and he would be unlikely to possess a full set of eyes, ears, hands and feet. Any resemblance to Errol Flynn or Douglas Fairbanks is, frankly, unlikely.

Cannon

Like small arms, naval artillery was developing throughout the sixteenth, seventeenth and eighteenth centuries. When Columbus made his voyage to the Caribbean, naval guns were the same guns that were used on land. A field gun would have its wheels removed and the barrel in its frame would be lashed down on the upper decks and there was no way to sight them.

The end of the sixteenth century saw the birth of naval artillery. Guns were now mounted on small two- or four-wheeled carriages, making them portable. The muzzle-loaded barrel was attached to the carriage with a trunnion or pivot, allowing the elevation to be adjusted.

Although chase guns were placed at the bow and stern of the ship, most of the guns were placed on the side of a ship and on the larger ships as many as fifty guns were carried. The main tactic for attacking another ship was to show the side of your ship to the foe and deliver a broadside, firing all of the guns down one side of the ship simultaneously. The key to success was to do this without allowing your enemy to do the same to you. Consequently, naval warfare became a matter of tactics.

In the seventeenth century naval ships began carrying as many as a hundred guns on three separate decks and huge forty-two-pounder guns were often the standard gun on the bottom decks. The 'pounder' rating of a gun referred to the size of shot it fires. A six-pounder fired a solid shot of lead which weighed approximately six pounds, and a thirty-two pounder fired a ball of lead that weighed approximately thirty-two pounds.

Naturally, the larger the shot, the heavier the gun, the larger the bore size and the more powder needed to propel it. For example, a two-pounder had a bore-size of 2 ½ inches; the gun weighed 600 pounds and it needed 3 ½ pounds of gunpowder. A six-pounder had a 3-inch bore, weighed between 1,000 and 1,500 pounds and needed 6 pounds of gunpowder. A twenty-four pounder had a 4 ½-inch bore, weighed between 3,000 and 4,000 pounds and needed 14 pounds of powder. And a thirty-two pounder had a 5-inch bore, weighed between 4,000 and 5,000 pounds and needed 18 pounds of powder. The weight ratio of powder to shot decreases as the shot gets larger and working out the precise amount of powder needed for any particular shot became an exact science in the eighteenth century when naval gunners also became masters in the science of trajectory.

Most of the weight of the gun was centred around the breech of the gun where the explosion takes place and most of the pressure is exerted. Large guns wore out relatively fast, usually being good for between 500 and 1,000 shots before being considered unsafe.

The weight of the cannon had to significantly increase as the size of the shot increased and it was easy to overload a ship. Strong decks were required to carry the weight of large guns and the ship's structure had to be strong enough to absorb the simultaneous and repeated recoil of the guns. It was also dangerous to carry heavy guns high above the waterline. Over-gunned ships could easily turn turtle and sink; the best-known example of this being perhaps the flagship of Henry VIII, the *Mary Rose*.

The biggest guns had an effective range of about 2,000 yards, although most engagements were fought at a range of 1,000 yards or less, and sometimes within pistol range, which was fifty to twenty-five yards.

Pirate sloops would usually carry just two cannon, one on either side of the main deck, as pirates were not keen on artillery duels. They did not want to damage a prize ship that might be their next home and, if possible, they tried to outrun the navy ships sent against them. They could not hope to match the skill of navy gunnery teams whose discipline was instilled with the lavish use of the cat-o'-nine-tails – neither discipline nor the cat-o'-nine tails appealed much to pirates.

They would usually fire a warning shot across the bow of a merchantman. If that failed to stop her, chain shot – cannon balls joined together with lengths of chain – would be fired through the rigging, in an attempt to dislodge a spar or two and slow the prize ship down enough to board her.

In the eighteenth century, most ships carried

cast-iron muzzle-loaders ranging from the small six-pounders to the large thirty-two-pounders, which would be carried on the lowest gundeck. Pirate ships would favour eight- or twelve-pounders which were easier to handle with an undisciplined crew.

On the crowded gun decks, recoil was a problem. Although the heavy wooden truck the gun was mounted in and its small wheels were designed to prevent them running backwards, they slipped easily across the smooth, wet, oaken decks. To get around this problem, the guns were secured to the sides of the ships by heavy breech ropes passed through or around the cascabels at the back of the gun. A system of ropes and blocks limited the recoil. Side tackle was also added, along with a small ramp behind the gun to help haul it back to the gunport once it had been reloaded.

Battle at sea: Danish pirate Peter Thordenskjold in a small hoy (l) takes on and defeats a much larger Swedish frigate.

Artillery Rounds

In the seventeenth century special shots or artillery rounds were developed especially for naval use. These were designed to destroy rigging and sails, or specifically to kill the crew.

One of the most effective was chain shot. Two or three cast iron balls were linked by a length of chain. The balls were loaded down the barrel one at a time. Once fired, their behaviour in the air was somewhat erratic, but when they hit something solid they caused major damage. If one of them broke through a deck, the other ball would rip back violently in the opposite direction. They would wrap themselves around the mast and reduce it to splinters, take out rigging and sails.

Bar shot – that is, long metal bars – were also fired into sails or at the side of ship. This made large gaping holes.

Bundle shot was similar to the bar shot, but designed to kill the crew. Several short iron bars would be bundled together with a length of rope so that they fit snugly down the bore of a cannon. Once fired, the rope would loosen and the iron bars would begin to spread apart. When they hit something these bars would begin spinning and tumbling, and would do serious damage on a crowded deck.

With canister or case shot, a large cask or metal container was filled with small iron balls or stones. When the canister round hit a ship, it would break apart, releasing a deadly rain. Grape shot was similar, but the iron balls – approximately one inch in diameter – were packed down the gun barrel between two wooden discs. When gun was fired, the discs would break apart and the rain of steel was released at the mouth of the gun. It was very effective at close range and was often used to repel boarders.

But sangrenel was probably the most deadly and feared of the anti-personnel rounds. A cloth bag was filled with jagged scrap iron. When the gun was fired, the bag disintegrated and jagged bits of iron flew in all directions. The wounds it produced were hideous and there was little possibility of removing jagged iron from a victim's body without killing or maiming the patient.

In the eighteenth century, naval gunners began heating solid iron shot until they were red hot before firing so that they would set fire to the ship they hit. This was a tricky operation, as the heat could set off the gunpowder prematurely, killing the gunners. To prevent this the barrel was dowsed with water. The inside was dried and the powder was added, followed by a plug of wood, then the hot cannon ball.

Explosive shells were also introduced in the eighteenth century. A cannon ball filled with gunpower and fitted with a timed fuse was fired from the gun. If the timing was right, the shell would explode when it reached the other ship.

Later cannons also began using a flintlock mechanism for firing instead of touching a flaming torch to the touch hole. The mechanism worked by pulling a lanyard instead of a trigger, a far more reliable and safe mechanism.

Swivel Guns

Swivel guns or patarero were small guns made of brass or bronze mounted on the poop deck and along the ship's rails to repel boarders or clear the decks of a prize ship just before boarding. Their mountings allowed the gun to swivel in a full circle to allow reloading. The rail mounting gave a steady platform for accurate fire and absorbed the recoil. They could also be removed quickly and moved to another part of the ship. Two handles welded to the barrel made them easy to carry to any point along the ship's rail where they might be needed. They could also be mounted in the ship's boats.

Nicknamed 'murderers', these guns would be loaded with pistol balls or scrap iron just before an engagement, but not mounted until the enemy began to close. It was then a simple matter to lift the lightweight cannon into its socket mount and let go with a mini broadside just as the enemy boarded. By not mounting the swivel guns until the last second, the enemy could not assess where the weakest place to board might be.

Swivel guns were relatively small, and ineffective at long range, but at close range against a man with a cutlass they were devastating. Quick to load, easy to aim and fire, the swivel-gun was one of the pirate's favourite weapons.

Sometimes, multi-barrelled rifles or volley guns were also mounted on the ships rails. These had a longer range. One man could put a volley of shots into the rigging, or they could be used to provide suppressing fire like a primitive machine gun. However, they took a long time to reload and, as some volley guns laid as many as twenty-five barrels side by side, they took up a lot of space. However, they were useful to prevent boarding parties crossing from one ship to another.

Other weapons

Bows and crossbows were used by the defenders manning fighting platforms mounted halfway up the masts of Spanish galleons, for fear that sparks from firearms would set the sails on fire. They were also useful sniper weapons in the hands of pirates.

Chemical warfare was also employed with the delightfully named 'stinkpots', pots filled with noxious chemicals, usually sulphur and its derivatives, which created clouds of foul-smelling odour when set on fire. Stinkpots were hurled at the deck of the victim's ship in hopes of causing the defenders to cough and gag, and to create confusion.

CHAPTER SIX

THE SHIPS

Although pirates would rarely, if ever, have a ship built especially for them, some ships lent themselves to piracy more easily than others. Chapter 6 examines a variety of sailing ships in use around the time of the Golden Age of Piracy, and shows which the pirates favoured, and why.

By and large, pirate ships were not purpose built. Pirates sailed in ships they stole and a large number of different types of craft were used. In those days, ships were classified according to the number of masts they had, how the sails were rigged and, in the case of fighting ships, how many gundecks they had.

Most ships used in piracy had two or three masts and each mast had its own name. The main mast is the middle mast of a three-masted ship, the front mast of a two-masted ship or the only mast on a one-masted ship. The mizzen-mast is the rear mast of a ship with two or more masts and the foremast is the front mast on a three-masted ship.

The sails can be either square-rigged or fore-and-aft rigged. With square rigging, the sails are hung from yardarms, or yards, that are carried athwart – at right angles to – the mast and trimmed with braces. A typical three-masted square-rigged ship would divide each of its masts in three – the lower mast, top mast and topgallant mast – each with a yard to hang sail. The advantage of square rigging sails is that they catch a lot of wind when it is coming from behind, but make it very difficult to beat upwind in a square-rigged ship.

In fore-and-aft rigging, the sails are attached to gaffs or stays extending from the mast in the midship line of the ship. This gives the craft increased manoeuvrability. Some ships also have lateen sails. These are a sails shaped like a right-angle triangle – the kind seen on modern racing yachts. Lateen sails again add to the manoeuvrability of the ship, allowing ships to sail in directions other than directly with the wind. However, they catch less wind than a square sail. Typically the lateen had a yardarm loosely affixed to a mast. This allows the sail to be shifted about to catch the wind. Square-rigged ships also carried a lateen-rigged foresail or jib mounted on the bowsprit – a spar jutting from the front of the ship.

Gaff sails hanging fore-and-aft from a gaff or spar extending from a mast on a ship were also used on square-rigged ships to improve manoeuvrability. Almost all square-rigged ships have supplementary gaffs on every mast. This allowed them to rig fore-and-aft in the event of storms with special sails called trysails.

In heavy seas or violent storms, the square-rigged sails could be torn from the yards by the strong winds. Worse, if the sails were not torn from the yards, the masts stood a good chance of breaking due to the added weight of the wet sails and force of the wind. And if the masts did not break, the ship risked capsizing – that is, rolling over in the water. So as a storm approached, the square-rigged sails would be put away and trysails would be used in their place.

The trysails were smaller and were attached only to the bottom portion of the mast. This reduced the possibility of the ship capsizing and also reduced the strain on tall masts. And as the trysails were rigged fore-and-aft they helped in the ship's manoeuvrability during the storm. Ships often carried a mixture of square-rigging and fore-and-aft rigging on different masts. When a vessel was ship-rigged it meant that it was square-rigged on all three masts. If it was brig- or barque-rigged it meant that it was square-rigged on the fore and mainmast, but fore-and-aft rigged on the mizzenmast – though, confusingly, brigs were often ship-rigged. Schooner- or sloop-rigged meant that all the masts were rigged fore-and-aft, although

sometimes an additional square-rigged top sail was carried on the mainmast.

Larger ships also varied in their deck arrangements. They came in two types – galley-built and frigate-built. Galley-built ships had a flush deck, with a large cabin under the quarterdeck at the rear which had loopholes for small arms. Frigate-built ships had a raised forecastle, so there was a well between it and the aftercastle. Both the forecastle and the aftercastle were fronted with sturdy beams and a strong door. The defenders would retreat into these 'closed quarters' when the ship was attacked and pour down small arms fire on the attackers in the well through loopholes.

The Sloop

Sloops were single-masted sailing vessels rigged fore-and-aft with a main sail and a jib. They were the ancestors of the modern yacht. Fast, light and agile, the sloop was the favourite of the pirates. They were easy to sail and could be operated with a small crew. As most of the rigging ran down the mainmast, the sails could be handled from the deck and only one man was needed aloft as a lookout.

Sloops came in all sizes from two-man turtle boats up to Royal Navy men-of-war that carried twelve large guns. Most were rigged as gaff cutters, with a gaff-rigged mainsail and two foresails. They could also hoist two square sails when running before the wind. Ideal for piracy because of their shallow draft – even a hundred-tonner drew just eight feet – they could navigate shallow waters out of reach of larger navy ships. They could sail well into the wind, allowing them to catch up with slow-moving merchantmen and outrun pursers. Sloops were also extremely seaworthy and could stay at sea when larger, square-rigged ships had to remain in harbour due to bad weather. Even when it was outgunned by larger ships, the sloop was still a dangerous foe as it had the manoeuvrability to avoid broadsides. But generally pirate ships avoided sea battles and relied on surprise and

Diagram of sailing ship, showing fore-and-aft rigged sails (tinted) and ship-rigged.

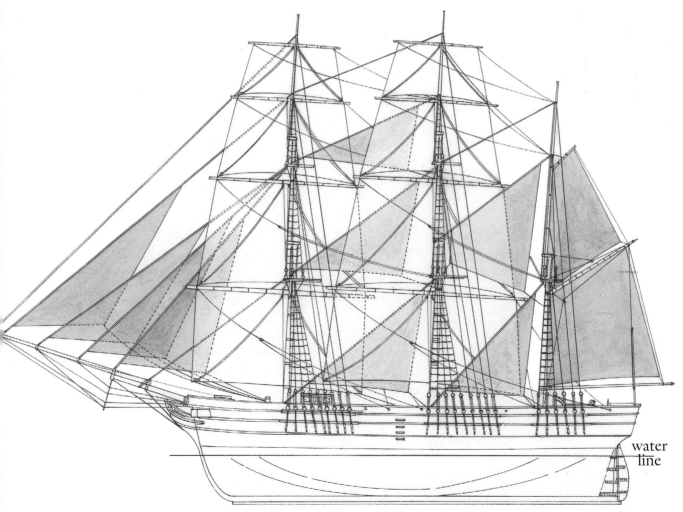

water line

Painting of the English schooner **SeaBreeze** *leaving Livorno harbour in 1864. The schooner's two masts with fore-and-aft rigging, and low draft made these ships a favourite with pirates.*

bluff. The pirates' ferocious appearance was usually more than enough for most other ships to surrender and a sloop with her six or seven guns was often a match for the brigantine with fifteen or twenty guns.

Most attacks on the American seaboard in the Caribbean in the early eighteenth century were carried out in sloops. The best were built in Bermuda and Jamaica. They were between 35 and 65 feet in length, with six to twelve guns on their single broad deck. Although few men were needed to sail them, pirates crews ran up to 150 on larger vessels. It is also notable that the Royal Navy's greatest successes in taking pirates came when they employed sloops.

The Hoy

A variation on the sloop was the hoy, a small cargo ship that was either sloop-rigged or square-rigged with a gaff sail. These immensely seaworthy craft were used for hauling cargo over a short distance and fishing, as well as smuggling and piracy. All ships of the time were armed in some fashion. But a pirate hoy would have between six and ten cannons, typically four- to eight-pounders, lashed to the top deck. A brace of swivel guns could be mounted fore and aft.

These were not the vessels to be used for long voyages and numerous strikes. These were hit-and-run ships. Once they had found a target they would quickly sail back to safe waters and find a place to stash the loot. The typical crew would be twenty or thirty and they would sleep below deck along with their contraband. If there were more, they would sleep on deck, among the cannon.

The Crumster

Another variation on the hoy was the crumster, cromster or crompster. This looked like a small three-masted galleon and was much prized among pirates.

Designed as a merchant ship, the crumster had a rear mast which carried a lateen or gaff sail. Sometime crumsters were used as warships, escorting larger galleons. While crumsters lacked the speed and manoeuvrability of the sloop, they would have at least twice the fire-power. When used as a warship, the crumster would have a gun deck which would carry between eight and sixteen guns, usually four- to twelve-pounders, and extra guns would be lashed to the top deck.

They would also have three or four times the crew of a sloop, usually more than sixty, depending on the number of cannons. Living conditions would be quite cramped, but the

important thing for the pirate was that a crumster could hold more loot.

The Schooner

Another vessel popular among pirates was the schooner. This had two masts, both usually fore-and-aft rigged, and a narrow hull which meant that it could reach eleven knots in a stiff breeze. At between ninety and a hundred tons, a schooner would draw only five feet of water, making her the perfect vessel to hide out in shallow coves. A typical schooner would carry eight cannon, four swivel guns and a crew of seventy-five.

The Barquentine

The barq, bark, barque, barkentine or barquentine was a small three-masted trading vessel, square-rigged on the foremast and fore-and-aft rigged on the mainmast and mizzen. They were used in Europe for coastal and cross-Channel work, but were never as popular in the Caribbean. Slow workhorses, they held little interest for pirates – except as plunder.

The Brigantine

Although, like the barq, the two-masted brig or brigantine was a workhorse, she was also the combat vessel of choice of many pirate captains. Larger than a barq, the brig was designed to be rigged square on the foremast with a gaff-rigged sail on the main mast, a square topsail above it and trysails and flying stay-sails between the masts, though often they were square-rigged on both masts. This made the brig immensely versatile. Square-rigged sails drove her best in quartering winds, while the gaff-rigged fore-and-aft sails were effective when sailing to windward. A typical brig was 80 feet long and displaced 150 tons. They would carry ten cannon and a crew of a hundred.

Pirates often converted three-masted square-rigged merchantmen they took as prizes into brigantines by removing the mizzen and moving the mainmast aft so that it could be rigged fore-and-aft. They would also lop off the forecastle, pilot's cabin, and much of the quarterdeck and railings to make the ship lighter and faster. Swivel guns would be added and gun ports cut in the sides. Figureheads and other identifying features would also be removed or replaced.

Italian brigantine, showing her combination of fore-and-aft rigging and square rigging.

Captain William Kidd was one of the few pirates to commission his own vessel. When he was still officially a privateer, he had the *Adventure Galley* build for him in the Thames River shipyard in Deptford. She was 124 feet long and displaced 287 tons with forty-six sweeps and was designed for speed and manoeuvrability. The latest in fighting vessels, she carried thirty-four guns and a crew of seventy men, though the crew was increased once Kidd became a proper pirate.

A hybrid vessel, she had a modern hull, but still employed the ancient method of propulsion, oar power. Under full sail – 3,200 square yards of canvas – she could make fourteen knots, but becalmed with two or three sailors straining at each oar she could make just three. She was a heavy ship for her size. Built for combat, her ribs were closer together than on a merchantman to withstand cannon blast.

Kidd commissioned a large captain's cabin where officers' meetings could be held, with a cubby nearby for the first mate. Otherwise there were no crew's quarters as such. At night, as many as 150 men would curl up where they could. There were no toilets, or heads. To relieve themselves, men would have to clamber out onto the bowsprit. There was no galley either, just a large stewpot on a hearth surrounded by brick. This could only be used in calm weather as it was located not far from the powder store. Fire was the great fear of all sailors. Wooden ships with huge expanses of canvas were particularly vulnerable and few sailors could swim, therefore no smoking or open flame was allowed below decks. Light for the powder room came from a lantern that was shone through a thick glass window from a tin-lined lightroom.

Venetian galley being caulked, c. 1850. Caulking was a method of keeping ships watertight by pressing a mixture of hot tar and old rope, known as oakum, into the seams.

The Galley

The galley was a long square-rigged sailing ship that also had a row of long oars or sweeps projecting from the sides. Each oar was pulled by two or three men. These were rarely the main means of propulsion, but gave the pirates the opportunity to attack from the leeward side, or escape into the wind. Sailing close-hauled, the sweeps to the leeward could be manned to point the ship's head closer to the wind. As pirate ships usually carried large crews for the purpose of fighting, manning the oars was rarely a problem.

The shot locker in the hold carried six tons of shot for the *Adventure Galley*'s twelve-pounders. Huge water casks, weighing a ton each, were carried amidships to help ballast the ship. Hoisting these and other stores aboard was done by forty men straining at a giant capstan, and raising the 3,000 lb anchor with its 6,000 lb cable by the same method could take an hour or more.

The Canoe, Pirogue, or Peroagoa

Europeans arriving in the Caribbean made copies of the native Carib Indians' canoes. Made from a single hollowed-out tree trunk, they could be up to a 100 feet in length and 6 feet in beam. Some were fitted with a keel so that they could carry sail, but normally they were paddled. They were used particularly by shore-based buccaneers, who used them to attack ships upwind, then escape into the shallows of a coral reef or mangrove swamp where they could not be pursued. Many pirates began their careers with a canoe, then worked their way up to a fully rigged ship. Henry Morgan, among others, used large canoes when travelling up rivers in central America to plunder Spanish settlements inland.

The Galleon

The Spanish galleon was the great prize ship for the pirates. The Spanish used them both as men-of-war and treasure or merchant ships. The most noticeable feature of the design of the galleon was that its hull sloped inward as it rose, tapering to a top deck that was narrow compared with the ship's beam at the water line. The purpose for this design was to concentrate the weight of its cannons close to the centre-line of the ship in an attempt to improve stability. Even so they rocked easily in high seas.

They were built to cross the Atlantic in large convoys, carrying goods out to the Spanish colonies and treasure back. Vulnerable to attack, they were heavily armed. Typically they carried seventy-four cannon, thirty-six on each side of the ship. The other two were mounted aft. They also carried numerous swing guns mounted along the rail that were used to repel borders. The crew would consist of around two hundred men, and galleons could also carry as many as forty paying passengers. However, the high castles at the forepeak and the stern where the officers and passengers were berthed made

them unstable. Galleons also had very short keels when compared to the length of the hull. The result was that a galleon pitched and rolled more easily than other ships – hence the Spanish Armada's vulnerability to attack from the smaller, more stable English ships in 1588. A galleon was not a ship you wanted to sail on if you were prone to sea sickness. However, the galleon was sleek and faster than many of her predecessors.

Most galleons were four-masted ships. The sternmost mast was known as the bonadventure mast and was rigged with lateen sails giving the galleon a top speed of about eight knots. When they were captured by English pirates, the carpenters set about them, sawing away much of their superstructure. This made them faster, more seaworthy vessels and useful for piracy.

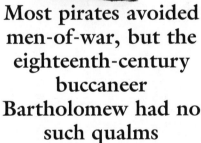

Most pirates avoided men-of-war, but the eighteenth-century buccaneer Bartholomew had no such qualms

To protect themselves from pirates, treasure ships would move in convoy or flotas typically with the strongest ships hauling the most treasure. Normally, the flotas would run rather than fight, but with a top speed of eight knots they could easily be caught by sloops and schooners. However, the formidable firepower of a galleon's broadsides was more than a match for any pirate ship. If a corsair actually got in close enough to attempt boarding, the galleon was equipped with razor sharp crescent blades on the outermost edges of its yards. These blades were designed to rip the adversary's sails to ribbons.

Galleons also carried a fighting platform half way up the mainmast and foremast. When an enemy ship attempted to board a galleon, archers from these platforms would release a shower of arrows and crossbow bolts onto the attackers. Firearms were not used in case sparks set the sails on fire.

Men-of-war

The Royal Navy sent numerous ships to suppress piracy. They were heavily armed and designed for combat and not for merchant service, though sometimes they were used to transport treasure or acted as escort to merchant ships. Sometimes they would be deployed strategically just beyond the horizon or in the

Corvette with three masts instead of the usual two. Although light in the water and fast sailers, corvettes were usually armed with no more that 12-pounder cannon; any larger would have shaken the ship to pieces.

shadow of merchant ships as a trap for would-be pirates. Most pirates avoided men-of-war, but the eighteenth-century buccaneer Bartholomew Roberts had no such qualms and would often take on a man-of-war if he knew she were carrying a substantial prize.

Men-of-war fell into three main classes depending on how many gun decks they had. Corvettes had one gun deck, frigates had one-and-half gun decks and ships of the line would have two or more gun decks. The number of masts on a man-of-war would also give some clue as to how many gun decks she had.

The Corvette

The corvette was sometimes called a 'sloop of war', but typically had two masts and was brig-rigged. A typical corvette would carry between ten and twenty guns, usually six- to-twelve pounders, on a single gun deck. A fast, light ship, it could attack quickly but could not bring an enormous amount of firepower to bear.

The Frigate

The frigate had three masts and was ship-rigged, but was noticeably smaller than a ship of the line. Typically she would have a full battery of guns on the gun deck and a light battery on a spar deck. A frigate would usually carry between twenty-four and forty guns ranging in size between twelve and twenty-four pounders.

The Ship of the Line

A ship of the line was the main battle ship of any navy and the largest of the men-of-war. She had three masts and was ship-rigged. Depending on the period, ships of the line carried between 32 and 144 guns arranged on three or sometimes four decks. In the mid-eighteenth century the typical ship of the line had seventy-four guns on three decks, though they continued to get bigger. However, there were also smaller ships of the line that would have just two gun decks. Typically the cannons they carried were heavier than those on other men-of-war – thirty-two to

forty-two pounders. The galleon, for all practical purposes, was also a man-of-war and was Spain's ship of the line.

Keeping Afloat

Maintaining their ships was a constant problem for pirates. In tropical waters weed grew on their hulls, making them slow and hard to steer, and marine borers were a constant threat to wooden ships. The most common were teredo worms, also known as shipworms or pileworms. They are actually soft-shelled molluscs rather than worms, but only a small part of the anterior end of the creature is covered by a shell. The rest is a long tube-like structure that, in some species, may be six feet long. The shell, which is white, carries file-like ridges that are used to saw into wood at a rate of about eight to twelve rasping motions a minute. The creatures eats the wood and secretes lime to line the inside of the burrow. The tube-like portion of the body extends back to the burrow opening, where the creature ingests food particles and oxygen from the water and discharges wastes and eggs. Laying up to a million eggs a year, teredo worms could honeycomb a hull on a long voyage. Other borers ate the planking layer by layer. To guard against this, ships were sometimes double-planked with a layer of felt and tar between.

Ships had to be careened regularly, at least every three months. They would be taken to a remote bay and stripped. The guns would be mounted on makeshift earthworks at the mouth of the bay in case they were attacked. The ship would then be beached, turned on her side and the bottom scraped. Holes would be patched and the hull would be smeared with pitch and tallow. This would be done on uninhabited islands, or places where the natives were friendly. Most of the Indian peoples of the Caribbean preferred the pirates to the settlers who tried to enslave them. They also enjoyed sharing a bottle of rum and a taste of the pirates' riotous living.

Early experiments in cladding the hull with lead failed as galvanic action between the lead and the iron nails or hoops ate the metal away. When they could afford to, pirates preferred to have barques and brigantines made from the worm-resistant cedar wood that grew in such abundance on the island of Bermuda.

*The capture of the **Liguria**, a pirate frigate, in 1798 by a frigate of the Royal Navy.*

CHAPTER SEVEN

LIFE ABOARD THE
PIRATE SHIPS

The eighteenth-century man of letters Dr Samuel Johnson said, 'No man will be a sailor who had contrivance enough to get himself into jail; for being in a ship is being in a jail with the chance of being drowned. A man in jail has more room, better food and commonly better company.'

The inmates of eighteenth-century jails would probably not have agreed with him, but life at sea could be unpleasant in the extreme. Wooden sailing ships were often damp, dark, cheerless places, reeking of bilgewater and rotten meat. It was not possible to caulk the planks so that they were completely watertight, and ships leaked constantly, even when the weather was fair. When the wind got up, water would cascade down the hatchways, leaving the lower decks awash. The pumps would have to be manned constantly and, once something was wet inside a ship, it could only be dried with difficulty. Men suffered from colds, cramps and catarrh, and when they were not breaking their backs hauling ropes and sails and pumping, they would go below and crawl into the forecastle, where they would share a damp blanket with a shipmate.

Pirates in the Caribbean were luckier than most ordinary seamen. Though they risked death in hurricanes, by and large the weather was warm and they could sleep out on deck, though usually they were packed tight, lying side by side on the steerage floor or, as one captain put it, 'kennelling like hounds on the deck'. To man cannon and board other vessels, pirate ships usually carried three or four times the crew of a merchantman. As many as 250 men would be packed on a ship just 120 feet long and 40 feet wide at the beam.

Even so, many Royal Navy seamen considered life on board a pirate ship heaven compared with the conditions they had experienced on board the ships of His Majesty, where the liquor was not confined to the officers. With the over-manning on a pirate vessel, there was plenty of leisure time to get drunk. Most naval ratings longed to desert to a pirate ship to escape the floggings and picklings – where salt or vinegar was rubbed into the open wound after a flogging – which were routine in the navy. In the Royal Navy, after a summary trial, a man could be hanged from the yardarm and his body left for the seabirds. Many ordinary seamen had been press-ganged into the service and were, consequently, never allowed ashore except in places so inhospitable that no one would think of deserting. While pirate and navy ships often had surgeons, these were generally unskilled, and an injured man frequently would not survive. If he did survive aboard a pirate, but could not work, he would be put ashore at the next port, wherever it might be. Although a pirate stood a good chance of departing this life at the end of a rope, he could at least look forward to a few years of freedom and high living. This was a greater life expectancy than in the navy.

For all seamen, disease was a constant danger. It was not unusual for a captain to lose half his crew during a voyage. In an effort to combat pestilence, the decks were scrubbed with vinegar and salt water, and if there had been a haul of French brandy, it was used as disinfectant. Pans of burning pitch or brimstone – sulphur – were taken below to fumigate the holds. But there were nooks and crannies that could never be cleaned or dried, and during a voyage, filth and debris accumulated in the bottom of the hull which became a breeding ground for hordes of rats, cockroaches and beetles.

As the pirates' diet consisted of almost nothing but meat, they were particularly vulnerable to scurvy. Caused by a lack for vitamin C – usually obtained from fresh fruit and vegetables – it caused swollen and bleeding gums, loosening of

the teeth, soreness and stiffness in the joints and lower extremities, bleeding under the skin and in deep tissues, anaemia and made wounds slow to heal. Seamen also suffered from malaria, yellow fever and dysentery, a particularly unpleasant condition when to go to the lavatory you have to climb out along the bowsprit. Bartholomew Roberts once lost over a hundred men while careening his ship on a swampy African river bank. Venereal diseases were so common that pirates boarding a prize ship would often head straight to the medicine chest and ransack it for the mercury compounds then used to treat syphilis, before plundering the ship for booty.

The food on board ship was usually atrocious. The fish and meat were rotten and the fresh water kept in huge casks in the hold stank, and the ships biscuit on ordinary merchantmen and men-of-war was full of black-headed weevil maggots. Many men could only bring themselves to eat in the dark. But things were worse for the crews of pirate ships. With so many men packed on board, it was impossible to carry enough stores to feed and

water them all. Pirates were constantly parched and on the verge of starvation, and hunger and thirst often drove them to make their most audacious raids.

When they plundered well-stocked merchantmen or went ashore, pirates had a taste for a robust concoction called salmagundi, from the French *salmigonis* meaning 'hotchpotch'. Fish, turtle meat, chicken, ham, pork, corned beef, pigeon, duck – any meat they could get their hands on – was diced and marinated in spiced wine, then it was mixed with pickled herring, anchovies, cabbage, mango, onions, palm hearts, hard-boiled eggs, olives, grapes and any pickled vegetables that were available. This was doused with oil and vinegar and seasoned with salt, pepper, garlic and mustard seeds. The whole lot was washed down with rum or beer – no doubt to take away its overpowering taste.

There were other treats to be pillaged from merchant ships. Some ships of that era carried a 'petty tally' – a small store of goodies such as almonds,

Cross-section of a three-decker sailing ship, looking forward from the stern to the bow. The crew would have slept in the hammocks on the lower deck, beneath the gun deck; the space allotted per man was 14 inches in the Royal Navy.

TER
NE

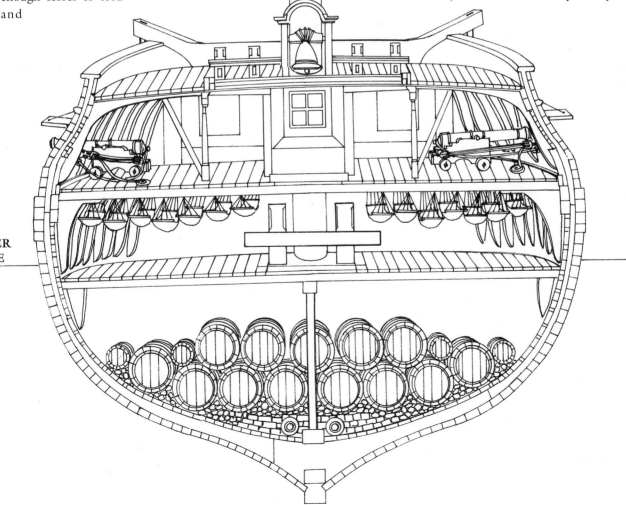

currants, spices, marmalade, sides of bacon and dried tongues of beef. 'For when a man is ill, or at the point of death, I would know whether a dish of buttered rice with a little cinnamon, ginger and sugar be not better than salt fish or salt beef,' wrote Captain John Smith, the founder of Jamestown and the lover of Pocahontas, in his 1627 book *A Sea Grammar*. 'And after a storm, when poor men are all wet, and some of them have not so much as a cloth to shift them, shaking with cold, few of those but will tell you a little sherry or aqua-vitae [liquor – usually whiskey, rum or brandy] is much better to keep them in health that a little small beer [weak or inferior beer], or cold water.'

For most of the time on board a pirate ship there was little for the pirates to do except play cards or dice, and fire guns, if they had any spare ammunition

Smith himself was captured by pirates on an expedition to New England in 1614 and escaped three months later.

For most of the time on board, there was little for the pirates to do except to play cards or dice, and fire guns, if they had spare ammunition. Drink, particularly rum and rum punch, were a solace. Some turned to prayer and the Bible. In 1727, when Bartholomew Roberts captured the frigate *Onslow*, the crew tried to press the ship's chaplain into becoming their parson. His duties, it was said, were to be 'to make punch and say prayers'. When the clergymen declined the position – and a share of the booty – the pirates let him go. 'However brutish they might be in other things, they bore so great a respect to his order, that they resolved not to force him against his inclinations,' wrote an eyewitness.

To amuse themselves, pirates held mock trials, mimicking what would happen to them if they were captured and came up before an Admiralty Court. In *A General History of the Pyrates*, Defoe relates a sham trial that took place on an uninhabited cay off the coast of Cuba. The judge, a pirate named George Bradley, sailing master of the *Morning Star*, sat in a tree with a tarpaulin over his shoulders by way of a robe, a shaggy cap on his head instead of a wig and large pair of spectacles on his nose. The officers of the ship carried handspikes as staves of authority and a hangman stood by with

a noose. The accused was then brought out 'making a thousand sour faces'.

A pirate playing the attorney general then said:

An't please your Lordship, and you gentlemen of the jury, here is a fellow before you that is a sad dog, a sad, sad dog; and I humbly hope your Lordship will order him to be hanged out the way immediately. He has committed piracy upon the high seas, and we shall prove, an't please your Lordship, that this fellow, this sad dog before you, has escaped a thousand storms, nay, has got safe ashore when the ship has been cast away, which was a certain sign he was not born to be drowned; yet not having the fear of hanging before his eyes, he went on robbing and ravishing man, woman and child, plundering ships' cargoes fore and aft, burning and sinking ship, barky and boat, as if the Devil had been in him. But this is not all, my Lord, he has committed worse villainies than all these, for we shall prove, that he has been guilty of drinking small beer, and your Lordship knows, there never was a sober fellow but what was a rogue. My Lord, I should have spoke much finer than I do now, but that, as your Lordship knows, our rum is all out, and how should a man speak good law that has not drank a dram. However, I hope, your Lordship will order the fellow hanged.

The judge was scarcely impartial. From his seat in the mangrove tree he said:

Harkee me, sirrah, you lousy pitiful, ill-looked dog; what have you to say why you should not be tucked up immediately and set a sun-drying like a scarecrow?

The judge then asked the accused to plead. He pleaded not guilty, so the judge threatened to have him hanged without a trial. In his defence, the accused said that he was an honest man who had been 'taken by one George Bradley' – the man who was now playing his judge – 'a notorious pirate, a sad rogue as ever was hanged, and he forced me, an't please your honour.'

Eventually, Bradley sentenced the accused to hang, giving three reasons:

First, because it is not fit I should sit here as judge and nobody be hanged. Secondly, you must be hanged, because you have a damned hanging look. And thirdly, you must be hanged because I am hungry; for know, sirrah, that whenever a judge's dinner is ready before the trial is over, the prisoner is to be hanged of course. There's the law for you, ye dog. So take him away, gaoler.

Soon after leaving the cay in August 1722, the *Morning Star* ran aground on Grand Cayman, though the crew got ashore safely. Her consort, the *Fenn*, put in to see that they were all right, but two men-of-war bore down on her. She cut her cable and made out to sea, only escaping when the crew took to the oars and rowed for their lives. A shore party was landed and rounded up forty of the *Morning Star*'s crew. But Bradley and others hid in the woods. Later, though, they surrendered to a Bermuda sloop.

Sometimes the pirates' pantomime proceedings became so heated that they ended in a riot. In 1717, there was one recorded case where the accused got so involved in the charade that he became convinced that he really was going to be hanged. He threw a grenade at the judge, then drew his cutlass and hacked the arm off the man playing the prosecutor, a pirate who called himself Alexander the Great.

As well as providing opportunities for excessive drinking and playacting, life on board freed the pirates from many of the features of ordinary life that they detested. There was no class distinction on a pirate ship and no one was set in authority over them. The captain was elected and had little power over his men.

'They only permitted him to be captain on condition that they could be captain over him,' said Defoe.

Major decisions were settled by a show of hands. A captain could easily be deposed and was accorded few privileges, apart from an extra share of the booty. Although Bartholomew Roberts was allowed the use of the master's

Pirates amuse themselves with a mock trial, as recounted by Daniel Defoe in A General History of Pyrates.

cabin and a small amount of china and silverware, any crewman could enter his cabin, day or night, help himself to Roberts' food and use his crockery and cutlery. However, there was a time when the captain came into his own.

'They chose a captain from amongst themselves, who in effect held little more than that title, excepting in an engagement, when he commanded absolutely and without control,' Walter Kennedy told the court when he was tried for piracy at the Old Bailey in 1721. Kennedy had been Roberts' quartermaster and took command of his ship, the *Rover*, when Roberts went after a brig off Devil's Island, Surinam.

'The captain's power is uncontrollable in chase or in battle, drubbing, cutting or even shooting anyone who does not obey his command,' wrote Defoe. The pirates picked for their captain 'one superior for knowledge and boldness... proof pistol, they call it'. Timid or incompetent captains were quickly deposed. One ship went through thirteen captains in just a couple of months. Pirates were only too well aware of the trouble a bad captain could get them into.

Crewmen aboard the *Rover* had had a good

run first under Captain Howell Davis, then under Bartholomew Roberts. But when Kennedy took over, they got separated from the rest of Roberts' fleet. Roberts blamed Kennedy, an Irishman, and refused to have any Irishmen in his crew after that. Kennedy sailed to Barbados and seized another vessel there. He narrowly escaped capture in Virginia, where some of his crew were captured and hanged. Taking a Boston sloop, Kennedy and a crew of volunteers set off back to his native Ireland, but strayed so far off course that he ended up in a creek in northwest Scotland. Leaving the ship at anchor, the crew went ashore posing as shipwrecked mariners.

Seventeen of them were arrested in Edinburgh, after throwing their gold about in riotous living. Two turned King's evidence and nine were hanged. Meanwhile Kennedy had made his way to London, where he opened a brothel in Deptford. But he fell out with one of his girls, who had him indicted for robbery and he was sent to Bridewell Gaol. The woman then found a former shipmate who identified him as pirate. He was transferred to the Marshalsea, which was then the Admiralty's jail. He was tried in the Old Bailey and hanged at Execution Dock in Wapping on 19 July 1721.

As well as being a bold fighter and a good seaman, a captain had to keep abreast of events. He needed to know about new colonies, new wars, new alliances and the general development of trade. This knowledge could mean the difference between life and death when selecting a prize. And when a ship was taken, those on board were interrogated for fresh information. The pirate captain also needed to know the value of things, so that he could divide the booty. Tact and diplomacy of a dizzying standard was needed to satisfy every man that he had his fair share. The captain also had to dispense justice, and fairness was seen as all important, one captain being deposed for excessive cruelty to his captives.

Law Amongst Pirates

However, there were strict codes about what could or could not be done on board a pirate ship. For example, pirates had to apply to the captain for permission to fight each other. These rules were agree by the men.

'Less law made for more justice,' said one ne'er-do-well.

Articles were drawn up and sworn to on a Bible or an axe. Bartholomew Roberts' were the most comprehensive (see facing page). Other articles varied. Those of Captain George Lowther stipulated that the first man to see a prize should receive the best pistols or small arms on board. They also required that 'good quarter shall be given when called for'. Some articles laid down that the punishment for murder should be for the murderer to be tied to the corpse and the two of them be thrown overboard. This punishment was also adopted by the Royal Navy. The articles of Captain John Phillips laid down that the punishment for carrying a candle into the hold without a lantern, smoking a pipe without a cap on it or striking another crewman was to be 'forty stripes lacking one on the bare back'. A common punishment for a minor offence was one stroke of the lash from each crew member.

There was the occasional instance of keelhauling. The victim was hoisted up to the end of the main yard, where he dangled by the wrists, where a weighted line was tied to his feet. This was then run under the hull and up to the other end of the main yard. A rag soaked in oil was tied over their nose and mouth to prevent them drowning. Then the victim was dropped into the sea, then hauled under the hull to emerge half-drowned upside down on the other side. In the process they would have been dragged over the barnacles that grew along the keel, which would have taken all the skin off their backs. The process would then be repeated three times. However, such barbarity was usually confined to the Royal Navy.

Marooning was a different matter. Few survived being put ashore on a deserted island far from civilization. Among those who did were a Captain William Greenaway and seven loyal crewmen who, in 1718, were put ashore after the crew of his sloop had mutinied. When Greenaway and his men refused to join the mutineers in a life of piracy, they were left stark naked on an uninhabited Bahamian island with no provisions. The island consisted of nothing but sharp coral and dense undergrowth and their prospect for survival looked poor. However, the pirates took pity on their former shipmates, returning with a sloop, and rowed them out to it. But then they slashed the sails and cut the rigging, leaving the marooned men worse off than before. They were now anchored a mile off shore without food or water.

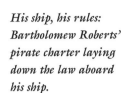

His ship, his rules: Bartholomew Roberts' pirate charter laying down the law aboard his ship.

1. *Every man shall have an equal vote in affairs of the moment. He shall have an equal title to the fresh provisions or strong liquors at any time seized, and shall use them at pleasure unless a scarcity may make it necessary for the common good that a retrenchment may be voted.*

2. *Every man shall be called fairly to turn by the list on board of prizes, because over and above their proper share, they are allowed a shift of clothes. But if they defraud the company to the value of even one dollar in plate, jewels or money, they shall be marooned. If any man rob another he shall have his nose and ears slit, and be put ashore where he shall be sure to encounter hardships.*

3. *None shall game for money either with dice or cards.*

4. *The lights and candles shall be put out at eight at night, and if any of the crew desire to drink after that hour they shall sit upon the deck without lights.*

5. *Each man shall keep his piece, cutlass and pistols at all times clean and ready for action.*

6. *No boy or woman to be allowed amongst them. If any man shall be found seducing any of the latter sex and carrying her to sea in disguise he shall suffer death.*

7. *He that shall desert the ship or his quarters in time of battle shall be punished by death or marooning.*

8. *None shall strike another on board the ship, but every man's quarrel shall be ended on shore by sword or pistol in this manner. At the word of command from the quartermaster, each man being previously placed back to back, shall turn and fire immediately. If any man do not, the quartermaster shall knock the piece out of his hand. If both miss their aim they shall take to their cutlasses, and he that draweth first blood shall be declared victor.*

9. *No man shall talk of breaking up their way of living till each has a share of £1,000. Every man who shall become a cripple or lose a limb in the service shall have eight hundred pieces of eight from the common stock and for lesser hurts proportionately.*

10. *The captain and the quartermaster shall each receive two shares of a prize, the master gunner and bosun, one and one half shares, all other officers one and one quarter, and private gentlemen of fortune one share each.*

11. *The musicians shall have rest by right on the Sabbath Day only. On all other days by favour only.*

They would have died there, if they had not found a broken hatchet blade on board. Greenaway, the only man that could swim, struck out for the shore with the hatchet blade around his neck. He cut down trees, made a raft and ferried berries, fruit and cabbage palms out to his men, and they set about mending the rigging and patching up the sails. A week later, they had just set off in the sloop when the pirates returned again. Taking to the raft, they paddled ashore and hid in the undergrowth while the pirates hacked down the mast of their sloop and sank her in deep water. They lived for the next eight days on berries, shellfish and stingrays, which they speared with sharpened sticks.

The pirates returned several times, but the maroons hid and did not answer when they called out to them. Eventually, the pirates offered them safe passage and the maroons

emerged. But it was a trick. Greenaway and two other crew members were forced into service with the pirates, while the other five were left on the cay.

The abandoned men survived the best they could for the next fortnight. Then the pirates returned once more and, possibly at Greenaway's urging, left at the water's edge a large cask of flour, a bushel of salt, pots and pans, an axe, a dozen knives, two muskets, shot, two bottles of gunpowder and three dogs of the type used to hunt hogs in the West Indies. They built themselves a hut and lived on roast pork, until pirates returned once more, burnt their hut down and ate their meat. But then the pirates promised never to return again and left them a bottle of rum. Soon after the pirates were captured by the Spanish. When Greenaway had told his story, they sent a boat and the remaining five men were rescued.

Daniel Defoe left a more famous account of marooning in Robinson Crusoe. It is a fictionalized version of the story of Alexander Selkirk. Selkirk sailed with the English buccaneer William Dampier who had renamed his ship *Bachelor's Delight* after seizing a cargo of young female African slaves. After a career in pirating around the West Indies, Central America and the Eastern Seaboard, Dampier circumnavigated the world, writing a diary as he went that meticulously plotted the great ocean currents. In the Pacific he rescued a Mosquito Indian who had been marooned on Juan Fernándes Island, 500 miles of the coast of Chile, three years before. During the War of the Spanish Succession – and Queen Anne's War that was taking place in North America at the same time – Dampier was commissioned as a privateer and, in 1703, led two ships, the *St George* and the *Cinque Ports*, on an expedition. The following year they rounded Cape Horn. After failing to take a Manila galleon, the two ships parted company. Selkirk was sailing master on the *Cinque Ports*, under Captain Stradling. They went to Juan Fernándes Island to refit and

careen. Selkirk and Stradling fell out and when, in October 1704, Stradling gave the order to put to sea, Selkirk protested that the ship was not seaworthy and demanded to be left on the island. Stradling took him at his word and sailed away without him. All that Selkirk had with him were 'his clothes and bedding, with a fire-lock, some powder, bullets, and tobacco, a hatchet, a knife, a kettle, a Bible, some practical pieces, and his mathematical instruments and books.'

The island was not quite the deserted spot that Defoe described as pirates occasionally put in there for wood and water. There were goats on the island, which Selkirk killed and ate. He made fire by rubbing two sticks of pimento wood together over his knee. When his clothes fell apart, he made a coat and hat from goat skin, which he sewed together using a nail instead of a needle. He tamed the island's feral cats, who provided him with company and killed the rats that used to chew his feet at night. He built two huts using branches covered with long grass and overcame solitude by reading the Bible, praying and singing psalms, saying that he was a 'better Christian while in this solitude than ever he was before'.

Meanwhile Dampier, wanting another crack at Spanish treasure ships, signed up as navigator on a privateering expedition led by Captain Woodes Rogers. They landed on Juan Fernándes Island on 2 February 1709 to be greeted by 'a man clothed in goat skins, who looked wilder than the first owners of them'. Dampier recognized Selkirk and recommended him as an excellent seaman to Rogers, who made him mate of this ship, the *Duke and Duchess*. They set sail on 12 February and, after capturing one of the Philippine ships, headed home via the Cape of Good Hope. Selkirk arrived back in London on 14 October 1711, having been away from England for more than eight years. His story was first told in Rogers' book *Cruising around the World*, which was published in 1712. His tale of being left alone in such a faraway place immediately seized the public imagination. And in 1719, the year after a second edition of Rogers' book appeared, Defoe's novel *Robinson Crusoe* came out.

Dampier died four years after they returned

When Selkirk protested that the ship was not seaworthy and demanded to be left on the island, Strandling took him at his word and sailed away without him

to London in March 1715, while Rogers was appointed governor of Bermuda in 1717, with the specific task of stamping out pirates. Those who asked for a pardon were given a small plot of land on Providence Island (now New Providence) and enough timber to build a house. Any who returned to their old ways were hunted down and hanged. Unfortunately, Rogers bankrupted himself trying to build the economy of the island and spent several years in debtors' prison in England. But he returned to the Bahamas and died in Nassau in 1729.

One of the enduring legends about pirates is that they disciplined errant crewmen and unwanted captives by making them walk the plank. This was very rare if it happened at all.

Alexander Selkirk tells Defoe the story of his experiences, which then form the basis for **Robinson Crusoe**. *Unattributed illustration in* Allers Familj-Journal, *18th November 1917.*

Robinson Crusoe with his family of domesticated animals. Coloured engraving after water colour sketches by Anelay and Huttula in an 1864 edition of **Robinson Crusoe.**

True, pirates in the seventeenth and eighteenth centuries would often feed unwanted captives to the sharks. And in ancient times when pirates preyed on Roman shipping in the Mediterranean, they would often play cruel games with their captives. When Romans identified themselves, the pirates would fall to their knees, beg forgiveness and tell their captives that they were now free to walk home. But the only place to walk was over the side and into the sea.

The idea of pirates making their victims walk the plank seems to date from 1769, when an ordinary seaman named George Wood was hanged for mutiny. On his way to the gallows in Newgate Prison, he told the chaplain that he and his fellow mutineers had forced a number of loyal crewmen 'to walk on a plank, extended over the ship's side, over the sea, in to which they were turned when at the extreme end'. However, the idea owes its currency to the work of the nineteenth century American author, artist, illustrator and pirate buff Howard Pyle.

The only pirate thought to have made his victims walk the plank was Major Stede Bonnet, sadistic even by pirate standards. Born in Barbados in 1689, he was the son of English plantation-owners and had served in the Army during the war of the Spanish Succession. Even though he had no experience of the sea, he

decided to become a pirate – though some say he put to sea because his wife was a shrew who nagged him, as good a reason as any. He bought a sloop, which he renamed the *Revenge*, fitted it out and took on a crew. Once out at sea, he announced his plan to become a pirate and told his crew that they could either join him or become the 'governors of the next deserted island we find'.

Fellow pirate Edward Teach – better known as Blackbeard – used to make fun of Bonnet's poor seamanship and once, when they met off the Carolinas, took Bonnet on board, got him hopelessly drunk and persuaded the *Revenge*'s crew to vote a Lieutenant Turner captain instead. When Blackbeard tired of the joke, he returned the *Revenge* to Bonnet, telling him to sail into Bath Town, Maine, and asked Governor Eden there for a pardon. Blackbeard said that he would follow Bonnet into port if all was well. But Blackbeard had no intention of retiring, and nor had Bonnet, who soon sailed again under the name Captain Thomas, renaming the *Revenge* the *Royal James*. He put ashore at Cape Fear River, North Carolina, with two prizes to careen on 27 September 1718. Colonel Rhett, who was hunting the pirate Charles Vane, heard that there were pirates in the river. Bonnet and his crew were captured and taken to Charleston, South Carolina, where

they were tried and found guilty. Despite his reputation for callous and brutal behaviour, the 29-year-old Bonnet did not go quietly. After an impassioned plea to the governor for clemency which, according to Defoe, particularly impressed the women, he was dragged to the gallows sobbing and pleading for his life. He was hanged on 12 November 1718.

Although Vane escaped the tender mercies of Colonel Rhett, he did not fare much better. He was another pirate with a reputation for cruelty and was known to have keel-hauled those who angered him. He was one of the few pirates who had no respect for the pirates' code, cheating his crewmen out of their fair share of their plunder. Once he tried, and failed, to take a ship under the command of a Captain Holford. Later Vane's ship broke up off Baracho Island in the Bay of Honduras and he was washed up on the beach. Unfortunately the first ship that came by was commanded by Captain Holford, who recognized Vane and left him where he was. A second ship picked him up, but she then caught up with Holford, who took Vane to Jamaica in irons. He was tried and hanged there on 29 March 1720.

As well as their mock trials, to maintain discipline, pirates held proper hearings of their own. Defoe recorded the trial of one Harry Glasby, 'a reserved and sober man' who had been forced into piracy by Bartholomew Roberts because of his skill as a sailing master. After jumping ship with two others in Hispaniola – a capital offence in the eyes of pirates – he was recaptured and was given a remarkably fair trial.

'Here was the form of justice kept up, which is as much as can be said of several other courts that have more lawful commissions for what they do,' said Defoe. 'Here was no feeing of council, and bribing of witnesses was a custom not known to them; no packing of juries, no torturing and wresting the sense of the law for bye ends and purposes, no puzzling or perplexing the cause with unintelligible canting terms and useless distinctions; nor was their sessions burdened with numberless officers, the ministers of rapine and extortion with ill-boding aspects enough to fright Astrea [the goddess of justice] from the court.'

The trial took place in the ship's steerage, where pipes, tobacco and a large bowl of rum punch were provided. Glasby and the other prisoners were brought out and the articles of indictment against them were read.

'They were arraigned upon a statute of their own making,' wrote Defoe, 'and the letter of the law being strong against them and the fact plainly proved, they were about to pass sentence when one of the judge moved that they should first smoke another pipe.'

While this was done, the prisoners pleaded movingly for their lives. But the court could not be prevailed upon to show mercy until one of the pirate judges, whose name was Valentine Ashplant, stood up, took the pipe out of his mouth and said that he had something to say in defence of one of the defendants. He kept it short and sweet.

'By God, Glasby shall not die,' he said. 'Damn me if he shall.'

'After this learned speech,' said Defoe, 'he sat down in his place and resumed his pipe.'

The motion was loudly opposed by the other judges in similar terms, but Ashplant was resolute and he made another speech in mitigation.

'God damn ye gentlemen, I am as good a man as the best of you,' he said. 'Damn my soul if ever I turned my back to any man in my life, or ever will, by God. Glasby is an honest fellow, notwithstanding his misfortune, and I love him. Devil damn me if I don't. I hope he'll live and repent of what he has done. But damn me, if he must die, I will die along with him.'

Then Ashplant pulled out a pair of pistols and pointed them at the other judges who, 'perceiving his argument so well supported, thought it reasonable that Glasby should be acquitted.'

The other two were granted no such reprieve. All their mitigation got them was the privilege of choosing the members of their own firing

> **Despite his reputation for callous and brutal behaviour, the 29-year-old Stede Bonnet did not go quietly, but was dragged to the gallows sobbing and pleading for his life**

squads. They were then taken out, tied to the mast and shot.

After his reprieve Glasby tried to run away again when the ship was in port, but got lost and had to return to the ship. This time he swore all sorts of oaths, but the pirates did not trust him and he was not allowed ashore again. Then, when Roberts was killed and his ship *Royal Fortune* captured by HMS *Swallow* off the coast of West Africa on 10 February 1722, Glasby was arrested and stood trial again at Cape Coast Castle, this time in an Admiralty Court. The court was told that he had been captured on board the *Samuel* in 1720. During his time with the pirates he had persuaded them to leave enough stores and instruments on board a prize ship for her to reach port when they released her after plundering her. He had never been seen loading or firing guns, and when the *Swallow* had caught up with the *Royal*

Fortune and Roberts was dead he had persuaded the pirates not to blow her up. He was acquitted and went on to speak in defence of others.

Who was Who Aboard a Pirate Ship

Sailing masters such as Glasby were always in demand, as many pirate captains did not have great nautical skills and they relied heavily on such skilled men. The sailing master was responsible for the setting of the sails. He also decided on the course, once the captain had picked a destination. With a good master, an eighteenth-century sailing ship with a weed-free hull could sail just a few degrees into the wind on either tack. That meant, if the vessel sailed for a period on one tack, then turned and sailed for the same period on the other, it was possible to beat

Eighteenth-century sextant, used in the navigation of ships to establish a position by the angle above the horizon of celestial bodies.

upwind. The only other alternative was to lower the boats and have oarsmen tow the ship to windward.

When pirates captured a new ship, it was important to capture the sailing master with her as each ship had its unique characteristics. His captors would treat him well and, if he joined the pirates, he would receive one and three-quarters share of the booty.

Navigators were in demand too. As navigation in the eighteenth century was hardly an exact science, the navigator was known on board as 'the artist'. The methods they used to plot their position was a complete mystery to most seamen and the artist was supposed to have a natural gift. Indeed, a lot of navigation depended on guesswork. Until the introduction of the marine chronometer in the 1760s, it was not possible to determine longitude with any accuracy. Using the stars it was possible to work out your latitude, so to travel to a specific destination a ship often set sail for the correct latitude, then followed it east or west. The Atlantic trade winds were well known, but the circulating ocean currents had not been charted by then.

Good navigators were few and far between. A fleet of pirate ships might have just one navigator between them. If he was any good he could bring a ship to a few miles upwind of her destination, then the ship could drift downwind into port. To arrive just a few miles downwind could be a disaster. In 1720 Bartholomew Roberts, usually an inspired seaman, set sail across the Atlantic from the West Indies to the Cape Verde Islands off western Africa. His crew came within sight of their destination, but could not make the last few miles against the trade winds. They had to run all the way back across the Atlantic to South America to try again. By the time they sighted Surinam they had been out of fresh water for two days and were on the point of death.

As on a Royal Navy man-of-war, the man actually responsible for steering the ship was the quartermaster. But on a pirate ship, he also served as first lieutenant, or a merchantman's first mate – though there was usually another titular lieutenant who would take command if the captain was killed. Defoe described the quartermaster's role as 'the trustee for the whole ship's company… like the Grand Mufti amongst the Turks to their Sultan, for the captain can do nothing which the quartermaster does not approve of. The quartermaster is a humble imitation of the Roman tribune, for he speaks for and looks after the interests of the company.'

The quartermaster was the strong man of the ship. It was his job to see that the captain's orders were carried out. He was also the ship's magistrate and he disciplined the crew and kept control of the captives which pirate ships often carried. He punished minor offences such as quarrelling and not looking after weapons properly – more serious offences had to go before a ship-borne court. The quartermaster was usually the only man who could inflict a flogging.

A good navigator could bring a ship to a few miles upwind of her destination, then the ship could drift downwind into port. To arrive just a few miles downwind could be a disaster

However, this was a detested form of punishment, common in the Royal Navy, and had to be authorized by a majority vote of the crew. Another duty was to preside over duels ashore between feuding crewmates. He also transacted the business of the ship, ashore or with other vessels.

The quartermaster was in charge of the selection and division of the plunder, receiving two shares of the booty along with the captain. He commanded the ship's boat in any particularly difficult or dangerous enterprise. And, like the captain, he was subject to the will of the crew. Chosen by a majority vote, he could also be deposed by it.

The bosun or boatswain was responsible for the maintenance of the ship, its tackle and stores, and the day-to-day running of the ship. He would be the most experienced seaman on board. He had to fix blocks and tackle – a skilled job in days when the weight of the things that had to be lifted depended on guesswork and lives depended on those guesses. It was his job to look after the ship, her canvas and cordage. The direction and manning of the work on the

sails, spars and rigging was under his command, and the maintenance and manning of the ship's boat was his responsibility. He also led work details and the landing parties that went ashore to forage for wood, water and food. It was said that an inexperienced captain could get by if he had a good master and navigator and a land-lubber could get by as a quarter-master if he had a good bosun.

Another important man on board was the ship's carpenter. He was responsible for the integrity of the ship's hull and soundness of her masts. He had to have a detailed knowledge of the ship's construction and be able to keep her afloat, even in the heat of battle. As head of a damage-control team, he would dash to any part of the ship that had sprung a leak and fix it, patching a hole, if neces-sary, with pitch and can-vas until the ship could be beached and the repair made good. Using the primitive ship's hand-pumps, it could take days to get rid of a large amount of water. A leak had to be stopped quickly, or the ship would sink.

The carpenter would use anything to hand to fix a leak. This often put him at odds with the bosun and sailing master, who wanted to jettison broken masts or fallen spars during action to improve the handling of the ship. But they could be just the materials the carpenter needed to brace a damaged hull by wedging them against stronger parts of the ship's struc-ture. As pirates had no access to dry docks, the carpenter was expected to remake sections of the hull with the ship upturned on a remote beach, and when they captured a prize the car-penter had to be on hand to survey it quickly to determine whether to keep the new vessel as their own, or let it sail away after they had plun-dered it.

With his set of sharp saws, the carpenter's second function was the amputation of dam-aged limbs. He was ably assisted in this by the bosun, whose largest axe was heated until it was red hot to cauterize wounds and stumps, and the sail-maker, who sewed up other wounds – or sewed the corpse into a canvas bag for burial at sea if the amputation was a failure. If pirates

It is thought that the origin of the name 'Jolly Roger' is the French joli rouge – 'pretty red' – a wry description of the blood-stained rag flown by early privateers

came upon anyone with any medical knowledge they would press him into service as a surgeon. Often any person who had some education and common sense was kept as a surgeon – and probably did no more harm than the profes-sionals at that time.

A skilled cooper was also required on board. In those days, the only watertight container that could hold more than a earthenware jar was a barrel and coopers had served a long apprenticeship under a master craftsman. Dry foodstuffs had to be sealed in barrels to prevent them being ruined by the damp. Fish and meats were pickled in brine or kept salted, and fresh water had to be stored in bar-rels. These had to be inspected regularly as running short of drink-ing water on a sailing ship usually resulted in catastrophe. At the first sign of a leak, the water would be poured out into another barrel while the first one was fixed.

To save space in the hold, empty barrels would be broken up and, when the ship came near a place where they could find fresh water, the cooper would have to quickly reassemble the hoops and staves to take supplies on board.

Pirate gunners would have been poached from men-of-war. Few sailors on merchant ships had the experience. Many would have started as a powder monkey at the age of ten or eleven, direct from the poorhouse or foundlings' hospi-tal. They would have worked their way up through each position in the gun crew before becoming the gunner captain – by which time they would probably be scarred with powder burns, profoundly deaf and may have lost a limb or two. On the gun decks of navy ships, accidents were commonplace. Gunners waved lighted fuses around while powder monkeys scampered around with buckets of gunpowder, but perhaps most dangerous of all was the recoil of the heavy cannon, which often tore apart the restraining tackling, leaving the 'loose cannon' to crush anyone in its path.

To escape from these conditions – as well as the iron discipline of the navy – many such men were eager to desert and join the pirates. As a pirate gunnery officer, he would be in charge of

the stowage of the guns and the safety of the magazine. His reward was an extra half share of the booty.

Other vital members of the crew were the musicians. They kept rhythm when the men were hauling halliards or sheets, or turning the capstan to haul in the anchor. They were also on hand to entertain the pirates during their leisure time. Some pirates were better known for their singing than their ability with the cutlass. Pirate musicians received one and a quarter shares of the booty. And captive musicians were seldom freed until a better musician had been taken. When the Orkney pirate John Smith moored in a creek to visit his girlfriend, his crew raided a local croft, but left behind the two daughters of the house, taking a piper instead. The local magistrates were alerted by the abduction. Smith and his crew were arrested and taken to London, where they were held in the Marshalsea. Smith was hanged at Execution Dock on 11 June 1725. One of his lieutenants was hanged at Greenwich, and another at Deptford, as a warning to others.

Into Action

Pirate ships would lurk among the cays in the Caribbean or up the twisted tidal estuaries of the Carolinas, where they could spot their prey before they themselves could be seen. On the open ocean, a lookout would constantly scan the horizon. From the top of a hundred-foot mast the horizon is twenty miles in all directions. The ship would then be shadowed and examined from a distance using a spyglass to determine what kind of ship it was, its nationality and its course. In those days, it was hard to tell whether the ship was a heavily armed naval vessel or a lightly armed merchantman as merchant ships often had false gunports marked out on their sides. Consequently a pirate ship might shadow its prey for several days before striking. The captain would then make an informed guess about where it was coming from, where it was bound, what it might be carrying and what sort of resistance they might expect. If the ship was a man-of-war, they would usually turn tail and run. Otherwise the crew would vote whether or not to attack.

The pirates were reluctant to fire on their intended victims as a sunken ship was no good to them. They would simply fire a warning shot and unfurl the Jolly Roger.

Pirate Flags

It is thought that the origin of the name 'Jolly Roger' is the French joli rouge – 'pretty red' – a wry description of the blood-stained rag flown by early privateers. The idea was to strike fear into the hearts of intended victims. The skull and crossbones – in white on black – first appeared in the Caribbean around 1700, when it was hoisted by the French pirate Emanuel Wynne. He added an hourglass, showing that time was running out. A number of pirates adopted the skull and crossbones as their ensign, embellished in various ways. Jack Rackham – known as Calico Jack – used the skull and cross cutlasses as his banner, while Thomas Tew's flag carried an arm and cutlass in a threatening pose.

Full skeletons were also popular. Bartholomew Roberts' flag showed a representation of himself with a skeleton drinking a toast to death. He had another flag which expressed the bloody vendetta that he was waging against Barbados and Martinique. It showed himself standing on two skulls, one marked ABH – 'A Barbadian's Head – the other AMH – 'A Martinican's Head'. True to his word, Roberts hanged the governor of Martinique from a yardarm in 1720.

Many pirates simply unfurled an oversized black flag. This was usually warning enough. Pirate ships carried large crews who drank a lot, especially before going into battle, as wounds are more easily borne when drunk. The sight of a hundred jeering drunks was enough to put the

Calico Jack Rackham's variation on a theme, with cutlasses instead of the usual crossbones.

fear of God into most merchantman's captains, especially as he knew that his small crew were reluctant to put up a fight and were probably eager to join the pirates.

Meanwhile the pirates 'vapoured' – they danced around growling, shouting war cries, clashing their cutlasses and waving other weapons. If they spotted the captain of the prize ship, they singled him out for abuse. The 'low and brutal' Captain John Russel hailed Captain George Roberts of the sloop *Dolphin* as he stood by to board her off the Cape Verde Islands in 1722 with the words, 'You dog. You son-of-a-bitch. You speckle-shirted dog. I will drub you, you dog, within an inch of your life – and that inch too.'

These were no idle threats. In 1719, a Captain Skinner surrendered to the pirate Captain Edward England off the coast of Africa. Once the pirates were on board, Skinner's former bosun who was among them said, 'Captain Skinner, is that you? The very man in the world I wish most to see. I am very much in your debt and you shall be paid in full in your own coin.'

The bosun then had the captain lashed to the windlass where he was pelted with broken bottles. Afterwards he was knocked around the deck by the pirates until they were tired. They then took pity on him, told him that he had been a good master, so he deserved an easy death – and they shot him in the head.

Normally captains who surrendered were allowed to go free after the ship had been plundered. Even if their ship was taken, they would be kept on as navigator. However, to encourage their prey to surrender, pirates deliberately fostered their fearsome reputations, meting out all manner of cruelty on those who resisted. Captain William Snelgrave, a English seaman who spent three weeks as a captive in 1719, witnessed the fate of a French captain who did not immediately strike his colours after the pirates had fired a warning.

'They put a rope around his neck and hoisted him up and down several times to the main yardarm, till he was almost dead,' he said. Pirates would 'sweat' their victims, forcing them to run around the deck while they jabbed at

An early pirate flag, belonging to one Edward Wynne. The hourglass was to signify to pirate victims that their time was running out.

Bartholomew Roberts, the infamous Welsh pirate, drinks a toast with death in his own version of the Jolly Roger.

them with pointed weapons. Teetotallers were forced to down a quart of rum in a single gulp or face a bullet in the head. Victims were pelted with broken bottles before they were shot. Catholic friars were flogged with a cat-o'-nine-tails for sport. Hemp used for caulking was stuffed in a victim's mouth and set on fire. In 1695, a Captain Sawbridge fell into the hands of the pirate Dirk Chivers. Irritated by the merchant captain's constant reproaches, Chivers had Sawbridge's lips sewn together. He was then put ashore where he soon died.

Armed with the knowledge that their victims were terrified of them, pirate captains could appeal to their reason. Captain Robert Culliford, who sailed with Captain Kidd, addressed a ship he knew to be full of specie with the words, 'Gentlemen, we want not your ship, but only your money. Money we want and money we shall have.'

If a prize ship refused to surrender at once, the pirate ship tried to attack from the stern so they would not risk a broadside and if the prize tried to escape they could shoot away the rudder, leaving the victim unable to steer. They would then clear the decks with a volley of musket fire, then board, brandishing their cutlasses.

Usually resistance was futile, but on 26 October 1686, the French pirate vessel, the *Trompeuse*, tried to take the small English frigate *Bauden* off St Jago Island. The Frenchman was a 300-ton vessel with 30 guns and 250 men. The *Bauden* displaced just 170 tons and carried sixteen guns and sixty-eight men. Thirty-eight of them were landlubbers, soldiers on their way to man the East India Company garrison in Bombay. Nevertheless the *Bauden*'s Captain John Cribb was determined to resist.

At 6am, Cribb spotted a sail three leagues – ten miles – to the west. He ordered the decks cleared and the guns double-loaded with shot. Powder chests were set up on the poop and forecastle, and the yardarms were lashed with chains to prevent them being cut away. Four six-pounders were run out on the quarter-deck and a six-pounder swivel gun was set up in the closed quarters so it could sweep the well if the pirates boarded. To hinder boarders further, the decks were greased with butter and strewn with dried peas and boards with nails through them.

At midday, the pirate ship, flying a French flag, was bearing down on the *Bauden*'s starboard quarter. A pirate clambered out on the bowsprit and ordered the *Bauden*'s captain to come aboard. Cribb refused. He said if the pirates had any business to discuss, they should come aboard the *Bauden*. The pirate replied in broken English that that was exactly what they intended to do.

'Welcome,' said Cribb. 'Win her and wear her.'

The pirates replied with a volley of small-arms fire. The men on the *Bauden* answered with a volley of their own from the waist of the ship. Then half withdrew into the forecastle and half into the aftercastle. From the forecastle, they fired the cannon at the pirate's bow. She veered, smashing her bowsprit into the *Bauden*'s mainmast. The guns at the rear in the steerage then fired. The impact pushed the rear of the pirate ship outwards, so her bowsprit became entangled in the *Bauden*'s rigging. The pirates then crawled along the bowsprit and lashed it to the *Bauden* so she could not get away. Others began to scale the *Bauden*'s sides, while the two ships blasted one another with cannon fire.

The pirates scaled the rigging and tried to cut the yards away. The chains prevented this, but the men in the rigging were vulnerable to small-arms fire. Cribb's men picked them off

Captain Robert Culliford, who sailed with Captain Kidd, addressed a ship he knew to be full of specie with the words, 'Gentlemen, we want not your ship, but only your money. Money we want and money we shall have.'

and they fell in the sea. The pirates dared not rush the aftercastle because of the swivel gun. Instead they concentrated their attack on the forecastle, where Cribb was. The pirates' cannon blasted three shots through the *Bauden*'s sides. One hit a powder chest, which exploded. The pirates cheered and swarmed onto the poopdeck with a poleaxe to hack down the ensign. But Cribb's men poured withering fire on them through the loopholes of the closed quarters and the pirates were forced to retreat. By this time, the battle had been raging for two hours.

Although by this time Cribb was badly wounded in the groin, he went out on deck to encourage his men. He was hit by a second bullet that passed right through his chest. Half-an-hour later, he was dead. The pirate captain had been killed too and his vessel was leaking badly. But the two ships were still lashed together and, for the next two hours, they continued pummelling each other with shot. Eventually the *Bauden* swept the deck of the pirate ship with a nine-pounder loaded with partridge – case-shot

– and double chain-shot. The game was now up. Fearing that they were about to sink, the pirates cut their ship free. As they moved off, the men of the *Bauden* came on deck to cry, 'Cheerio.'

They could see that the pirate ship was listing badly, keeping one side high to stop water flooding in through the shot holes. By their reckoning, at least sixty pirates had been killed and the chain-shot would have maimed many more. More than a thousand rounds of shot had been exchanged. The *Bauden*'s rigging had been shot away and she had been severely damaged along the port side. Eight men were dead, including Captain Cribb and the first mate. Sixteen were wounded, including the bosun, the quartermaster, the gunner and ordinary seaman Richard Salwey, who later wrote an account of the action.

'I, the writer of this,' he wrote, 'have received besides bruises, one small shot which went in a little way below my small ribs and struck down to my bladder about five inches where it still remains in my body. But, blessed be God, I feel no pain save on the change of weather.'

However, it was rare for a solitary ship to beat off the pirates. And even if they did manage a stout defence, it did not necessarily mean that the captured captain would be killed. In August 1720, Captain James Macrae of the *Cassandra* inflicted between 90 and 100 casualties on the pirates when he was attacked by Edward England aboard the *Fancy* and former Royal Navy lieutenant John Taylor in the *Victory*. During a fierce gun battle Macrae ran the *Cassandra* aground and escaped into the jungle, even though he had a musket ball lodged in his head. The pirates now had his ships and the £75,000-worth of valuables he had on board and they put out a £2,000 reward on Macrae's head.

Foolishly Macrae returned to his ship ten days later. Taylor was for killing him when one of his crew stepped forward and said, 'Show me the man that offers to hurt Captain Macrae and I'll stand to him, for an honester fellow I never sailed with.'

The man had a wooden leg, heavy whiskers

and a belt stuffed with pistols, and it is thought that he was the model for *Treasure Island*'s Long John Silver.

England gave Macrae the badly damaged *Fancy* and returned half his cargo. After forty-eight days – much of which he spent becalmed – Macrae reached India. He later rose to become the governor of Madras. The kindness England showed to Macrae enraged the other pirates, who marooned him on Mauritius with a pistol, powder and a keg of water and sailed off with Taylor on board the *Cassandra*. England made himself a raft and drifted five hundred miles to Madagascar, where he died some years later a penniless beggar.

Taylor went on to take the greatest single prize in the golden age of piracy. On 26 April 1721 – Low Sunday, the Sunday after Easter – the *Cassandra* under Taylor and the *Victory*, now under the French pirate La Buze, saw the Portuguese East Indiaman *Virgem de Cabo* (Virgin of the Cape) at anchor in the harbour at Saint-Denis on the island of Bourbon (now Réunion) in the Mauritius group, undergoing

repairs after losing her mast in a gale.

The owner of the *Cabo* was Dom Luis Carlos Ignaico Xavier de Meneses, the fifth Count of Ericeira and the former viceroy of Goa, who was on his way home to Portugal. Seeing the newcomers were flying English flags, the Cabo saluted them and assumed they would return the compliment, as was customary, once they had anchored. Instead they sailed up with one on either side of her, struck their ensigns and hauled up the Jolly Roger. And instead of firing a salute they opened up a broadside, pounding the *Cabo* from both sides.

The *Cabo* had a crew of 130, but had only 21 cannon and 34 muskets. They faced 200 pirates armed to the teeth. Taylor's men hurled grenades on to the deck and swarmed aboard. Thirteen of the *Cabo* crewmen immediately changed sides. The rest put up little resistance, except for the Count of Ericeira, resplendent in a scarlet coat. He continued to fight off the pirates with the stub of his sword which had been broken in the fighting until Taylor gave the order to stop.

Treasure Island, by Robert Louis Stevenson, 1886. Stevenson's classic adventure novel was first serialised as **The Sea Cook: or, Treasure Island in Young Folks** *and then published in book form in 1883. The frontispiece of the 1886 illustrated edition shows a map of Hispaniola with instructions for finding pirates' treasure.*

The count was treated with great respect for his bravery and was allowed to keep his broken sword, even though the hilt was encrusted with gold and diamonds. The pirates also told him he could keep his personal effects, but he proudly refused, saying that that he wanted to be treated the same as his crew. As a result, his collection of priceless Oriental manuscripts and ancient books was torn up to make cartridges and wadding.

The governor of Bourbon paid a £400 ransom and the count was rowed ashore to a twenty-one-gun salute and three rousing cheers of 'Vive le Roi!' from the pirates. As well as losing the fortune he had amassed in Goa, he had also lost a consignment of diamonds worth over half a million pounds belonging to the king. As a result he was banished from court for ten years.

The *Cabo* also had on board silk, porcelains, spices and other goods. The haul came to well over £1 million. When the booty was shared out, each man got £4,000 plus forty-two small diamonds. One man complained bitterly that he had been given one big diamond rather that forty-two little ones, so he took a hammer and smashed it to pieces – boasting later that he had obtained more than forty-two small diamonds as a result.

Some of Taylor's men took their money and settled down in Madagascar, while others took a French pardon and settled on Réunion. Taylor sailed for the Caribbean with 140 men to seek a pardon from the governor of Jamaica. This was refused. Instead, he obtained one from the Spanish and was later to sail for the Spanish coastguard out of Portobelo. He was never brought to justice. Legend has it that he ended his days trading in logwood from Honduras, finally dying of old age in Cuba.

Brought to Justice

Those few men who survived the privations, diseases, shipwrecks, maroonings and seabattles of pirate life might have decided that it was time to retire. Their captain would write them a 'ticket',

The British authorities made sure that the gallows were in sight of the sea-approach to the harbour, so the crews of passing ships could see the corpses of executed pirates turning in the wind

saying that they had been pressed into service, they had never taken the articles of piracy and they had not shared in the booty. This seldom worked. Most ended their lives by way of a rope, one way or another. The British hanged pirates, while the Spanish preferred garrotting.

The British authorities made sure that the gallows were always in sight of the sea-approach to the harbour, so the crews of passing ships could see the corpses turning in the wind. The trial and execution of pirates was the job of the Admiralty, though colonial governors often captured, tried and executed pirates on the Admiralty's behalf. All land below the high water mark fell under the jurisdiction of the Admiralty, so the gallows were erected there.

The hangings were a public event and the execution of a famous pirate drew a large crowd, though spectators often had mixed feelings. Some applauded the fact that the seas would now be safer and trade more profitable; others admired these men who had bucked the system and lived life as they pleased. Afterwards the corpse was usually allowed to rot in the noose until the rope rotted through. But at London's Execution Dock, there were simply so many hangings that bodies were disposed of after the tide had washed over them three times. Sometimes bodies of famous pirates were preserved in tar, so that they could be displayed for years as a gruesome warning. In Boston, after a pirate had been hanged on the foreshore, his body was cut down and displayed on Nix Maze, an island in the harbour.

For many pirates, death by hanging was a price worth paying for a few years freedom on the seas. By and large, they met their ends bravely. Denis Macarty escaped the gallows once by taking Woodes Rogers' pardon at Providence in the Bahamas in 1718. But he could not give up his old ways and, later, joined the famous pirate Calico Jack Rackham. He was captured along with Rackham off Jamaica in 1720. Found guilty of piracy, and about to be hanged, he said, 'My friends said I would die with my shoes on. To make 'em liars, I kicks them off.' And he did.

Rackham was captured hiding below decks. Before he was hanged, he was visited by Anne Bonny who had fought on bravely. She told him dismissively, 'If you had fought like a man you wouldn't now have to hang like a dog. Do straighten yourself up!' Anne herself escaped the gallows because she was pregnant.

Not all pirates were against the death penalty. As another woman pirate and associate of Calico Jack, Mary Read, expressed it:

if it was put to the pirates, they would not have any punishment less than death, the fear of which kept some dastardly rogues honest; that many of those who now cheated the widows and orphans, and oppressed the poor neighbourhoods, who have no money to obtain justice, would rob them at sea, and the ocean would be crowded with rogues, like the land.

She too escaped the noose because she was pregnant.

When Captain Richard Thomas was asked to repent on the gallows, he replied,

Yes, I repent that I had not done more mischief, and that we did not cut the throats of them that took us, and I'm extremely sorry that you ain't hanged as well.

Bartholomew Roberts escaped the gallows to die in a gun battle off West Africa on 10 February 1722 at the age of forty – not a bad age in the eighteenth century. Of lowly birth in Wales, he explained his attitude to piracy and the noose, saying simply:

In honest service, there are commonly low wages and hard labour; in this – plenty, satiety, pleasure and ease, liberty and power. Who would not balance credit on this side, when all the hazard that is run for it, at worst, is only a sour look or two on choking? No, a merry life and a short one, that's my motto.

Execution of a pirate at Wapping Dock, London.

CHAPTER EIGHT

CAPTAIN KIDD AND THE
LURE OF THE ORIENT

After the death of Henry Morgan, Captain Kidd took over his mantle as the world's most notorious pirate. William Kidd was born in Greenock, Scotland, around 1645. It is thought that he was the son of a Presbyterian minister and that he went to sea early in life, though nothing is known of him until 1689.

The previous year, the Glorious Revolution had ousted James II and put William of Orange, a Dutch prince, on the throne of England. This brought England into conflict with France in 'King William's War', otherwise known as the War of the Grand Alliance, or the War of the League of Augsburg.

When the war broke out, Kidd was on a ship anchored off St Christopher (St Kitts) in the Leeward Islands whose sovereignty was disputed. The English and Dutch crewmen overpowered their French comrades and took the twenty-gun ship to Nevis, an English possession. The ship was renamed *Blessed William* with Kidd as its captain. More English volunteers were taken on, bringing the crew up to eighty or ninety.

At the time Thomas Hewetson was in command of the local privateer squadron. Hewetson had set sail from England in 1688 with the intention of establishing a colony in Chile, but had failed to make it through the Straits of Magellan. His fifty-gun flagship, the *Lion,* and two other vessels then headed for the Caribbean to make their fortunes as buccaneers. They were anchored off Barbados in July 1689 when one of the ships blew up. Most of his men deserted and Hewetson was about to sail home as an escort for a merchant convoy when he heard of the war with France. With '350 lusty men', he took a commission from the governor of Bermuda Sir Robert Robinson. Hewetson became 'commander in chief of all

the vessels in the Leeward Islands', where Kidd and the *Blessed William* had their base.

When the Comte de Blénac, a buccaneer of noble birth who became French governor of the Antilles, had attacked the English colony on St Christopher, Hewetson set sail for Marie Galante, off Guadaloupe, 'to reduce it, securing plunder for himself and fellow adventurers'. They arrived on 30 December 1689 and spent five days sacking the island, taking their plunder back to Nevis. There they learnt that an expedition under Sir Thomas Thornhill had been cut off after attacking the French colony on St Martin. They arrived to find the English troops ashore being besieged by five French warships under the command of Jean-Baptiste Ducasse.

Ducasse was a veteran Hugenot privateer. He had gone to sea as a young man with the Compagnie du Sénégal which transported slaves across the Atlantic. In September 1678, during the Franco-Dutch war, he had taken a Dutch slaving station on the African coast and later became a lieutenant in the French Navy. He led a campaign against pirates and Dutch slavers, before attacking the Dutch colony of Surinam in 1688. He played a crucial role in the French attack on the English colony on St Kitts and 'laid the southern part of the island in ashes'.

At St Martin, Ducasse had arrived with 700 men in the nick of time to save the French colony from Thornhill's invasion force, trapping the English forces ashore. When Hewetson arrived, the two squadrons fought a fierce gun battle. Eventually Ducasse was forced to with-

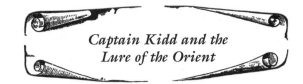

draw and Hewetson evacuated Thornhill's men, taking them back to Nevis. Hewetson praised Kidd as a 'mighty man' who had fought as well as anyone he had seen. But Kidd's men were less than happy that they had been employed as regular naval forces at St Martin, limiting their opportunity for plunder. Many deserted. And when Kidd went ashore on 2 February 1690, mutineers under William Mason stole his ship and made off with £2,000 worth of the booty looted from Marie Galante.

Hewetson took another commission from the governor of Barbados, then sailed for the Spanish. Meanwhile, the governor of the Leeward Islands, Christopher Codrington, gave Kidd a ship recently captured from the French and renamed *Antigua*. He raised a crew and set off after the *Blessed William*, which had sailed to New York. Kidd arrived there in March 1691, but Mason and his men had already sailed for the Indian Ocean after working briefly as a privateer for Jacob Leisler, a German merchant who had seized power in New York after the fall of James II. Kidd joined the English forces who were about retake the colony, using the *Antigua* to ferry guns and ammunition for them. When New York was back in British hands, Kidd was rewarded with £150 and a share of the French ship the *Saint Pierre*, taken by Mason under one of Leisler's commissions.

On 16 May 1691 Kidd married the twice-widowed Sarah Bradley Cox Oort just days after her second husband John Oort died, leaving her a considerable fortune. Eleven days later he set sail after a French privateer reported off Block Island in Rhode Island Sound. But then he seems to have temporarily lost his taste for the sea. For a couple of years, he settled down with his new wife. They had two children and traded in real estate. In 1693, he sold a property on Dock Street and moved his family into a mansion at 119-121 Pearl Street. A respectable member of the community, he bought a pew in Trinity Church, which boasted among its congregation the new governor of New York Benjamin Fletcher.

In 1694, Kidd sat as foreman of the jury that acquitted fellow New York Scot Colonel Robert Livingston, whose ship the *Orange* had been caught trading with the French on Saint Domingue. This, along with the exploits of Thomas Tew that were the talk of the American colonies at the time, seems to have inspired Kidd to return to privateering.

Thomas Tew and the Amity

A native of Rhode Island, Thomas Tew had moved to Jamaica in the 1680s, where he made his living as a sea rover. In December 1692, he bought a privateer commission from Isaac Richier, the lieutenant-governor of Bermuda, to attack a French slaving station at Gorée on the Gambia River in West Africa. He bought a share in the seventy-ton *Amity*, which carried eight guns. Crewed by sixty hard-bitten men, he set out in January 1693, accompanied by a sloop under Captain George Dew. During a storm Dew's vessel sprang its mast and he turned back, leaving Tew to go on alone. It was then that Tew made a proposal to his crew. He suggested that, instead of attacking the French, they make their way to the Indian Ocean, where the pickings would be rich and they stood little

Captain Kidd attacks mutinous gunner William Moore with a bucket in a dispute over attacking a ship flying English colours. Moore died from his injuries, the crime for which Kidd was hanged.

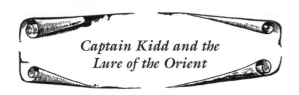

Flag of Thomas Tew, the pirate whose exploits may have inspired Kidd to take up privateering again.

ing expeditions first in the Mediterranean, then in the Caribbean. The *Victoire* was attacked by HMS *Winchelsea* off Antigua. During the battle, the *Winchelsea* suddenly exploded. Most of the *Victoire's* officers had already been killed and Misson took command with Father Caraccioli, a priest he had met in Rome, as his mentor. Caraccioli was a proto-Marxist and a huge influence on Misson, who invited the crew to join him on a 'socialist' pirating expedition. After taking ships off the Windward Islands and selling their plunder in Boca Chica and Portobelo to re-equip the vessel, they set sail for West Africa. There they took a slaver and invited the slaves to join the crew, while Misson lectured his men on the evils of slavery.

At Table Bay on the Cape of Good Hope, they took an English ship whose crew, with the exception of officers, were eager to join his socialist experiment. Engaging a Portuguese ship off Zanzibar, Caraccioli lost a leg. According to Defoe, Misson and Caraccioli then set up a pirates' haven called Libertilia on Madagascar. They released their captives and gave them monetary compensation and a ship to leave in, if they wanted to go. In the Arabian Sea, Misson seized a ship carrying 1,600 pilgrims bound for Jiddah, but let them go on their way after taking a hundred girls to boost the female population of Libertilia.

After meeting Misson at St Mary's, Tew sailed with him to Libertilia, where he took part in the government of the pirate colony. He also undertook missions to resupply the colony. Taking a slaver in the South Atlantic, he liberated the slaves at Libertilia to swell the population. But after battles with the Portuguese and the Madagascans, in which Caraccioli was killed, Misson and Tew decided to abandon their libertarian experiment. They loaded their loot onto their two sloops and headed for North America. But in a high wind off the coast of South Africa, Misson's sloop capsized and sank with all hands.

The *Amity* set sail back across the Atlantic. Avoiding Bermuda, Tew headed for his native Rhode Island, where the locals were dazzled by his haul of gold, silver, jewels, ivory, silks and spices worth some £100,000. He was given a hero's welcome – by everyone except the governor, John Easton, a devout Quaker. Tew offered him £500 for a commission to exercise 'perhaps where the commission might never be seen or heard of'. Easton refused, so Tew went

chance of being caught. This course, he said, would 'lead them to ease and plenty, in which they might pass the rest of their days; that one bold push would do their business, and they might return home, not only without danger, but even with reputation'.

The crew, it was said, cried out, to a man, 'A gold chain, or a wooden leg, we will stand by you.'

They altered course for the Cape of Good Hope and sailed into the Indian Ocean. After a couple of weeks they came upon a rich merchant vessel belonging to the Great Mogul of India, which was heading for the Red Sea. After a fusillade, Tew took the vessel without a single loss and sailed to St Mary's, an islet off Madagascar. This was the bolt-hole of Adam Baldridge, a Jamaican buccaneer who had fled there in 1685 after being wanted for murder in Jamaica. Establishing a defensible harbour there, he became known as 'king of the pirates' in the outlaw colony which at its peak numbered 1,500.

Tew divided the booty and careened his ship. His men got between £1,200 and £3,000 apiece and his quartermaster and twenty-three of his men settled in Madagascar, a favourite spot for pirates to retire because of the accommodating brown-skinned women there. However, the natives of Madagascar eventually rose up against Baldridge and his musket-toting cut-throats. Baldridge fled with his treasure to New York, where he lived into old age.

Tew and the *Amity* teamed up with the French pirate Captain Misson, who had sailed on the French man-of-war *Victoire* on privateer-

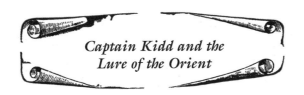
to New York where he was fêted by the Governor Benjamin Fletcher, who attended Trinity Church alongside Kidd. Tew's wife and two daughters attended gala evenings at the governor's mansion, swathed in silks and jewels from the plunder. The governor gave Tew a gold watch, while Tew gave the governor £300 for a commission.

Back in Newport, Tew prepared the *Amity* for another voyage. As his future seemed assured, Tew took the opportunity to send money to his backers in Bermuda – fourteen times their original investment it was said – explaining that he could not return there because he had sprung a mast.

By this time, Tew's exploits were so well known that young men from all over New England left their families and their masters and flocked to join up with him. Some even took to stowing away. Tew set out again in November 1694. Again he made his way around the Cape of Good Hope and into the Red Sea, but it was not until September 1695 that they came across another of the Great Mogul's treasure ships. This time things did not go so smoothly. During the battle a shot tore open Tew's belly. He held his bowels in with his hand, but when he grew weak and dropped them, it 'struck such terror into his men that they suffered themselves to be taken without further resistance'.

Tew's career may have come to the usual sticky end, but the son of Rhode Island tavern-keeper William Mayes was already following in Tew's footsteps. In December 1694, Mayes obtained a privateering commission from the deputy governor of Rhode Island, John Greene Jr, a man known to be corrupt. Mayes had political connections as he was married to Sarah, the daughter of Samuel Gorton, the former president of the colony. The Board of Trade in London pointed out that Greene had no powers to issue such a commission and had taken no bond against Mayes' good behaviour. When Greene said that he knew of no such statutes, the Board of Trade expressed disbelief that anyone so ignorant could have been appointed to the post of deputy governor.

The Customs house in Newport were told that Mayes had set sail in his sixty-ton brigantine *Pearl* with six guns and fifty men 'on a trading voyage to Madagascar'. The Board of Trade said that no commerce existed with the island and that, at best, he was going to trade with the pirates on the island, but that the chances were he intended to do a little piracy himself. But by this time, Mayes had sailed. Later, in his defence, it was said that Mayes had traded in Madagascar, but had then been robbed by Henry Every.

Born in Plymouth, England, in 1659, Every saw action as a midshipman, a first mate and a sailing master in the Royal Navy until he was discharged. In 1693, he signed aboard a heavily-armed private frigate at Gravesend. She was named *Charles II*, after the king of Spain, and was part of an expedition to salvage Spanish wrecks and attack French possessions in the Caribbean. Spain was allied with England against France at the time. The commander of the expedition was John Strong, who had learnt the salvage business with Sir William Phips, who went on to become the governor of Massachusetts. They stopped at the Spanish port of Corunna in early 1694, where Strong died. He was succeeded by Charles Gibson with Every as first mate.

The death of Strong delayed the expedition and the *Charles II* lay at anchor in Corunna for three months while the English crew grew restive. One night, Every led a mutiny and slipped out of port. The next morning he cast Captain Gibson and sixteen loyal hands adrift in an open boat with the words 'I am a man of fortune and must seek my fortune,' and he too headed for the Indian Ocean.

The Board of Trade refused to believe that Every had robbed Mayes. Instead they believed that Every persuaded Mayes to join him in an attack on the Mogul trader *Ganj-i-sawai* off Bombay on 8 September 1695, netting some £200,000. They then fled across the Atlantic. Every went to the Bahamas where the corrupt local governor Nicholas Trott took a £1,000 bribe to allow Every and his crew to land. He

Tew's exploits became so well known that young men from all over New England left their families and their masters and flocked to join up with him

sold the *Charles II*, now renamed the *Fancy*, to Trott, who stripped her and allowed her to drift onto a leeward shore a few days later so the surf would destroy the evidence. Every and his pirate crew then melted away. Only one of them, it seems, faced justice, after a fashion. It is said that crewman Joseph Morris stayed behind on the Bahamas, where he lost his reason after 'losing all his jewels upon a wager'.

Mayes headed to New York, where he arrived in 1699 with a ship laden with booty. Presumably his powerful political connections allowed him too to melt back into civilian life. In 1702, he seems to have taken over his father's tavern, the White Horse in Newport, Rhode Island.

However, there was one man who had a mind to put an end to the activities of Tew, Misson, Mayes, Every and the like. It was Captain Kidd's old friend Robert Livingston. Kidd had sailed to London in 1695 in the hope of getting a privateering commission. This was not forthcoming, but he met up with Livingston, who had a scheme for ending Red Sea piracy – and making a tidy profit at the same time. The idea was to send a specially commissioned privateer to the Indian Ocean to catch the pirates. It would be funded by seizing the pirates' treasure. What better commander could there be for such an expedition than Captain Kidd, a respectable New York merchant and former privateer who had already done service for the crown?

They put the scheme to the Earl of Bellomont, who had just been appointed governor of New York and New England. He used his influence with the Whig government to come up with two commissions. One was a letter of marque allowing Kidd to capture ships and goods belonging to the current enemy, France. The other allowed Kidd to capture pirates and impound their goods. Tew and Mayes were among those named.

Kidd was to be equipped with a purpose-built frigate, the 287-ton *Adventure Galley*, carrying thirty-four guns. This was to be paid

> **Mayes headed to New York, where he arrived in 1699 with a ship laden with booty, and seems to have taken over his father's tavern in Newport**

for by a band of influential backers, including several close friends of the king. They put up four-fifths of the money while Livingston and Kidd put up the other fifth. The king promised to contribute £3,000, but never came up with the money.

The articles signed by Bellomont, Kidd and Livingston stipulated that sixty per cent of the booty should go to the backers, fifteen per cent to Kidd and Livingston and just twenty-five per cent to the crew – rather than the sixty per cent specified in most privateering agreements.

Usually the crown took ten per cent off the top of any booty. But it was arranged for Kidd to land the plunder in New England, where Bellomont was about to take up his position as governor, so there would be no royal duties to pay. If Kidd and Livingston came up empty handed, they would have to pay the whole cost of the expedition. The men too were taken on a 'no purchase, no pay' basis. Purchase here meant booty, so if they did not take any prizes they got no money.

The deal was not particularly advantageous to Kidd. He had to sell the *Antigua* and a third of his interest to a speculator to find his stake. He knew that French ships were few and far between in the Indian Ocean and pirates were, at best, elusive. He also knew that he ran a great risk with the law. Privateer crews often mutinied and turned to piracy if there was no plunder. But, Kidd wrote later, 'Lord Bellomont assured me again and again the noble lords would stifle all complaints.'

Indeed, his backers were among the most powerful men in the land – Lord Keeper of the Great Seal and later Lord Chancellor Sir John Sommers; Secretary of State, the Duke of Shrewsbury; First Lord of the Admiralty, Lord Orford; and Master General of Ordinance, the Earl of Romney. Kidd was invited to their palatial homes and told that it would be disloyal to refuse the King's commission. Later, as Kidd protested to one of his backers, Bellomont 'added threats to his wheedles'. Kidd wrote:

I, thinking myself safe with the King's commission and the protection of so many great men, accepted, thinking it was in my Lord Bellomont's power as governor of New York to oppress me if I continued to be obstinate. Before I went to sea I waited twice on my Lord Romney and Admiral Russell. Both hastened me to sea and promised to stand by me.

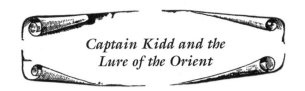

As an added precaution, Kidd did not take on the usual ruffians who had little to lose if they turned pirate. He recruited seventy men, most of whom were married and had settled families in England. He then planned to sail first to New York, and then to pick up eighty more men with wives and families in New England.

On 1 March 1696, Kidd set sail from Deptford. The voyage was a disaster from the start. There was no love lost between Kidd and the Royal Navy. At the time, it was unheard of for a privately-owned ship to be sent against pirates: that was the Navy's job. As Kidd was departing Greenwich, he neglected to salute a passing Navy yacht, as was the custom. Taking offence, the yacht fired a gun, to remind them of their duty. Kidd's men, manning the yardarms, promptly turned their backsides and slapped them in derision. The incensed captain of the yacht promptly press-ganged Kidd's hand-picked crew, replacing them with unhandy landsmen from the yacht.

On the way across the Atlantic, they captured a French fishing vessel, which helped pay for their provisions in New York. However, the eighty crewmen he needed were not forthcoming and, to attract them, Kidd had to up the crew's share of the profits to the customary sixty per cent – without informing his backers. One of the crewmen who signed up was Kidd's brother-in-law Samuel Bradley. Another came all the way from Philadelphia. But generally they were not the respectable family men Kidd had hoped for.

'Many flocked to him from all parts,' wrote Fletcher who was still governor of New York, pending the arrival of Bellomont, 'men of desperate fortunes and necessities, in expectation of getting vast treasure. It is generally believed here that if he misses the design named in his commission, he will not be able to govern such a villainous herd.'

Kidd reached Madeira by mid-October, then visited the Cape Verde Islands. On 12 December 1696, about a hundred miles north-west of Cape Town, he unexpectedly ran into a Royal Navy squadron under Commodore Thomas Warren. Kidd demanded that Warren give him some sails to replace those he had lost in an Atlantic storm, insisting that his royal commission entitled him to aid. When Warren refused, Kidd threatened to take the sails from the first merchantman he met. Relations between Kidd and Warren grew fraught and

Kidd became convinced that Warren intended to press thirty of his men into naval service. That night, while they were becalmed, the *Adventure Galley* rowed away from Warren's squadron.

Kidd sailed into the Indian Ocean without stopping at Cape Town, where he would almost certainly have been arrested. When Warren put in there, he reported that Kidd intended to turn to piracy. At Johanna Island (Anjouan) in the Comoros, Kidd met an East Indiaman flying a Royal Navy pennant and ordered her captain to strike it, saying that only he had the right to fly a Navy pennant by virtue of his royal commission. The East Indiaman grew so fearful of Kidd that she kept her guns trained on the *Adventure Galley* all the time she was in port, even threatening to board her. The *Adventure Galley* moved on to nearby Moheli Island, where she careened. During her stay fifty of her men died from disease.

Captain Kidd buries his treasure on Gardiner's Island off the US Atlantic coast, as seen by Howard Pyle, **Harper's Monthly.**

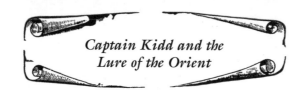

By this time, Kidd had been at sea for more than a year. Apart from the one fishing boat they had taken on the way to New York, they had seen no Frenchmen and no pirates, and neither Kidd nor his crew had earned a penny. Provisions were running low and the ruffians Kidd had recruited in New York were now openly advocating piracy.

On 27 April 1697, Kidd headed north. In July, he anchored at Perim, an island at the mouth of the Red Sea. This was a favourite spot for pirates to wait in ambush for the convoys coming out of Mocha, the chief port of the Yemeni coffee trade. He sent reconnaissance boats through the straits,

The *Adventure Galley* then fired a broadside into the Arab boat, hitting her in the hull, the sails and the rigging

which reported that fourteen or fifteen ships were ready to sail. For three weeks, he rode at anchor waiting for them. Although seizing Arab vessels was technically piracy, such things were usually winked at. Kidd had powerful and important backers, who could pull strings, and who were unlikely to be sympathetic if he came home empty-handed. And if he did not take a prize soon, his crew would mutiny.

The convoy sailed out of Mocha on the evening of 14 August. None were flying French colours. Some even flew Dutch and English flags. Worse, the convoy was escorted by the thirty-six-gun English East Indiaman *Sceptre* under Edward Barlow.

The following morning one of Barlow's men reported that there was one too many ships in the convoy. Barlow then spotted Kidd. 'He showed no colours,' Barlow wrote in his log, 'but had only a red broad pennant out without any cross on it.'

This Barlow took to be an order to surrender or no quarter would be given.

'Had not our ship happened to have been in their company, he had certainly plundered all their head-most ships of their wealth,' said Barlow.

The *Adventure Galley* closed on a large Arab merchant ship. Barlow waited until he was nearly alongside, when he hoisted his English ensign and fired off two or three guns. The *Adventure Galley* then fired a broadside into the Arab boat, hitting her in the hull, the sails and the rigging. The *Sceptre* moved in, but the

Adventure Galley took off under sail and oar, outrunning the English ship.

In August, off Goa, Kidd came upon another Arab vessel and boarded it. His men took a bale of pepper and a sack of coffee, which he let them keep for their mess. The ship had an English captain called Parker, whom Kidd took as his pilot. He also took her Portuguese first mate as an interpreter.

Word quickly spread around the ports of the Indian Ocean that Kidd had taken to piracy and when the *Adventure Galley* put in at Karwar on the Malabar Coast two English officers of the East India Company came on board and demanded the release of Parker and the Portuguese mate. Kidd denied all knowledge of the two men. They were, in fact, locked in the hold. After the two officers left, a crewman who did not like the way things were turning out jumped ship, and later made a deposition to the East India Company station in Bombay (Mumbai) that Kidd was 'going on the ill design of piracy'.

In his report, the chief factor of the East India Company at Karwar said that Kidd was a 'very lusty man' who treated his men very harshly, regularly threatening to knock their brains out with a pistol butt. They in their turn were in awe of him because of his commission from the king.

'They are a very distracted company,' the chief factor wrote, 'continually quarrelling and fighting among themselves, so it is likely they will in a short time destroy one another, or starve, having only sufficient provisions to keep them at sea for a month more.'

The East India Company's agent at Calicot (Kozhikode) refused Kidd wood and water, even though Kidd insisted that 'he was sent out by the King of England'.

Soon after, Kidd spotted a merchant ship sailing northwards along the coast, but when they came within six thousand yards they saw she was flying English colours. The *Adventure Galley*'s gunner William Moore proposed they plunder her anyway. Kidd refused.

'I dare not do such a thing,' he said.

But Moore became insistent.

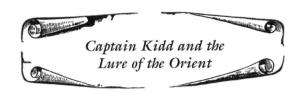
'We are beggars already,' he said.

They stopped her. She turned out to be the *Loyal Captain* bound from Madras to Surat. And when her papers proved to be in order, Kidd let her go.

This infuriated the crew, who were on the point of mutiny. Some brought out their guns, but Kidd faced them down. He said that he had not come to take English ships or other lawful vessels. Many were ready to jump ship.

'If you desert my ship you shall never come aboard again,' he told them, 'and I will force you to Bombay and I will carry you before some of the Council there.'

But Moore, the gunner, was not satisfied by this.

Kidd picked up an iron bucket and hurled it at Moore's head, hitting him just above the right ear: Moore died the next day

'Captain, I could have put you in the way to have taken the ship, and have never been the worst for it,' said Moore.

This sent Kidd 'into a passion' – so much so that teenage deckhand Hugh Parrot took refuge below decks. But Moore and others did not.

'You have brought us to ruin,' Moore told Kidd, 'and we are desolate.'

'Have I brought you to ruin?' Kidd asked. 'I have not done an ill thing to ruin you. You are a saucy fellow to say those words.'

According to a sailor named Palmer, Kidd did not say 'saucy fellow' but 'lousy dog'.

'If I am a lousy dog,' said Moore, 'you have made me so.'

Kidd was now beside himself with rage.

'Have I ruined you, you dog!' he screamed and he picked up an iron bucket – worth eight-pence in lawful English money, as the prosecutor later pointed out – and hurled it at Moore's head, hitting him just above the right ear and injuring him badly.

As his shipmates carried the wounded gunner below decks, Kidd called after them, 'Damn him. He is a villain.'

Next day Moore died of a fractured skull.

At the end of November, twelve nautical miles from Calicut, they spotted a sail and bore down on her. Kidd ran up the French flag and the other ship, the *Maiden*, did the same. But when he boarded her, the Dutch captain explained that the ship was Moorish. He and

the two other officers were Dutch; the rest of the crew were Arabs. However, Kidd discovered that the *Maiden* carried a French pass, making her, he argued, a legitimate prize.

'By God, have I catched you?' he said. 'You are a free prize to England.'

In fact, the ship was Indian-owned. The French pass meant nothing as it was usual for vessels to carry passes from any nation whose navy happened to be operating in the area. Indeed, the captain had a number of other passes in his possession. But Kidd needed a prize. The *Maiden's* Arab crew were cast adrift in a long-boat and with the connivance of the Dutch officers, the cargo was sold off ashore and the proceeds shared out among Kidd's men. For the first time in two years, they had seen some money. However, under the articles Kidd signed, this should have been held back until adjudication was made by an Admiralty Court, and the backers had got their share.

On 28 December 1697, with the *Maiden*, now renamed *November*, in tow, the *Adventure Galley* took an Arab ketch off the Malabar Coast, netting a sack of coffee and some sweets. Two weeks later, he seized butter, beeswax, rice, iron, opium and gunpowder from a Portuguese ship. Then on 30 January 1698, the lookout spotted the four-hundred-ton *Quedah Merchant*, an Armenian vessel with an English captain named Wright, bound from Bengal to Surat with a rich cargo of silk, muslin, sugar, guns, iron, saltpetre and gold coins. She was making heavy weather some thirty nautical miles off Cochin. Kidd loaded the *Adventure Galley* with sail and, four hours later, caught up with her. He put a shot across the *Quedah Merchant's* bows and, again, hoisted the French flag. Kidd then ordered the ship's captain to come aboard. Instead Wright sent his French gunner. This convinced Kidd that he had taken a French ship. So he ran up the English flag and claimed the *Quedah Merchant* as a prize.

Again the merchant ship had a French pass, signed by the director general of the Royal French East India Company in Bengal only two weeks before. But that did not make her a French ship. In fact, her Armenian owners were on board and offered to ransom her for £3,000.

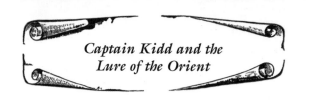
Instead, Kidd sold some of her cargo ashore for £10,000 and divided it among the crew. The *Adventure Galley*, the *November* and the *Quedah Merchant* then set sail for Madagascar.

Only five or six days into the voyage did it become clear who the master of the *Quedah Merchant* was. Kidd was horrified to discover that Wright, an Englishman, was in command. He called a ship's meeting and addressed the crew from the quarterdeck.

'The taking of this ship will make a great noise in England,' he warned, and he proposed handing her back to Captain Wright. But the crew would have none of it.

On 1 April 1698, Kidd and his tiny fleet sailed into the harbour of St Mary's off Madagascar and, for the first time on the voyage, set eyes on another pirate ship. She was the *Mocha Frigate*, an East Indiaman taken by the mutineer Robert Culliford. Kidd, still eager to do his duty, ordered his men to board the *Mocha Frigate*. But they just laughed, saying that they would rather fire ten shots at him than one at Culliford and his men.

All but thirteen of Kidd's men deserted to Culliford, including Joseph Palmer and Robert Bradinham who later testified at Kidd's trial. They shared out the rest of the booty from the *Quedah Merchant* – generously giving Kidd a privateer's cut, forty per cent of the plunder, rather than the two shares given to a pirate captain. They sacked and burned the *November*, then stripped Kidd's other two ships and burned his log.

When Kidd refused to condone their life of piracy, they threatened him with murder and he barricaded himself in his cabin. A prisoner on board his own ship, Kidd sweated it out in his stifling cabin for weeks until he finally capitulated and sworn an oath to Culliford.

'Before I would do you any harm, I would have my soul fry in hell-fire,' he said.

His life was spared, along with that of his brother-in-law who had been sickly since the epidemic that had taken fifty men fifteen months previously. In mid-June, Culliford sailed with most of Kidd's crew and his guns. Kidd decided to head back to America. He was eager to see his family and believed that he had enough left in jewels, silver and gold to pay off his backers. But the *Adventure Galley* was now stuck on a sandbank and half full of water. Kidd burnt her for her iron. Then he fitted out the *Quedah Merchant* for the journey home.

Recruiting a crew was no easy task in St Mary's and she did not set sail until 15 November 1698.

Kidd was three days out from St Mary's when the East India Company's headquarters in Surat sent a letter to the Lords Justices in London accusing Kidd of piracy. Instead of defending him, Kidd's high-placed backers now found him a liability. In parliament, the Tory opposition ripped into the Whig grandees who had funded his expedition. There was no doubt in anyone's mind that it had been a failure. Kidd had not cut piracy in the Indian Ocean. Rather, he had added to it. And all news of Kidd that had reached London was damning. The government despatched a Royal Navy squadron to capture Kidd and the Admiralty sent a circular to all colonial governors, ordering them to arrest him, so that 'he, and his associates, be prosecuted with the outmost rigour of the law'. Then, with the object of isolating Kidd, they offered a pardon to all other pirates east of the Cape, except him and Captain Every.

Meanwhile, Kidd crossed the Atlantic, making landfall at Anguilla in the Leeward Islands in April 1699. He sent a boat ashore and learnt that he and his men had been declared pirates and were the subject of a global manhunt. His crew wanted to dash the *Quedah Merchant* on the reef and disperse, but Kidd surmised that they were too notorious to go on the run. He still believed that his powerful backers could straighten things out, so he made for New York, where he thought that he could count on the protection of Lord Bellomont.

As Kidd sailed north, it became all too obvious that the *Quedah Merchant* was too big and too distinctive to escape detection. In the Mona Passage, he came upon a trading sloop called the *Antonio*. She was neat, fast and anonymous, and Kidd bought her for 3,000 pieces of eight. He moored the *Quedah Merchant* up the Higuey River on Hispaniola and transferred most of her booty – including his own personal treasure of silks, jewels, silver plate and gold – onto the *Antonio*. Leaving most of his crew to guard the *Quedah Merchant*, he set out for New York with a crew of twelve.

On 10 June 1699, he rounded Long Island and moored in Oyster Bay. He sent a letter to an old friend of his in New York, the lawyer James Emmott. Emmott came out to the ship, then went to Boston where Bellomont was

installed as governor, carrying with him the two French passes Kidd had taken from the *Maiden* and the *Quedah Merchant*. He met Bellomont late on the night of 13 June and proposed that Bellomont offer Kidd a pardon, handing over the two French passes as evidence that Kidd had been attacking enemy ships.

Bellomont then sent a letter to Kidd which was carried by Duncan Campbell, the Boston postmaster and a friend of Kidd. It read:

I have advised with His Majesty's Council and showed them this letter, and they are of the opinion that, if you can be so clear as you (or Mr Emmott for you) have said, then you may safely come hither. And I make no manner of doubt but to obtain the King's pardon for you, and for those few men you have left who, I understand, have been faithful to you, and refused as well as you to dishonour the commission you have from England. I assure you on my word and honour, I will perform nicely what I have promised.

However, Bellomont confided to London that he was double-dealing.

'Menacing him had not been the way to invite him hither, but rather wheedling,' he wrote.

Kidd then sent a number of gifts to Bellomont's wife, including a beautiful enamelled box with diamonds set in gold. He sent a flurry of gifts to others in an effort to ingratiate himself. The rest of the booty he buried in discrete caches around the orchard of Gardiner's Island at the eastern end of Long Island, obtaining a receipt from the owner John Gardiner. This was his insurance policy. If he was free, he could return to collect the buried treasure. If not, it would make a useful bargaining counter.

After a reunion with his wife and children at Block Island, Kidd sailed with his family to Boston. Arriving there on 2 July, he took rooms in a boarding house and sent Lady Bellomont another gift – £1,000-worth of gold bars in a green silk bag. This was a mistake. His largesse could be construed as a bribe and, with these gifts, he seemed to be treating the plunder as his own personal property, rather than taking it to an Admiralty Court where it could be divided properly among his backers.

The following day, Kidd reported to Bellomont, who asked for a detailed account of his movements. Kidd said that his crew had burnt his log. On 6 July, he was due to return to the Massachusetts Council to testify. But before hearing what he had to say, the Council issued an arrest warrant. Kidd was arrested outside Bellomont's front door, calling for his benefactor's assistance as the police closed in.

Kidd was confined to Boston's austere Stone Prison. Bellomont denounced him as a 'monster' and he was treated like a wild animal. His lodgings were ransacked and Gardiner was ordered to dig up Kidd's buried treasure. Kidd could not provide an accurate inventory of everything he had buried – which was lucky for Gardiner, who failed to hand over a large uncut Golconda diamond. However, 1,111 ounces of gold, 2,353 ounces of silver, more than a pound of gemstones, forty-one bales of merchandise and fifty-seven bags of sugar were recovered and sent, under close guard, to the Treasury in London.

Kidd and his men had already suffered the rigours of winter in Stone Prison before HMS *Advice* arrived on 6 February 1700 to take them to England. Kidd was locked in a steerage cabin; his men chained in the gunroom. On 11 April they arrived in the Thames Estuary. Kidd was transferred to the royal yacht *Katherine* and taken with an escort of musketeers to the Admiralty. But at Greenwich, it was found that he was too sick to be taken out of his cabin. He held out a gold coin to be given to his wife and asked for a knife so he could kill himself. When this was refused he begged to be shot, rather than hanged.

As if he was not ill enough, he was taken to Newgate prison in the City of London. Already five hundred years old, it was squalid even by the standards of the time. Inmates slept two or three to a bed. The place was crawling with lice that crunched underfoot 'like shells on a garden path,' as one prisoner put it. Open sewers ran

At Anguilla in 1699, Kidd went ashore to discover he and his men had been declared pirates and were the subject of a global manhunt

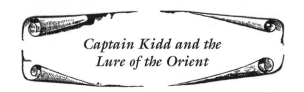

through the cells, creating a smell so overpowering that visitors would carry bunches of flowers to bury their noses in, and prisoners were washed with vinegar before they appeared in court. Despite this, the prison was run as a

French pass taken by Kidd from the Quedah Merchant, *and intended to be used in his defence at his trial. Both this document, and a similar pass taken from the ship* Maiden, *mysteriously vanished before Kidd's trial.*

private business and prisoners had to pay for their board and lodgings.

In May 1700, the jailer reported to the Admiralty that 'Captain Kidd was troubled with great pain in his head, and shaken in his limbs, and was in great want of his clothes.' This was hardly surprising, as he had been allowed no exercise for nine months. He could not discuss his case or prepare a defence. He could not even write to his wife and his only visitors were an aged uncle and aunt. Then suddenly on 27 March 1700, he was called before the bar of the House of Commons. The Tories hoped that his testimony would lead to the impeachment of his Whig backers. But instead of denouncing them as villains who had betrayed him, he simply protested his innocence which, by implication, exonerated them too. Some MPs admired his courage. Others found him boorish. One thought he was drunk. Another said simply, 'I had thought him only a knave, now I know him to be a fool as well.' He was returned to Newgate to await his trial at the Old Bailey which began on 8 May.

The Admiralty appropriated £50 for his defence, but neglected to send it to his lawyers until the night of 7 May, so they had just one brief consultation with their client before the trial began. Even though the proceedings were complicated – there were four separate trials on six indictments before six justices – the whole

thing was over in three days. Kidd was not allowed to testify in his own defence. The only opportunity he got to speak was when he – not his counsel, the court ruled – cross-examined Palmer and Bradinham, two of the crewmen who had deserted him at St Mary's. The crewmen who had stayed with him were not allowed to testify and the two French passes that had been handed over to Bellomont had been mysteriously mislaid.

The first indictment against him was not for piracy at all, but for the murder of the gunner William Moore. Kidd pleaded provocation.

'I had not design to kill him,' he said. 'It was not designedly done, but in my passion, for which I am heartily sorry.'

The jury took just one hour to find him guilty.

Palmer and Bradinham were the only witnesses in the matter of his piracy and that of the nine other defendants. As neither Kidd nor his co-defendants could testify, and he could not produce the missing French passes, Palmer and Bradinham's testimony could not be rebutted.

'This man contradicts himself in a hundred places,' said Kidd of Bradinham during his cross-examination. 'He tells a thousand lies.'

'Will you ask him any more questions?' the Solicitor-General asked.

'No, no. So long as he swears it, our words cannot be taken,' said Kidd.

Later, as the trial drew to a close, Kidd interjected, 'Mr Bradinham, are not you promised your life to take away mine?'

The jury took half-an-hour to find Kidd and six of his co-defendants guilty. The other three were acquitted.

When asked whether there was any reason why he should not suffer death according to law, Kidd replied, 'I have nothing to say, but that I have been sworn against by perjured and wicked people.'

Then the sentence was read: 'You shall be

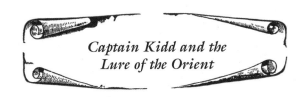

taken from the place where you are, and be carried to the place from whence you came, and from hence to the place of execution and there be hanged by your necks until you be dead. And the Lord have mercy on your souls.'

'My Lord,' protested Kidd. 'It is a very hard sentence. I am the innocentest person of all, only I have been sworn against by perjured people.

On 23 May 1701, Kidd was taken to Execution Dock in Wapping to be hanged. The first rope broke and he had to be strung up a second time. A heavy man, he would have died quickly. When his body had stopped twitching, he was cut down and left for the tide to wash over him three times. He was then painted in tar, bound in chains and put in a metal harness that would keep his skeleton intact while his flesh rotted away. The body was then displayed hanging from a gibbet that cost £10 to build at Tilbury Point, where anyone sailing in or out of the Thames could see it.

Only one of the men convicted with Kidd was hanged: the other five were released. Two of them, James Howe and Nicholas Churchill, paid £315 each for their freedom. They sailed out of the Thames, past Kidd's rotting corpse,

on their way back to Pennsylvania. On the way, they stopped off to dig up £2,300 in gold that they had helped their late captain bury.

Palmer and Bradinham were rewarded with full pardons. Culliford, their pirate captain, was tried the same day as Kidd and found guilty of piracy. But as he had surrendered under a royal pardon, he was released after a year.

Kidd's widow married a third time and lived another forty-three years in New Jersey. His daughters also married and bore children of their own.

Three months before Kidd's execution Bellomont had died 'wore out in spirit, and put an end to his life by the fatigue he underwent to serve His Majesty,' his widow complained. The French passes he had been given by Kidd for use in Kidd's defence were later discovered in the Public Record Office in London.

The booty recovered from Gardiner's Island was forfeit to the crown. Sold off at auction, it fetched £6,742. The money was spent on one of the buildings that now houses the National Maritime Museum in Greenwich. But many people think that there is more of Captain Kidd's buried treasure out there somewhere.

Captain Kidd on trial for his life before the bar of the House of Commons, 1701. Convicted of the murder of his gunner, William Moore, Kidd was hanged at Wapping on 23 May 1701.

CHAPTER NINE

THE SUPPRESSION OF PIRACY

Although the early buccaneers of the 'Golden Age' of piracy could undoubtedly be a cruel and ruthless body of men, they had some scruples when it came to choosing ships to attack. The same could not be said for the pirates who followed in their wake, men such as Charles Vane, Calico Jack Rackham and Edward Teach, better known to the world as the infamous pirate Blackbeard.

The year after Captain Kidd was executed the War of the Spanish Succession broke out, pitting Spain and France against the Grand Alliance of Prussia, Austria, the Netherlands, Hanover, Portugal and the newly united Britain. The British pirates of the Caribbean sailed once again as privateers. Meanwhile the French buccaneers – or filibusters – found themselves escorting the treasure ships of their old enemies, the Spanish.

In North America, the war was known as Queen Anne's War as the British tried to oust the French from their colonies there. In May 1702, the newly-crowned Queen Anne issued a proclamation authorizing privateers to seize enemy vessels. Pirates quickly signed up for these licences to plunder. Between 1704 and 1707, a fleet of thirteen privateers operating out of New York seized thirty-six enemy ships, making a profit of £60,000 at the cost of the lives of 260 men. In 1708, privateering became even more profitable, when the British parliament renounced its ten per cent claim on all prizes. By the end of the war in 1713, British and colonial privateers had taken more than 2,000 prizes, most of them French, and a new generation of privateers had grown up, ready to used their new found skills in peace-time piracy. The majority were English, Britain using the war to expand its sea power and colonial empire, at the expense of the French and Spanish.

The pirates now needed a new home. Port Royal had fallen into the sea and Saint Domingue was now out of bounds because of the new-found relationship between France and Spain. They moved to New Providence Island in the Bahamas, at that time practically uninhabited after being repeatedly sacked and burned by the French and Spanish during the war. The harbour there was too shallow for large men-of-war to enter, but deep enough for the fast shallow-drafted sloops favoured by the pirates. It was ringed by hills that gave an excellent view of an approaching enemy or a passing prize. The surrounding reef teemed with fish, lobsters, conch and turtles. The well-wooded interior contained fresh water springs and an abundance of wild pigs, pigeons and fruit.

The pirate Henry Jennings dropped anchor in New Providence in 1710. Charles Vane, Thomas Burgess, Thomas Barrow, Benjamin Hornigold and the infamous Blackbeard followed, using the harbour as a base to waylay merchantmen sailing in and out of the Caribbean. In April 1714, Governor Pulleine of Bermuda complained that three teams of buccaneers in open boats, with around twenty-five men to a boat, had robbed Spanish vessels of £60,000 in booty in just eight months. Hornigold was mentioned as one of their captains and, by 1715, he was in possession of a sloop equipped with ten guns and a crew of

135 men. The Bahamas quickly became a market where anything could be bought and sold and the pirates became so confident that in June the Chief Justice of New Providence, Thomas Walker, had to flee to South Carolina when Hornigold threatened to kill him.

In July 1716, Governor Alexander Spotswood of Virginia complained to London that 'a nest of pirates are endeavouring to establish themselves in New Providence and by the additions they expect and will probably receive, may prove dangerous to the British commerce, if not timely suppressed.'

Governor Robert Johnson of South Carolina tried to crack down on them. A ship he commissioned took Hornigold's ship and destroyed it. But Hornigold himself escaped and was soon operating out of New Providence again.

Spotswood also mentioned that one of the ringleaders was Thomas Barrow.

'He is the 'governor' of Providence and will make it a second Madagascar,' said Spotswood. New Providence soon became the largest concentration of pirates ever seen in the Caribbean. Two thousand of them were living on board ship in the harbour or in the shantytown on shore. The only permanent buildings were the taverns where the pirates boozed and gambled away their prize money – otherwise, they spent it on the prostitutes who worked out of tents made from sail canvas.

In this pirate paradise, the beach was strewn with refuse and the harbour filled with more than forty abandoned hulks. And there was no law, except that of the fist and the cutlass.

'I am a free prince,' the brazen Captain Bellamy told the skipper of a merchant ship he captured off South Carolina in 1717, 'and I have as much authority to make war on the whole world as he who has a hundred sail of ships at sea and an army of one hundred thousand men in the field.'

New Providence pirates raided up the Eastern Seaboard as far as Maine.

'North and South America are infested with these rogues,' said the governor of Bermuda.

'There is hardly a ship or vessel coming in or going out of this island that is not plundered,' complained the governor of Jamaica. 'This in great measure I impute to the neglect of the commanders of His Majesty's ships of war.'

At the time, the Royal Navy was ill-equipped to take on the pirates. Since the end of the war,

it had been chronically undermanned due to sickness, death and desertion, and often ships were forced to stay in port eight months of the year. Navy captains also had little interest in suppressing piracy as, under Admiralty law, they were allowed to charge twelve and a half per cent of the value of a cargo for escort duty. When shippers complained, the Navy offered to transport the goods in their own ships at a more competitive rate.

While both the Navy and the pirates were happy with this arrangement, the colonial governors were not: it inhibited the growth of the economy of the colonies in North America and the Caribbean.

'The pirates continue to rove across these seas,' wrote the governor of New England, 'and if sufficient force is not sent to drive them off, our trade must stop.'

However, when London sent more ships,

A pirate ship chases booty in this somewhat romanticized nineteenth-century illustration.

their captains quickly signed up to their comrades' money-making scheme. Private enterprise now took a hand. A group of London merchants formed a consortium and leased the Bahamas from the Crown, hiring the Dorset privateer Woodes Rogers to lead an expedition there. He had recently completed a round-the-world trip that had brought in £800,000. Unfortunately Rogers himself had only received £1,600, considerably less than the debts he had incurred. But such misfortune did not dampen his imperial ardour, and in 1717 he was appointed 'Captain-General and Governor-in-Chief in and over our Bahama Island in America'. His job was to suppress piracy by any method to hand, including the issuing of the King's pardons, though his ambition was to establish more British settlements and promote trade in remote oceans. He was offered no salary, only a share in the profit any new colony might make.

On 11 April 1718, he set off down the Thames on board his 460-ton flagship, the East Indiaman *Delicia*. He took with him 100 foot-soldiers to man the garrison and 250 colonists – farmers from Switzerland, the German Palatinate and Hugenots – along with their stores, materials and tools, and £2 10s-worth of tracts from the Society for Promoting Christian Knowledge, in the vain hope that these would help the pirates mend their ways. In the Channel, the *Delicia* was joined by the navy sloops HMS *Shark* and *Buck*, and the frigates *Rose* and *Milford*.

On the afternoon of 24 July, Rogers' fleet arrived off the bar outside New Providence. Some of the original English settlers rowed out from Harbour Island forty miles away to greet their new governor. They told him that there were around a thousand pirates in New Providence, but most of them would be prepared to return to the fold in exchange for a royal pardon. Hearing that Rogers was on his way, the diehards – notably Blackbeard – had already decamped. Only the notorious pirate Charles Vane remained.

That night the *Shark* and the *Rose* took on local pilots and sailed into the harbour. Vane saw them coming, filled a recently captured French

In 1717 the governor of Jamaica complained: 'There is hardly a ship or vessel coming in or going out of this island that is not plundered.'

merchantman with explosives, set her ablaze and sent her out towards them. The ship exploded, sending the two Royal Navy vessels tacking back out to deep waters. Vane escaped through the narrow channels at the east end of the harbour the next morning, threatening to return and take his revenge by burning the *Delicia*.

Rogers stepped ashore on New Providence on the morning of 27 July. He was greeted by a dishevelled guard of honour drawn up by Thomas Burgess and Benjamin Hornigold. Three hundred boozy pirates fired a salute over his head and gave a rousing cheer for George I, who had become king of England in 1714. Then from the crumbling ramparts of the town's ruined fort Rogers read aloud his commission and the proclamation pardoning the pirates. As word spread, more pirates put into New Providence to receive the king's pardon. Along with it they received a plot of land, provided they cleared it and built a home within a year. In all, over 600 pirates took the King's pardon and SPCK tracts were given to waverers.

Rogers build a small eight-gun redoubt at the eastern end of the harbour, then set about building a larger fort to guard the main, western entrance. Everything seemed to be going according to plan. But that summer was particularly hot and an epidemic of fever – attributed by some to the rotting hides of cattle slaughtered for food – swept through the island. It killed off many of the immigrants, shattering the chances of establishing a self-sufficient farming settlement. And when the sailors on board the warships began coming down with the fever too, the Royal Navy set sail.

A new war threatened between England and Spain and the island was under danger of attack from Cuba and from a number of the New Providence pirates who had gone back to their old ways. Rogers responded by commissioning Burgess and Hornigold as privateers and organizing the pardoned pirates into three militia companies. The pirates, however, proved next to useless in this role.

'These wretches can't be kept to watch at night,' Rogers complained, 'and when they do they come very seldom sober, and are rarely

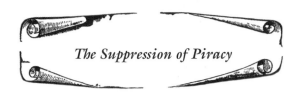

awake all night, though our officers and soldiers very often surprise their guard and carry off their arms, and I punish, fine, or confine them almost every day.'

However, the worry that Charles Vane might return to New Providence was soon removed. A few months after leaving harbour Vane was voted out of his captaincy for failing to engage a French ship. He was replaced by 'Calico Jack' Rackham, and cast adrift in a sloop. Although Vane worked his way back up the pirate hierarchy, seizing larger and larger ships, he met an untimely – for him, at least – fate at the end of a rope in Jamaica in 1720. Meanwhile Blackbeard busied himself in the Carolinas and showed no inclination to return either.

Blackbeard

Official records maintain that Blackbeard's real name was Edward Teach, though contemporary accounts call him Tach, Tash, Tatch or, even, Thatch. These may have been aliases, or may simply reflect the literacy standards of the day.

Defoe said his real name was Edward Drummond. He was born in Bristol – though some say Jamaica or Virginia – and sailed as a privateer during the War of the Spanish Succession. He joined Hornigold's ship as a pirate in Jamaica in 1716 and soon distinguished himself in combat. Later that year, when Hornigold took a French ship off the island of St Vincent, he gave its command to Teach, who renamed it the *Queen Anne's Revenge*. But when news of the imminent arrival of Rogers reached New Providence, Hornigold and Blackbeard went their separate ways. Hornigold took the pardon, while Blackbeard took to sea on his own account.

Blackbeard was tall, strong, brave, wild and, like many pirate captains, a flamboyant dresser. He was swathed in coloured silk sashes that hung down from his shoulders. Each carried a flintlock – three pairs in all – cocked and primed. Daggers and cutlasses were stuffed into the belt around his waist. According to Defoe, his trademark beard, 'like a frightful meteor, covered his whole face and frightened America

Captain Woodes Rogers and his men landing in California, 1710. Woodes Rogers' voyage round the world, including the rescue of Alexander Selkirk from Juan Fernandez, took the British flg into waters in which it was practically unknown.

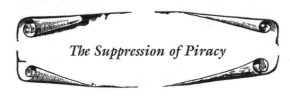

Wild, staring eyes, pistols in his belt, burning fuses in his hair – it can only be Blackbeard, the terror of the Caribbean.

sixteen when he married her and, after he had satisfied himself with her, according to Defoe, it 'was his custom to invite five or six of his brutal companions to come ashore, and he would force her to prostitute herself to them all, one after another, before his face'.

This may had been part of the diabolical image Blackbeard liked to maintain with his crewmen, as well as his victims. One day at sea, he suggested to his shipmates that they should make a 'hell of our own and try how long we can bear it'. With two or three crewmen who accepted the challenge, he went down into the hold, where they sat on the large stones used as ballast. Pots of brimstone – that is, sulphur – were brought down and set on fire. They sat there in the dark surrounded by sulphurous fumes until the half-suffocated crewmen cried out for air and the hatches were opened. According to Defoe, Blackbeard was 'not a little pleased that he had held out the longest'.

When he clambered back on deck, one of the crew cried out, 'Why, Captain, you look as if you were coming straight from the gallows.'

'My lad,' roared Blackbeard, 'next time we shall play at gallows and see who can swing longest on the string without being throttled.'

Sometimes his games went too far. One night, while he was drinking with his navigator Isaac Hands, he pulled a pistol under the table surreptitiously. Then he blew out the candle, cocked and fired – hitting Hands in the knee and crippling him for life. Another crewman had only escaped a similar fate because he had gone up on deck for some air. When asked why he had done such a thing, Blackbeard replied that if he did not kill a crewman now and again people would forget who he was.

After leaving New Providence, Blackbeard found sanctuary with the governor of North Carolina, Charles Eden. While the rest of the American colonies now discouraged piracy as a hindrance to trade, North Carolina had no exports to speak of and encouraged pirates to offload their plunder there. Blackbeard openly careened his ship in the Cape Fear and Pamlico rivers and sold his booty at bargain-basement prices in Bath on the Pamlico. Eden even gave Blackbeard and his crew a pardon under the Act of Grace, in exchange for a share of the loot.

However, in the spring of 1718, Blackbeard blockaded Charleston, the capital of South Carolina, for a week, seizing eight or nine ships going in or out of the harbour. He took a mem-

more than any comet that has appeared there for a long time'. The wild mat of black hair grew down to his chest and up his cheeks almost to his eyes. He braided it in narrow plaits, each tied with a colour ribbon. His hat was festooned with slow-burning fuses – hemp soaked in saltpetre and lime water. He lit these just before going into action, making him a truly terrifying sight.

He was also a great drinker and believed that a drunken ship was a happy ship. One day in his journal he noted: 'Such a day – Rum all out – Our company somewhat sober: Rogues aplotting – Great talk of separation – So I'd look sharp for a prize.'

Luckily a booze-laden merchantman happened along, which he took. The next entry read: 'Such a day – took one, with a great deal of liquor on board, so kept the company hot, damn'd hot, then all things went well again.'

Unlike earlier pirates he was also fond of women and often took the wives and daughters of planters. According to contemporary accounts, he had one wife and a child in London and at least a dozen wives scattered around various ports, one of whom he bought for five hundred pounds. His last wife was just

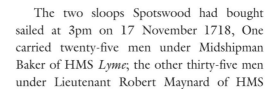
ber of the governor's council and his four-year-old son hostage and threatened to kill them and send their heads to the Governor Robert Johnson and 'burn the ships that lay before the town and beat it about our ears' unless Johnson sent medical supplies. The governor sent a chest containing £300- or £400-worth of medicines. It seems these were the mercury compounds then used to treat syphilis. Soon after Stede Bonnet, who had once sailed with Blackbeard, fell into Johnson's hands. Bonnet's pleas for clemency fell on deaf ears, as we have seen, and he hanged.

In the eighteen months since Blackbeard left New Providence, he had seized more than twenty prizes between Virginia and Honduras. However, his men began to outstay their welcome in North Carolina. The good people of Bath wanted their trade, but not their loutish behaviour – especially after they seized a trading sloop in the river. But Governor Eden did nothing. He even officiated at Blackbeard's fourteenth marriage, to the 16-year-old daughter of a Bath planter.

However, Governor Alexander Spotswood of neighbouring Virginia decided to take action when he heard that Blackbeard and his flotilla was intending to establish a base at Ocracoke, North Carolina, and build a fort there. He had at his disposal two men-of-war, HMS *Lyme* and *Pearl*. He sent agents to spy on Blackbeard and employed a local pilot, who told him that the waters around Ocracoke were took shallow for his men-of-war to navigate. So Spotswood bought two shallow-draft sloops and, together with his captains, he drew up a plan of attack in secret – 'for fear of Blackbeard's having intelligence, there being in this country an unaccountable inclination to favour pirates'. Ocracoke was also outside his jurisdiction and any attempt to arrest Blackbeard there was usurping Eden's authority. However, publicly, he persuaded the Virginia assembly to post a £100 reward for the death or capture of Blackbeard, £40 for any other pirate captain, £20 for pirate lieutenants and £10 for ordinary buccaneers – within the jurisdiction of Virginia and North Carolina.

The notorious Blackbeard once remarked that if he did not kill a crewman now and again, people would forget who he was

The two sloops Spotswood had bought sailed at 3pm on 17 November 1718, One carried twenty-five men under Midshipman Baker of HMS *Lyme*; the other thirty-five men under Lieutenant Robert Maynard of HMS *Pearl*. At dusk on 21 November, they approached Ocracoke and spotted Blackbeard's sloop *Adventure*, together with a prize moored some way up the inlet.

Blackbeard was not surprised to see them. Despite the secrecy surrounding the expedition, Blackbeard had been warned that something was afoot by North Carolina's corrupt Customs collector Tobias Knight. But while Maynard anchored among the shoals and readied his men and arms for battle in the morning, Blackbeard and his crew of just eighteen spent the night getting drunk. The navy men could hear them singing and carousing across the still water.

At first light, Maynard set sail. Once the navy sloops came within range of the *Adventure* Blackbeard opened fire. Maynard unfurled his ensign and bore down on the pirate, forcing Blackbeard to cut his cable to escape. Maynard made after him, but Blackbeard's sloop ran aground. The navy sloops drew more water than the *Adventure*, so Maynard had to heave ballast over the side and jettison the drinking water to get near him.

As they did this, Blackbeard roared out across the water, 'Damn you, you villains, who are you? And from whence you came?'

'You may see by our colours that we are no pirates,' Maynard shouted back.

Blackbeard then told him to come over on his boat to see who he was. Maynard responded, 'I cannot spare my boat, but I will come aboard you as soon as I can, with my sloop.'

This enraged Blackbeard, who took a swig of liquor, and bellowed, 'Damnation seize my soul if I give you quarter, or take it from you!' Maynard replied that he expected no quarter – and would give none.

Blackbeard got his sloop afloat again, unfurled his black flag and fired a broadside of small shot. The heavily-laden navy sloops only had one foot freeboard at the waist, where his

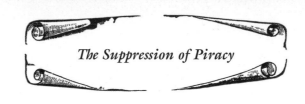

men sat at the oars. On Baker's sloop, the *Ranger*, nine men, including Baker himself, were killed and the rigging was damaged. She drifted helplessly and played little part in the rest of the engagement.

In Maynard's sloop, twenty-one of the thirty-five men were killed or wounded. Maynard ordered the rest below, in case Blackbeard fired another broadside, while he and the helmsman lay low on the deck. Blackbeard then came alongside and threw hand grenades made of bottles full of powder, scrap iron and shot, with a quick fuse sticking from the mouth. Once this had burnt down, the grenade was thrown. They exploded with a loud bang, causing a great deal of confusion and a lot of smoke. But Maynard's men were safe below decks.

Seeing few men on deck, Blackbeard cried out to his men that they were 'all knocked on the head, except three or four; let's jump on board and cut them to pieces'.

Blackbeard leapt on board with fourteen men. He came face to face with Maynard. The two men fired at each other at point-blank range. After all the liquor he had consumed, Blackbeard's hand was not as steady as perhaps it might have been. He missed: Maynard did not. His men had emerged from the hold and a pitched battle ensued.

The gunshot wound seemed to have had little effect on the drunken Blackbeard. With a single blow from his cutlass Blackbeard broke Maynard's sword in two. When Maynard stepped back to cock a pistol, Blackbeard raised his cutlass again to swing at the defenceless lieutenant, but one of Maynard's men slashed Blackbeard across the throat and neck. Maynard escaped with a slight cut across the fingers.

Maynard fired the pistol, hitting Blackbeard in the side. But, though he was spouting blood, the pirate still was not done. He and his fourteen men fought on against Maynard and his twelve 'till the sea was tinctur'd with blood around the vessel'. According to Defoe, Blackbeard suffered twenty-five wounds, five of them gunshot. But finally, as he raised another pistol to cock it, he keeled over and fell dead on the deck.

By that time, eight of Blackbeard's men were dead. The rest, though wounded, jumped overboard and cried for quarter. The *Ranger* now caught up with the action. She boarded the *Adventure* and took the men there, who also asked for mercy – 'though it was only prolonging their lives a few days'.

'Here was the end of that courageous brute,' said Defoe, 'who might have passed in the world for a hero, had he been employed in a good cause. His destruction, which was of much consequence to the plantations, was entirely owing to the conduct and bravery of Lieutenant Maynard and his men.'

Blackbeard's head was cut off and hung from Maynard's bowsprit as his sailed back to Virginia. It was said that Blackbeard's headless corpse swam around his ship three times before it sank. Maynard also took with him a letter from Tobias Knight he found in Blackbeard's possession warning him of Spotswood's plans. Spotswood reported this to the Board of Trade in London, but Knight protested that the evidence against him was 'false and malicious'. He stayed in office, as did Governor Eden until he died of yellow fever three years later.

The matter of the reward took four years to resolve. The captains of the *Lyme* and *Pearl* insisted that the money be shared out among all the crewmen of both ships. Maynard said that only the men who had fought should share in the reward. Eventually those who fought got £1 13s 6d. The rest got 9s 6d, while Maynard got two shares for leading the raid.

The death of Blackbeard marked the end of piracy based in American coastal waters. However, news of his rampage had inspired some of Woodes Rogers' reformed pirates to revert to their old ways. Two days out of New Providence, three ships Rogers had sent to Hispaniola for supplies mutinied. He sent Hornigold out to catch them. Hornigold brought back just thirteen men, three of whom died of their wounds.

The remaining ten were tried by a vice-admiralty court which Rogers, strictly, had not authority to convene. Its eight judges included two reformed pirate captains, Peter Courant and Thomas Burgess. Nine of the defendants were found guilty and condemned to death. The other one was acquitted on the grounds that he had been forced to join the pirates.

Two days later, at 10am on 12 December 1718, they were taken out of their irons. With their hands tied in front of them, they were marched out of the fort down onto the beach where a gallows had been erected. They were stood on casks and nooses tied around their necks. There they waited for forty-five minutes

while prayers were said, psalms recited and the crowd – largely of former pirates – was addressed.

The men, who ranged in age from eighteen to forty-five, reacted very differently to their impending death. Two dressed in ribbons for the occasion. One wore old clothes and refused even to wash. Twenty-four-year-old William Dowling, who had murdered his own mother in Ireland, was unrepentant and 22-year-old Thomas Morris shouted from the gallows that he only wished he had been a greater plague. Thirty-four-year-old William Lewis, an ex-boxer, was drunk. Forty-year-old John Augur was remorseful and drank a small glass of wine on the gallows, toasting the success of the Bahamas and their governor. The contrite William Ling, 30, drank only water. At the last moment 18-year-old George Rounsivil was reprieved on the grounds that his 'loyal and good' parents lived in Rogers' home county of Dorset. A rope tied to the casks was then pulled and the remaining eight men dropped.

Rogers gave Hornigold the credit for capturing the recidivists. In a letter to Secretary of State James Craggs in London two weeks later, he wrote, 'I am glad of this new proof Captain Hornigold has given the world to wipe off the infamous name he has hitherto been known by, though in the very acts of piracy he committed most people spoke well of his generosity.'

Ironically he suffered a pirate's death. Cast away on a desert island, he succumbed while five of his crew escaped on a canoe they had built.

The hanging of the eight mutineers marked the end of piracy in the Bahamas. With lavish handouts of food and liquor, Rogers managed to extract a fortnight's more or less continuous labour from the reformed pirates of New Providence to complete the building of a new fort. By January 1720, it bristled with fifty guns.

On 24 February, four Spanish warships carrying 1,300 troops anchored off the eastern approach to the harbour. Rogers had just one infantry company and a militia of 500 hard-drinking ex-pirates to defend the island. However, when the Spaniards tried to invade on the night of 25 February, two sentries armed with muskets were enough to see off boatloads

Modern artwork of Blackbeard, with his ship, the **Queen Anne's Revenge***, in action behind him.*

Blackbeard's flag, featuring devil-horned skeleton with hourglass in one hand and spear in the other poking at bleeding heart motif.

He hunted ships, mainly Spanish, around the Caribbean. When he heard from the crew of one prize that there was a new war between England and Spain, he sent some of his crew to Jamaica to see if he could obtain a pardon there. The governor's reply was to send a Royal Navy squadron after Calico Jack. He escaped with most of his crew, but his flagship, the *Kingston*, was taken.

With two small boats, Jack took a Spanish prize off Cuba and sailed it to New Providence where he received a pardon from Rogers. There he met Anne Bonny, the wife of another pardoned pirate.

Anne had been born in Ireland, the illegitimate child of a prominent lawyer, William Cormac, and Peg Brennan, the family maid. The birth caused a scandal and Cormac took Peg and their daughter to start a new life as a merchant in South Carolina. He quickly became wealthy and, by the time Anne reached marriageable age – then 12 – she was surrounded by suitors. But as well as being rich and a beauty, Anne also had a violent temper. She stabbed a servant girl with a knife and, when a young man tried to rape her, she beat him up. She fell for a ne'er-do-well named James Bonny, who took her to New Providence, where he turned informer and she met the swaggering Jack Rackham.

Calico Jack wooed her with expensive baubles and offered to buy her from her husband – a common practice then, though of doubtful legality. But James Bonny would have none of it and complained to the governor, who threatened to have Anne flogged if she did not return to her husband. Rackham decided that the only way he could have his Anne was to go back to pirating. They got their chance when the *Curlew*, a merchant sloop renowned as the fastest in the Caribbean, anchored in the harbour at New Providence.

Jack gathered together a handful of his old crewmen. Then at midnight, when the watch changed, they slipped aboard. Anne, dressed as a sailor, confronted the two men on watch and threatened to blow their brains out if they offered the slightest resistance. And silently the *Curlew* slipped out of the harbour. They put into Cuba, where Anne gave birth. Leaving the infant there, they took to plundering coastal traders and fishing boats all around the Caribbean.

Taking a Dutch vessel they forced a number

of raw Spanish troops. Though they moored in Bahamian waters for some time, they did not attempt to set foot on the Bahamas again.

With no base, the numbers of active pirates quickly dropped off. Up until then contemporary estimates of the pirate population put the number between 1,000 and 2,000 at any one time. This range seems generally accurate. From records that describe the activities of pirate ships and from records and projections of crew sizes, it appears that 1,800 to 2,400 Anglo-American pirates prowled the seas between 1716 and 1718, l,500 to 2,000 between 1719 and 1722, and 1,000 to 1,500, declining to fewer than 200, between 1723 and 1726. In the only estimate we have from the other side of the law, a band of pirates in 1716 claimed that '30 Company of them', or roughly 2,400 men, plied the oceans of the globe. In all, some 4,500 to 5,500 men went, as they called it, 'upon account'. Between 1716 and 1726, their adversary, the Royal Navy, employed an average of 13,000 men.

Calico Jack and Anne Bonny

Former New Providence pirates were still making trouble, however. Charles Vane's quartermaster John 'Calico Jack' Rackham began making a name for himself after ridding himself of his captain, whom he had always despised for his cruelty. He picked up his strange nickname because he, rather sensibly, preferred to wear cotton clothing in the tropics, rather than the rich silks and velvets favoured by other pirates.

of the crewmen to sign articles and join them. One of them, a handsome young Dutch boy, was very much to Anne's liking. It turned out that he was neither Dutch nor a boy. When Calico Jack caught them together, he threatened to kill them both. It was only then that Anne's new friend 'suffered the discovery of her sex to be made by carelessly showing her breasts, which were very white'.

Jack's new female crew member was an Englishwoman named Mary Read. Like Anne, she had been born illegitimately and her mother, to disguise the fact, had dressed her as a boy. Later, she signed up as a cabin boy on a man-of-war. After that she became a foot soldier, then fought with distinction as a dragoon in Flanders during the War of the Spanish Succession. During the fighting, she fell in love with her tent mate, a Flemish youth who returned her passion and insisted on marrying her. The newlyweds became innkeepers in Holland and, for the only time in her life, Mary wore women's clothes. When her husband died suddenly of fever, she disguised herself as a sailor and signed on board a Dutch ship – the ship that was taken by Calico Jack. The three of them kept her secret, until Mary fell for a crewman and married once again.

In October 1720, the pirates of the *Curlew* swarmed on board a merchantman off Jamaica, screaming, cursing and brandishing their cutlasses. At their head were two hellcats wearing jackets and long pants. Dorothy Thomas, a female passenger, noticed something unusual about them.

'By the largeness of their breasts,' she said, 'I believed them to be women.'

Soon after, while Calico Jack's crew were celebrating by getting drunk, they were challenged by a privateer sloop from Jamaica who had a commission to take pirates. The men were too drunk to fight and hid in the hold. But Anne and Mary fought off the boarders like wildcats, using pistols, cutlasses and boarding axes. When they realized things were going badly, Mary fired into the hold, screaming at the cowards to 'come up and fight like men'. She killed one pirate and wounded others. But eventually they were overpowered.

The pirates were tried in Spanish Town, Jamaica. Mary's husband was acquitted on the grounds that he had been forced to become a pirate. But Calico Jack, Anne, Mary and eight other crewmen were found guilty and sentenced

to be hanged. When asked whether they had anything to say, Anne and Mary replied, 'Milord, we plead our bellies.' Both were pregnant and, under English law, no court has the power to condemn an unborn child, no matter how guilty the mother.

However, Mary Read died in prison of white fever. After Calico Jack was hanged at what is now known as Rackham's Cay near Port Royal, Anne Bonny gave birth, but used her charms to win two more reprieves. It is thought that her wealthy father bought her release. Still not yet twenty, she became the mistress of Robert Fenwick, a former successful Red Sea pirate, who lived at Fenwick Castle near Charleston, South Carolina. Later she ran away with a young lover, but Fenwick caught up with them. He forced her to help hang the lover and promise never to run away again.

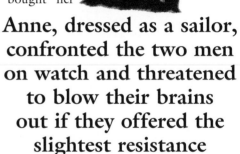

Anne, dressed as a sailor, confronted the two men on watch and threatened to blow their brains out if they offered the slightest resistance

Black Bart

The last great pirate of the golden age – and probably the greatest – was Bartholomew Roberts. Born in Pembrokeshire, Wales, in 1682, 'Black Bart' was another pirate known for his extravagant dress. When he died in battle he was wearing a crimson damask waistcoat and breeches, a scarlet plumed hat and a massive gold chain with a jewelled cross slung around his neck. He carried two pairs of pistols in a silk sling over his shoulder, though his preferred weapon was a razor-sharp cutlass that he kept tucked in his belt.

A reluctant pirate – only coming to it at the age of 37 – he was a devoted Christian, forbidding gambling and leading his men in prayer. He was also that rarest of thing for the pirate – a teetotaller.

He saw action on board a navy ship or a privateer during the War of the Spanish Succession, then became a merchant seaman. During the time of Blackbeard's exploits he was the mate of a Barbados trading sloop. By his mid-thirties he was a master mariner but, being of humble birth, stood no chance of becoming

a ship's captain, unless he turned pirate.

In 1719, he was sailing as second mate on board the slaver *Princess* down the Guinea Coast when the ship was taken by the famous Welsh Pirate Captain Howell Davis. Davis himself had started as mate on a slaver, when his ship, the Bristol snow *Cadogan*, was taken by the Irish pirate Edward England. England took some of his cargo, then gave Davis the ship, along with sealed orders only to be opened on reaching a certain latitude. These gave Davis dubious title to the vessel and suggested that he sail for Brazil. Instead he sailed to Barbados, where he was jailed. Although no one really believed his story, he was released after three months. He sailed for New Providence, where Woodes Rogers gave him a sloop and a commission to take pirates who were operating off the coast of West Africa. But when Davis crossed the Atlantic he turned pirate himself.

When the Portuguese governor of the island of Mayo invited Davis and his men ashore as his guests, Davis captured and sacked the fortress. At Gambia Castle, Davis tricked the governor into believing that his ship was a British man-of-war, then put a pistol to the governor's head and took the castle without a fight. He teamed up with Thomas Cocklyn and Oliver La Bouche, who had both taken a pardon in the Bahamas in 1717. Together, they took a ship of twenty-four guns off Sierra Leone. Cocklyn was later hanged.

By the time Davis took the *Princess*, he had taken many prizes carrying gold, ivory and slaves – the Atlantic slave trade was now reaching its height. Davis took pride in never having

The pirate Mary Read reveals to her astonished victim that he has been defeated by a woman in this 1853 engraving by Huart after A Debelle in Histoire des Pirates et Corsaires.

to force a seaman to join him and Roberts reluctantly agreed to sail with him on his pirate ship, the *Royal Rover*. Over the next six weeks, they took a number of prizes including a Holland-bound ship with a rich cargo and the governor of Accra aboard.

At Princes Island (now known as Bioko or Fernando Po), Davis again tried to disguise his ship as a British man-of-war. Unfortunately, the governor had heard about the incident at Gambia Castle and ambushed Davis's party. Davis was shot in the stomach and died a few minutes later. The *Royal Rover* fled out to sea. The pirates held a meeting to elect a new captain. An expert in all aspects of seamanship and naval warfare, Roberts was the obvious choice. It was only then that he reconciled himself to his new profession.

'It is better to be a commander than a common man,' he said, 'since I have dipped my hands in muddy water and must be a pirate.'

Although he was short in stature, he was a commanding presence. According to Defoe, 'When Roberts saw there was no managing of such a company of wild ungovernable brutes by gentle means, nor keep them from drinking to excess, the cause of all their disturbances, he put on a rougher deportment and a more majesterial carriage towards them. And if any seemed to resent his usage, he told them they might go ashore and take satisfaction of him, if they thought fit, at sword and pistol, for he neither valued nor feared any of them.'

When a crewman insulted him to his face, Roberts shot him dead. When another man named Thomas Jones, hearing of it, cursed him, Roberts stabbed him with his sword. Though wounded, Jones then picked Roberts up, threw him over a cannon and beat him up. This caused consternation on board ship. One faction sided with Roberts, another with Jones. At a meeting, it was decided that the dignity of the captain must be upheld. As it was an honorary position bestowed by free vote, no man on board was entitled to violate it. Although his wound had not yet healed, Jones was sentenced to two lashes from each of the 180-man crew. Afterwards, he and some of his supporters jumped ship.

Robert's first act as captain was to devastate the Portuguese settlement on Princes Island to avenge the killing of Davis. Then in the Bight of Bonny – also know as the Bight of Biafra – he took a Dutch merchantman and a Royal African Company slaver. Holing up on the tiny island of Annobon, 200 miles off the coast of Gabon, he persuaded the crew to sail for Brazil. He set a course for the island of Fernando de Noronha, which was just 6 miles across, 2,600 miles away, arriving there twenty-eight days later in a remarkable feat of navigation. There they watered and repaired the *Royal Rover*, ready for a Brazilian foray.

In September 1719, they found forty-two Portuguese merchantmen forming up into a convoy ready to be escorted across the Atlantic to Lisbon by two men-of-war. They were laden with gold, sugar, tobacco and hides. The *Royal Rover* sailed into the middle of the fleet, boarded the most heavily-laden ship, plundered her cargo – including 40,000 Portuguese gold moidores, worth around £54,000 – and made off before the escorts had even raised anchor. From there they headed to Devil's Island of Guiana, then a Spanish possession later to become the notorious French penal colony, where they traded the booty for money and women. After an orgy of self-indulgence lasting several weeks, they sailed into the Caribbean, but were chased out by the Royal Navy and the islands' privateers. They sailed on up the American coast to Newfoundland where they spotted twenty-two merchant ships at anchor in Trepassey Bay. Roberts had one ten-gun sloop with a crew of sixty. Between them the merchantmen had forty guns and 1,200 men.

Nevertheless, Roberts sailed into the bay with drums beating and trumpets blaring. Not a shot was fired in self-defence as the merchantmen's crews piled into their boats and rowed for shore, leaving Roberts and his men to plunder at will. He also attacked the fishing fleet of 150 in Trepassey sinking many of them, and when a flotilla of a half-dozen Frenchmen sailed in he attacked them too, taking a large brigantine, which he renamed the *Royal Fortune*, mounted twenty-eight guns on her and made her his flag-

A reluctant pirate, Black Bart was a devoted Christian, forbidding gambling and leading his men in prayer. He was also a teetotaller

ship. Even the governor of New England was in awe of Roberts' audacity at Trepassey. He wrote, 'One cannot withhold admiration for his courage and daring.' But that may have been because the victims were French.

He cannot have been so sanguine when Roberts took a number of prizes off the New England coast. The *Boston Newsletter* of 22 August 1720 carried eyewitness accounts of several passengers of the sloop *Samuel* who were threatened with death if they did not hand over their valuables. The pirates, they said, tore open the hatches 'like a parcel of furies' and broke open everything they could lay their hands on. What they did not want, they threw over the side.

They stole £10,000-worth of goods, along with sails, rigging, powder and guns. The chief mate, Harry Glasby, was dragged from his hiding place and pressed into service aboard the *Royal Fortune*. The pirates cursed and swore and told the *Samuel*'s captain, 'We shall accept no Act of Grace, may the king and parliament be damned with their Act of Grace for us, neither will we go to Hope Point' – that is, Execution Dock – 'to be hanged a-sun-drying.'

They let it be known that they would only accept a pardon when they had made enough money. Seven or eight hundred pounds in cash seems to have been the goal. Some retired when they had made that much. Most did not.

'If we are captured,' they told the captain of the *Samuel*, 'we will set fire to the powder with a pistol, and all go merrily to hell together.'

The Caribbean was no longer a good place for a pirate to be, but Roberts stopped off at Deseada Island in the Lesser Antilles to take on water and provisions, before heading back to Africa. He meant to stop at Brava Island, the southernmost of the Cape Verde Islands, but the winds pushed him too far north. Finding it impossible to beat upwind to Brava, he was forced to take the northeasterly trades back across the Atlantic to try again. By this time they had just one hogshead, or large cask, of water left. It contained 54 gallons (63 gallons US) of water for his crew of 126. The *Royal*

> ### 'We shall accept no Act of Grace, may the king and parliament be damned with their Act of Grace for us, neither will we go to be hanged a-sun-drying.'

Fortune would not touch land for 2,000 miles. Roberts rationed his men to one mouthful of water every twenty-four hours. Some got so thirsty that they drank seawater or their own urine and died of 'apyrexies' and 'fluxes' – fever and dysentery.

Eventually they ran out of water altogether. But the next day, soundings indicated that the seabed was shelving. That night they anchored in just seven fathoms – forty-two feet – of water. Soon after daybreak, the lookout spotted land. They launched their boat and, that evening, it returned with fresh water from the Maroni River in Guiana.

Not wishing to repeat the experience of this disastrous Atlantic crossing, the *Royal Fortune* embarked on a campaign of piracy in the Caribbean under the very noses of the Royal Navy. They sailed into the harbour of St Kitts, looted the shipping and took on stolen sheep, while the guns of the fort fired on them.

'Between 28 and 31 October, these pirates burned or sunk fifteen French and English vessels and one Dutch interloper of forty-two guns at Dominica,' complained the governor of the French Leeward Islands.

Basing himself in the area of St Lucia, Roberts inflicted such a toll on the ships coming out of Martinique that the governor had to beg for help from the governor of Barbados. It was to show his contempt that Roberts designed his new jack. According to the governor of Bermuda, Roberts' French prisoners were 'barbarously abused, some were whipped almost to death, others had their ears cut off, others they fixed to the yardarm and fired at them as a mark and all their actions looked like practising of cruelty'. But when the governor of Martinique sent to the governor of the British Leeward Islands for the protection of the Royal Navy, the captain of HMS *Rose* responded tartly, 'You know, sir, you have no power to give me orders, but I will concert any affairs that shall be for my King's service, and I am sorry I am forced to say I wish you'd do the same.' And he sailed off.

However, reports of the barbarous behaviour of Black Bart's men sickened people and

diminished the romantic appeal of pirates. This led to the Piracy Act of 1721, which extended the penalties for piracy to anyone who 'shall trade with, truck, barter or exchange' with the outlaws.

By this time, Roberts had brought trade in the Caribbean to a halt. He now had two captured vessels carrying his loot, but their holds were full and he was unable to exchange his plunder for gold in any of the British colonies of the Caribbean or North America. So, once again, he set out to cross the Atlantic. He made landfall in Senegal, then sailed on to Sierra Leone where he spent six weeks careening and refitting his ships. Although all the trade there was supposed to be under the control of the Royal African Company, there were a number of independent merchants who were happy to deal with Roberts and other pirates.

One of the richest was John Leadstone – an ex-pirate known as Captain Crackers – who had three guns outside his door with which he saluted visiting pirates. Another was Benjamin Gun, who ran a port on the Rio Pungo and achieved immortality as Robert Louis Stevenson's Ben Gunn in *Treasure Island*. While the coast of West Africa was too disease-ridden and unhealthy to became a second Madagascar, these men did good business exchanging brass pots, pewter pans, old guns and English gin for slaves, which they then sold to the independent merchantmen who defied the monopoly of the Royal African Company. These traders warned Roberts that two Royal Navy men-of-war – HMS *Weymouth* under Captain Mungo Herdman and HMS *Swallow* under Captain Chaloner Ogle – were patrolling in the area and would return to Sierra Leone at Christmas.

Undeterred, Roberts set off southeastwards along the coast at the end of August 1721. Off Sasstown, Liberia, he captured the Royal African Company frigate *Onslow*, which he took as his flagship, renaming her *Royal Fortune* and increasing her guns from twenty-five to forty. In the creeks of the Calabar River in the Bight of Bonny, he stopped to careen his ships again and when the locals refused to trade with him he attacked them, fighting so ferociously that he was remembered in their oral history two hundred years later. At Cape Lopez at the southernmost end of the Gulf of Guinea, Roberts turned west again. It was now Christmas and he figured that the British men-of-war would be back in Sierra Leone, leaving unprotected

waters behind them. However, the Navy had been delayed at Princes Island where a hundred of their men had died of malaria and venereal disease. They were further delayed at Cape Coast Castle, in what is now Ghana, where they press-ganged merchant seaman as replacements.

Roberts crossed the Gulf of Guinea and made landfall in the Ivory Coast. Then he began pirating eastwards once more, sailing directly into the path of the men-of-war. He sailed past Cape Coast Castle, where the two

Eighteenth-century engraving of Anne Bonny, female pirate and partner-in-crime of Mary Read.

Key to Wreck Locations Attached

X marks the spot on this speculative map of buried pirate gold throughout the Caribbean and the Mexican Gulf.

navy ships were anchored, and on 11 January 1722 sailed into Whydah (now Ouidah, Benin), which was the greatest slaving port on the coast, and set about plundering it. Eleven slave ships moored there surrendered without a shot. These were ransomed for eight pounds of gold dust each, which was worth about £500 at the time. However, one captain refused to pay. Against Roberts' orders, his ship was set on fire and eighty slaves were given the terrible choice of burning to death or jumping, fettered in pairs, into the water to drown or be torn to pieces by sharks.

Two days later, the pirates intercepted a message from Cape Coast Castle, warning the Royal African Company's agent in Whydah that pirates were heading their way – with HMS *Swallow* on their tail. Roberts put to sea immediately. Beyond Whydah, the coast was swampy and there were no European settlements, so Roberts headed back to the tiny island of Annobon, but he missed it and made landfall back at Cape Lopez.

The *Swallow* and the *Weymouth* arrived in Whydah two days after Roberts had left. Captain Ogle guessed that he had gone south and headed off after him. At dawn on 5 February 1722, the *Swallow* was searching the inlets around Cape Lopez when, in this vast area of swamp and lagoon, Captain Ogle was surprised to hear cannon fire. Ogle followed his ears and found the *Royal Fortune*, with her consorts *Great Ranger* and *Little Ranger*, anchored near Parrot Island.

When Roberts spotted the *Swallow*, he mistook her for a large merchant ship. He ordered the captain of the *Great Ranger*, James Skyrme, to pursue the prize. Ogle took off, running before the wind, until he reckoned that they were out of earshot. Then he allowed the *Great Ranger* to catch up with him. The pirate ship was festooned with flags, the topmost being the Jolly Roger. Skyrme fired his bow chaser guns, forcing the *Swallow* to come to. Then he ordered his men to boarding stations, whacking sluggards with the flat of his cutlass.

It was only when they were within musket range that Skyrme realized that a terrible mistake had been made. The man-of-war turned to starboard, ran out her lower guns and fired a devastating broadside. This spread confusion through the pirate ship. They lowered the Jolly Roger, then ran it up again. They made to flee, then turned to fight, returning a broadside at the *Swallow*.

Waving their cutlasses the pirates readied themselves to board the *Swallow*. This was a reversal of the usual order of things. The Royal Navy vessel was carrying no cargo. However, the navy seamen aboard were eager to get their hands on the vast treasure their unwitting quarry was carrying. They kept up a withering fire, shooting off one of Skyrme's legs. The main-topmast of the *Great Ranger* was shattered and came crashing down on the deck. For hours the two ships slugged it out on the rolling Atlantic swell and under the boiling sun of the equatorial noon. With his sword still in his hand, badly bleeding and half-mad with pain, Skyrme directed the fighting. He repeatedly urged his crew to board the *Swallow*. But it was a move they would not or could not make.

By 3pm, ten pirates lay dead. Twenty were wounded, sixteen severely. Others had deserted their posts. Amazingly the *Swallow* had not suffered a single casualty. The *Great Ranger* had been so badly shot up that it could now neither fight nor flee and Skyrme was forced to ask for quarter. He struck his pirate colours and threw them into the sea so they could not be used as evidence against him.

But some of his men were not ready to be taken. True to their word, half a dozen of them ran down into the magazine in the steerage with the aim of blowing them all to kingdom come. One of their number named John Morris fired a pistol into barrel of gunpowder. Fortunately, the barrel was half empty: nevertheless, the resulting explosion killed Morris, and the rest of the men, the clothes burnt off their backs and the skin off their faces, were too badly injured to make another attempt to blow up the ship.

The navy then boarded the *Great Ranger* and found a hundred men on board – fifty-nine English, eighteen French and twenty-three African slaves. There was no gold on board, but the decks ran with blood and the injured lay about everywhere. The *Swallow*'s surgeon, John Atkins, who supplied much of the information for Defoe's account of the incident, came on

board to tend the wounded. One of the injured was Roger Ball, who died of his wounds the next day. Another was William Main. Seeing a bosun's whistle hanging around his neck, Atkins said, 'I presume you are bosun of this ship.'

'Then you presume wrong,' Main answered, 'for I am bosun of the *Royal Fortune*, Captain Roberts, commander.'

'Then, Mr Bosun, you will be hanged, I believe,' said Atkins.

'That is as your honour pleases,' said Main.

Atkins then asked how the powder had caught fire.

'By God,' he said, on being told, 'they are all mad and bewitched, for I have lost a good hat by it.' It had been blown out of the cabin galley into the sea.

'But what signifies a hat, friend?' asked Main.

'Not much,' replied Atkins. Proving better pillagers than any pirate, the navy seamen were stripping Main of his remaining clothes when Atkins asked him whether Roberts' company were 'as likely fellows as these'.

'There are 120 of them,' said Main, 'as clever fellows as ever trod shoe leather. Would that I were with them. No doubt of it.' Then he looked down to see that even his shoes and stockings were gone. 'By God,' he said wryly, 'it is the naked truth.'

The *Great Ranger* was quickly patched up and Captain Ogle sent her off with the injured under guard to Princes Island. The rest of the prisoners were taken below, shackled and pinioned, then Captain Ogle turned back towards Cape Lopez and the other two ships of Roberts' fleet with morale on the man-of-war running high.

On the morning of 10 February 1722, Roberts was eating a hearty breakfast of salmagundi in his cabin on board the *Royal Fortune*, when he received word that a strange sail was approaching. He took little notice. His ships had been at anchor for five days waiting for Skyrme to return and there was little for the seamen to do but drink. The men on the deck nursing their hangovers noticed that the vessel approaching was flying a French ensign. She was almost upon them when a navy deserter from the *Swallow* recognized his old ship and raised the alarm. Roberts came up on deck. He ordered the men from the *Little Ranger* to come on board, and they cut the cables and

made off. He learnt from the deserter that the *Swallow* sailed best 'upon the wind' – that is, when the wind struck her abeam. So Roberts raised a full set of sails and ran before the wind. He could easily have outrun the man-of-war, but instead turned about and headed directly for the *Swallow*. This was a typically audacious manoeuvre and it has been said that he wanted to gauge the warship's firepower. If so, he succeeded all too well.

At 11am, the two ships came within range of each other. The *Swallow* got in first with a broadside. Roberts was seen to slump against a gun carriage. The helmsman, a hand named Stephenson, ran to his assistance, but could not see any wounds on him and told him to stand up and fight like a man. It was then that he noticed grapeshot had hit Roberts in the throat, killing him. Stephenson burst into tears.

A sudden death in battle is likely what Roberts would have chosen for himself. 'Damn to him who ever lived to wear a halter [noose],' he often said. His body, with his arms and ornaments, were thrown overboard, as he had requested. What remained was his reputation. In his two-year career as a pirate Roberts had taken over 400 ships.

Spanish gold doubloons and a lump and bar of the precious metal, all found in the wreck of the Spanish ship **Nuestra Senora de las Maravillas,** *lost off the Bahamas in the 17th century.*

With the death of Roberts, the heart went out of his crew. There was no nominated second in command, so Harry Glasby, the sailing master, took over. He persuaded Roberts' men not to blow the ship up and tried to get them to surrender. A number of the veterans of Howell Davis' command, who had been pirating for four years by then, could not face the prospect of the noose and refused. They kept up fire on the *Swallow*, who was overhauling them. But most of the pirates decided the best thing to do was get drunk.

At 1.30pm, the damaged mainmast crashed to the deck, so it was not necessary to strike their colours and at two they asked the navy for quarter. They threw incriminating documents, such as the signing-on papers that showed the men were volunteers, overboard. But Roberts' pirate flag was tangled up in the rigging and they were unable to dispose of it. Later, when the navy came on board, they managed to retrieve it. The navy boarding party also found large quantities of gold dust and plundered goods below deck. Then John Mansfield, a pirate who had deserted from the man-of-war *Rose* and had joined the Roberts crew 'for drink rather than gold', really gave the game away.

After lying in a drunken coma throughout the battle, he awoke to see the *Swallow* lying alongside, cried, 'A prize! A prize!' and urged his shipmates to board her.

The crew of the *Royal Fortune* joined the men of the *Great Ranger* in the hold of the *Swallow*. There were 254 prisoners in all, including seventy Africans. Fifteen of them died on the way to Cape Coast Castle where the remainder were thrown in the slave hole, a cavern blasted from the solid rock under the ramparts. Four more died there awaiting trial, leaving 169 to face an admiralty court. The eighteen Frenchmen from the *Great Ranger* were acquitted on the grounds that, as foreigners, they had been forced.

All the pirates pleaded not guilty and any who could provide evidence that they had been forced were acquitted, even if they had served with Roberts for a long time. Seventy-four men, including the sailing master, Harry Glasby, were found not guilty. Fifty-four were sentenced to death, two of whom were later reprieved. Seventeen were sent home to the Marshalsea, though all but four died on the way. And twenty were sentenced to seven years' hard labour in the Royal African Company mines on the Gold Coast. None survived.

So fifty-two men, including Captain Skyrme who had miraculously survived the loss of his leg, lived to face the gallows outside the castle ramparts. They were hanged in batches, the first being the 'House of Lords' as Roberts' original crew styled themselves, each taking a title. In prison, Lord Sutton asked the jailer to have the man he was shackled to removed, or to have his prayer book taken away, because his prayers were disturbing his lordship's peace.

'What do you propose by so much noise and devotion?' Sutton asked the man.

'Heaven, I hope,' he replied.

'Heaven, you fool?' said Sutton. 'Did you ever hear of any pirate going thither? Give me hell, it's a merrier place. I'll give Roberts a salute of thirteen guns at the entrance.'

Lord Sutton was not on such good form the day they hanged him because he had dysentery.

However, the rest of the House of Lords put on a good show. One of their lordships told Surgeon Atkins, acting as chaplain, 'We are poor rogues and so must be hanged, while others, not less guilty in another way, escaped.'

Another, who was well up on the etiquette of hanging, complained that their hands were manacled behind them, when they should be tied in front, while others called for bread and water. And Lord Sympson spotted a woman named Elizabeth Trengrove, who had been a passenger on one of the ships they had taken, in the crowd and exclaimed, 'I have lain with that bitch three times and now she has come to see me hanged!'

Others were more contrite. Atkins kept a log and recorded that William Williams was 'speechless at execution'.

More than a third of the condemned men came from the west of England, the rest from Wales, London and the north. The average age was 28, while the average age of the House of Lords was 30. Only four men were over 40 and four under 20 – the oldest 45, the youngest 19.

The hangings went on for a fortnight and the last batch of fourteen were hanged on 20 April 1722. The bodies of eighteen of the worst villains were dipped in tar, hung in chains, bound in metal straps and hung from a gibbet – as Kidd's had been in England 21 years before.

The death of Captain Roberts was greeted with profound relief around Britain's mercantile empire which now stretched from New York and Jamaica to Bombay. Captain Ogle was knighted, the only British naval officer to be honoured specifically for actions against pirates. He was also a wealthy man due to the gold dust he had taken from Roberts' cabin and had neglected to hand over to the authorities. It was inevitable that a man of such initiative would rise to become an admiral.

Although with the expansion of the British empire there were now more potential prize ships than ever on the oceans of the world, the golden age of the pirates was over. Britannia – more specifically the Royal Navy – now ruled the waves, not the Jolly Roger.

CHAPTER TEN

THE SWASHBUCKLING CONTINUES

Although the so-called 'Golden Age' of piracy lasted less than half a century, piracy itself would prove to be longer-lived. However, in the hundred years after the death of Captain Roberts there was something of a lull. Then in the early nineteenth century, there was a new outbreak. The cause, as before, was peace.

Although there were sporadic outbreaks of piracy after the passing of the 'Golden Age' – in 1769, for example, a gang of seagoing thugs from Hove in Sussex were sentenced to death at the Old Bailey for boarding a Dutch coaster off Beachy Head and robbing it of sixty men's hats – by and large, ships were left to sail to their destinations unmolested. The end of the Napoleonic Wars, the War of 1812 and the Latin American wars of liberation, however, and the naval unemployment they brought in their wake, left seaports around the Atlantic, once again, awash with unemployed privateers. At the same time, the spread of the industrial revolution swelled the number of cargo vessels that plied the sea lanes of the Atlantic and the coastal waters of the Americas.

Basing themselves in the coves and cays around Cuba and Puerto Rico, the new generation of pirates were a pale reflection of the dashing sea rovers who had gone before them. The cargo ships they preyed on carried not the gold, silver and silks of the Aztecs, Incas and Moguls, but coal, cotton-ware and iron goods. In 1822, pirates boarded the brig *Washington* and took $16 from Captain Lander's trunk. They ordered the cook to hand over the potatoes, then stole cooking utensils, the ship's compass, a hailing trumpet, most of the crew's clothes and some twine before departing. But Lander and his crew were lucky. They escaped with their lives.

Without the protection of the Royal Navy, the newly independent United States was par-

ticularly vulnerable. In 1820 alone, twenty-seven American vessels were attacked in the Caribbean and the Atlantic, with a heavy loss of life and cargo. Maritime insurance rates doubled, threatening to strangle new nation's trade. Congress gave President James Monroe sweeping powers to deal with the sea-borne menace and demanded the death penalty for all pirates.

By the following summer six US warships and three gunboats were patrolling in the Caribbean and the Gulf of Mexico. On 16 October the US brig *Enterprise* under Lieutenant Commander Lawrence Kearney caught up with the four pirate schooners commanded by one Charles Gibbs, a particularly unsympathetic character. Born in Providence, Rhode Island in 1794, Gibbs had sailed on the sloop *Hornet* against the British in the War of 1812. He was on board the *Chesapeake* when she was taken by the British frigate *Shannon* in 1813, and he was held in Dartmouth jail until a prisoner exchange. Returning home, he tried his hand at running a grog shop and failed, so he sign on board a privateer sailing out of Buenos Aires. The crew mutinied. Putting the officers ashore in Florida they voted Gibbs their captain. They then went on the rampage, taking more than twenty vessels and killing all their captives so there would be no witness – except for a young Dutch girl who they abused for two months before offering her the choice of taking poison or suffering a more violent death.

Surprised by a British sloop while plundering in Cuban waters, Gibbs escaped overland

Walking the plank in Howard Pyle's Book of Pirates. *Although a popular image of pirates at work, there is little evidence that any pirates actually subjected their victims to this particular ordeal.*

with $30,000. He then fought in a war between Brazil and Buenos Aires and served as a lieutenant on the Argentine ship *25 de Mayo*. He was captured by the Brazilians, but later released. Then he served the Dey of Algeria in the Ottomans' defence against the French. Returning to the US, he signed on board the *Vineyard* out of New Orleans, then took over the ship, murdering the master and mate, and went on the rampage yet again. He was as savage as ever, once chopping off a captured captain's arms and legs. On another occasion he burnt an entire merchant crew to death.

When Kearney caught up with Gibbs, his crew of one hundred were plundering three merchantmen off Cape Antonio, Cuba. After a fierce fight, the pirates were routed. Forty pirates were captured. The rest – including Gibbs – beached their vessels and fled into the jungle. Later, Gibbs was caught. He was transported back to Rhode Island, where he was tried and hanged in April 1831.

Although newspapers applauded Kearney's success – 'It is probable that this fortunate and well managed affair will check, if it does not break up, piracy in this quarter,' said one – attacks continued throughout 1822 and 1823. According to one estimate, 2,000 pirates were

operating in the Caribbean again. The American men-of-war were too big to chase them over the shallow reefs and sand banks of the area, so Congress commissioned a special West India Squadron, under Commodore David Porter, to deal with the problem. He was given $500,000 – a massive appropriation for the time – to establish a purpose-built anti-pirate force. He bought eight fast shallow-draft schooners and the Connecticut steamer – the first time a steam-driven ship had been used in action. To attack pirates ashore he needed landing craft, so he bought five flat-bottomed barges with twenty oars apiece. And he bought a decoy ship which looked like an unarmed merchantman but carried six guns.

When, at last, the mate of the *Black Joke* fell into a drunken sleep, de Soto put a pistol to his head and blew his brains out

Porter's anti-piracy fleet was manned by 1,150 sailors and marines and had its headquarters in Norfolk, Virginia. In April 1823, it caught up with the Cuban pirate known as Diabolito – 'Little Devil' – in his two-masted schooner *Catalina* and, in a ferocious battle, killed seventy of his men. Porter's pirate killers quickly put an end to piracy in the Caribbean but the notorious Benito de Soto was still in action on the Atlantic until 1828.

De Soto had first sailed from Buenos Aires several years earlier on the Portuguese slaver *Defensor de Pedro*. When they moored off the African coast and the captain went ashore to collect more slaves, the first mate suggested to de Soto that they mutiny and take over the ship. De Soto agreed and the two of them tried to talk the rest of the crew into joining them. Twenty-two said they would, while the other eighteen were against the plan. Without consulting the mate, de Soto rounded up all the arms on board and seized the ship. A boat was lowered and those against the mutiny were given a stark choice – join the mutiny or row for shore, which was some ten miles away, with the one pair of oars de Soto allowed them. The eighteen dissenters got on board and struck out for shore. Had the weather stayed calm they would have made it by dusk. But a storm blew up. De Soto simply headed off in the *Defensor de Pedro* – now renamed the *Black Joke* – and everyone on board agreed that the men on the boat could not survive.

That night the former mate, who was now the ship's new captain, led a drunken celebration on board the *Black Joke*. When, at last, the mate fell into a drunken sleep, de Soto put a pistol to his head and blew his brains out. He told the crew that he had done this for their benefit. He was now their leader and, if they did what he told them, he promised them a harvest of gold.

The ship was already half full with slaves. Some were for throwing them overboard. Instead de Soto headed for the West Indies where he sold them – all except for one boy who he kept as a cabin boy. This proved his downfall.

With her hold now empty, the *Black Joke* was free to plunder other vessels. One victim was an American brig. After her cargo had been pillaged, all hands were herded into the hold and the hatches battened down. The only exception was a black man who was left on deck for the sadistic amusement of de Soto and his crew. They set fire to the brig and watched the hapless African scramble through the rigging in a forlorn attempt to escape the flames as the mocking crowd cheered him on. Eventually he fell exhausted, crashing through the charred hatch to be burnt to death with his shipmates, while de Soto's crew cheered all the harder.

At dawn on 21 February 1828, de Soto spotted a vessel near Ascension Island. It was the merchantman *Morning Star* on her way from Ceylon to England. At first, he thought she was a French ship, but a French crewman named Barbazan assured him she was British.

'So much the better,' said de Soto, 'we shall find more booty.'

He ordered the sails to be squared and ran before the wind, chasing the *Morning Star* which was about two leagues ahead. Seeing she was in danger, the *Morning Star* raised more canvas. De Soto cursed and, when his black cabin boy asked him if he wanted his morning cup of chocolate, he struck him violently with his telescope. Meanwhile Barbazan cleared the decks ready for action, armed the men and gave them breakfast. As the *Black Joke* gained on the *Morning Star*, de Soto began to calm down. He drank his chocolate in a single draught and ate some cold beef. Then he sat down on the deck and smoked a cigar. Less than a quarter of an hour later, the

Morning Star was within range. Without getting up, de Soto ordered the British colours to be hoisted and had a gun fire a blank cartridge. When this did not bring the *Morning Star* to, he cried out, 'Shoot the long gun and give it to her point blank.'

The gun was fired, but the shot fell well short. De Soto jumped to his feet and cursed the gunners for their incompetence. He ordered them to load the gun with canister shot, then took the match himself. He did not shoot immediately, but waited until he was abreast of his quarry. Then he ran up the Colombian colours, seized a 'speaking trumpet' or loud-hailer and cried out, 'Lower your boat this moment and let your captain come on board with his papers.'

On board the British ship, the women passengers were in tears and there was general alarm. One crewman had been killed and there was much damage. The *Morning Star* carried no guns and the crew did not even have small arms, but the captain did not slacken his sail. However, as the *Black Joke* drew within fifty yards it became clear that there was no way the *Morning Star* could outrun her.

A passenger volunteered to go over to speak to the pirates and a boat was lowered. But when de Soto learnt that he was not the captain, his crew beat the man cruelly and sent him back, telling him that if the captain did not return immediately he would blow the *Morning Star* out of the water. The passenger went back to the *Morning Star* and, this time, the captain did as he was told. When he boarded the *Black Joke* with the mate, he was taken to see de Soto who, with one blow of his cutlass, cleft the captain's head to the chin bone, saying, 'Thus does Benito de Soto reward those who disobey him.' Meanwhile the mate was taken to the forecastle where he was despatched by Barbazan.

Barbazan and five men were then sent over to the *Morning Star* with orders to kill everyone on board and sink her. There were to be no witnesses. The six were athletically-built men, carrying cutlasses, pistols and long knives in their belts. As they rowed over to the *Morning Star*, de Soto stood at the rail of the *Black Joke* with his cutlass, still red from the blood of the murdered captain, raised above his head. Beside him stood a man with a match, ready to fire the long gun if the boarding party met any resistance.

As the boarders approached, the women on board the *Morning Star* clung to their husbands in terror. Some of the men tried to give them words of comfort, but when the pirates boarded the ship they began slashing right and left with their cutlasses at anyone within reach, uttering dreadful oaths. The screaming women ran and hid as best they could, while the pirates slaughtered some of the men on deck and drove others below. Bleeding, beaten and terrified, the surviving men lay huddled together in the hold, while the pirates began pillaging the ship. They broke open every trunk searching for valuables. Money, plate, charts, nautical instruments and 'seven parcels of valuable jewellery' which formed part of the cargo' were carried back to the *Black Joke* while de Soto directed operations from the deck of his ship that lay alongside.

De Soto stood at the rail of the *Black Joke* with his cutlass, still red from the blood of the murdered captain, raised above his head

A sick officer, Mr Gibson, was dragged from his berth and his cabin ransacked. He died shortly after. The clothes of the other passengers were stripped from their backs. The remaining men were locked in the round house, with the exception of the steward who was to serve food and wine to the pirates. Though he served champagne in the best crystal, the steward found himself seized violently by the throat and came face to face with the point of a knife. A pirate had broken a glass as he drank and, feeling a shard between his teeth, accused the steward of trying to poison him – forcing him to down the rest of the bottle just in case.

The steward was then ordered to tell the pirate where the captain kept his money. He answered that he may as well ask him to produce the philosopher's stone. So the pirate put a pistol to his chest and fired. But the gun misfired and, when the pirate re-cocked it, he found it knocked aside by Barbazan. The steward was then sent to the hold with the other men.

Barbazan and his men had been ordered to kill everyone on board. But once the pirates were full of liquor, they decided to rape the women first. From the hold the men could hear their wives' piteous cries.

When the pirates heard de Soto's shout, ordering them to return to the *Black Joke*, they locked the women in a cabin, heaped heavy

BENITO SOTO

The only known image of the feared Benito de Soto, captain of pirate ship the **Black Joke**.

lumber on the hatches of the hold and began drilling holes in the ship's planks below the water line. Then they left the ship, which was sinking fast.

However, the women managed to break out of the cabin. When they came on deck, it was nearly dark and they could see, at some distance, the pirate ship sailing away from them. They hid themselves until it was pitch black, then they hauled the lumber off the hatches to release the men. By this time there was six feet of water in the ship. The sailors quickly set to with the pumps and they managed to keep her afloat. However, the pirates had sawn through the masts and cut away the rigging, so there was no way they could sail her. Fortunately for the *Morning Star*, another ship came by the next day and took them aboard.

It was only later that de Soto learned that whose on board the *Morning Star* had not been slaughtered, only left to drown. So he circled back to finish the job. By this time, the *Morning Star* had sunk and, seeing no trace of her, de Soto concluded he was safe. He then took off towards Europe, boarding and plundering a small brig along the way. This time there was no mistake. Before sinking the ship, he killed everyone with the exception of one man who knew the course to Corunna, where they were bound. When they reached the coast of Spain and sighted a port, de Soto asked him, 'My friend, is that the harbour of Corunna?'

'Yes,' replied the man.

'Then you have done your duty well,' said de Soto, 'and I am obliged to you for your services.' Then he drew a pistol, shot the man and had his body thrown over the side.

Arriving in port, de Soto posed as a regular trader and sold off the booty, then, after obtaining false papers, set out for Cadiz. A fair wind brought the *Black Joke* in sight of port by nightfall. She anchored outside the harbour with the intention of entering next day. But that night a gale blew up, pushing her directly on to the shore. De Soto tried to beat to windward, but the ship could not clear the point and they ran aground. In the morning the crew, who were lucky to be alive, lowered the boats and rowed for shore. Once on the beach, de Soto decided that they must sell the wreck and buy another ship, so that they could return to pirating. They walked to Cadiz, where de Soto made out that he was first mate to a fictitious captain who had perished in the accident and a few days later he managed to sell the wreck for $1,750. The contract was signed but the money not yet paid, when suspicion arouse from inconsistencies in the various stories that the pirates told. Six were arrested. Six others escaped to Caracas, where they were arrested later. Meanwhile, de Soto and another man fled to Gibraltar. But with neither passports nor permission from the governor they were denied entry to the fortress, and were forced to take lodgings at an inn on the neutral ground between Spain and Gibraltar. But after a couple of nights, de Soto grew restless, and hatched a plan to enter Gibraltar with false papers. His companion, a Frenchman, thought that this was a reckless move and escaped aboard a passing vessel. His description was circulated widely. He was a tall, stout man with a fresh complexion and fair hair. His countenance, it was said, was mild and gentle. This was though to be Barbazan. He was one of the worst villains of the pirate crew and the only one to escape punishment.

De Soto entered Gibraltar with the forged pass and stayed at a rundown inn in the area inhabited by Spaniards, Jews and Moors. It was run by a man named Basso, who grew suspicious of de Soto because he wore expensive clothes – a white hat of the best English quality, silk stockings, white trousers and a blue frock coat – while his face was deeply tanned by the sun and wind. The maid also said that she found the dirk under de Soto's pillow every morning when she made the bed. He was eventually arrested, and when his room was searched, the trunk and clothes taken from Mr Gibson, the sick officer dragged from his berth to die, were discovered, along with a pocket book contain-

ing the handwriting of the *Morning Star*'s captain, whom de Soto had murdered and the dirk, which belonged to another passenger.

De Soto was kept in a tiny cell in the garrison at Gibraltar for nineteen months while the case against him was assembled. Those who had seen him in his cell had said he was sallow and pitiable, but at his trial he appeared livid and ferocious. The clinching testimony at this trial was given by the one victim he had let live – his African cabin boy. De Soto was found guilty of piracy and sentenced to death.

His crewmen arrested at Cadiz, along with those taken in Caracas, were also tried, convicted and executed. Their limbs were severed and hung from tenterhooks as a warning to others.

De Soto continued to protest his innocence up until the day before his execution, then he made a full confession and handed over the razor blade that he had kept hidden in the sole of his shoe with the intention of committing suicide. As he marched out to the gallows he seemed genuinely contrite. He walked firmly at the tail of the cart, gazing alternately at his coffin which was on it and the crucifix he carried in his hands. Occasionally he pressed the crucifix to his lips as he repeated the prayers that the padre attending the execution whispered in his ear.

The gallows had been erected on the beach at the edge of the neutral zone between British and Spanish territory. There he climbed up onto the cart. When it was found that the noose was too high, he climbed up onto the coffin so that he could get his head in. As the wheels of the cart started to turn, he muttered, 'Adios todos' – farewell, all – and leaned forward to help his fall. His death was witnessed by the cabin boy who was then returned to Africa.

The last recorded act of piracy on the North Atlantic took place on 20 September 1832, when the American brig *Mexican* bound from Salem to Rio de Janeiro carrying $20,000 in silver was taken by the pirate schooner *Panda*. When pirates asked their captain Pedro Gilbert what they should do with their captives, he said, 'Dead cats don't mew. You know what to do.'

The crew of the *Mexican* were locked in the forecastle. The pirates slashed the rigging and the sails, then set the ship ablaze. However, after the pirates had left, the crew escaped, dowsed the flames, but left enough smoke to fool the pirates until they were over the horizon. After six weeks at sea, the *Mexican* man-

aged to make it back to Salem. HMS *Curlew* caught up with the *Panda* off West Africa. During the ensuing engagement, the *Panda* exploded and sank. Pedro Gilbert and his crew were captured by the British and taken to Boston by HMS *Savage*, where they were tried. During the trial the 19-year-old mate of the Mexican, Thomas Fuller, became so angry that he broke off from giving his testimony to attack one of the defendants who had beaten him. Gilbert was hanged behind Leverett Street Jail on 11 March 1835.

Piracy continued in the Far East, and to this day it flourishes in the Philippines, the Malacca Strait, the South and East China Sea, off the east coast of Africa and in the rivers and coastal waters of Brazil, and according to US authorities, drug-related piracy still occurs in the Caribbean. The days of the 'Golden Age' of piracy, however, where a hand-picked crew of desperadoes aboard a sleek, fast schooner could descend upon a fat merchantman, fire a broadside, board her in the smoke and make ten years' pay in twenty minutes are long gone

James Monroe, fifth United States President (1817-1825), from the painting by Fenderick. Given wide-ranging powers by Congress to put an end to piracy, Monroe was by and large successful in his aim.

FURTHER READING

Alleyne, Wayne, *Caribbean Pirates*, Macmillan Caribbean, London, 1986

Berckman, Evelyn, *Victims of Piracy*, Hamish Hamilton, London, 1979

Black, Clinton V., *Pirates of the West Indies*, Cambridge University Press, Cambridge, 1989

Botting, Douglas, *The Pirates*, Time-Life Books, Alexandra, Virginia, 1978

Burg, B.R., *Sodomy and the Perception of Evil: English Sea Rovers in the Seventeenth-Century Caribbean*, New York University Press, New York, 1983

Carter, Marina, *The Pirates of the Cayman*, Pink Pigeon Press, London, 2001

Cordingly, David, *Life Among the Pirates*, Little, Brown and Company, London, 1985

Cordingly, David, *Pirates*, Salamander Books, London, 1996

Dallas, Ron, *Pirates: Terror of the Seas*, Excalibur Press, London, 1991

Defoe, Daniel, *A General History of the Pyrates*, Dover Publications, New York, 1999

Dow, George Francis, and Edmonds, John Henry, *The Pirates of the New England Coast 1630–1730*, Dover Publications, New York, 1996

Downe, Robert, *Who's Who in Davy Jones' Locker*, Southgate, Hereford, 2001

Edmunds, George, *Kidd: The Search for his Treasure*, Pentland Press, Durham, 1996

Exquemelin, Alexandre-Oliver, *Exquemelin and the Pirates of the Caribbean*, Heinemann, Oxford, 1993

Grant, Neil, *The Buccaneers*, Angus & Robertson, London, 1976

Johnson, Captain Charles, *Pirates*, Creation Books, London, 1999

Lane, Kris E., *Blood and Silver: A History of Piracy in the Caribbean and Central America*, Signal Books, Oxford, 1999

Lucie-Smith, Edward, *Outcasts of the Sea*, Paddington Press, London, 1978

Marley, David, *Pirates and Privateers of the Americas*, ABC-CLIO Inc, Santa Barbara, California, 1994

Mitchell, David, *Pirates*, Thames and Hudson, London, 1976

Marine Research Society, *The Pirates Own Book: Authentic Narratives of the Most Celebrated Sea Robbers*, Dover Publications, New York, 1993

Pennell, C.R., ed., *Bandits at Sea: A Pirates Reader*, New York University Press, New York, 2001

Rediker, Marcus, *Between the Devil and the Deep Blue Sea*, Cambridge University Press, Cambridge, 1987

Ritchie, Robert C., *Captain Kidd and the War Against the Pirates*, Harvard University Press, Cambridge, Massachusetts, 1986

Senior, C.M., *A Nation of Pirates*, David & Charles, London, 1976

Smith, Aaron, *The Atrocities of Pirates*, Prion Books, London, 1997

Stanley, Jo, ed., *Bold in her Breeches*, HarperCollins, London, 1995

Thrower, Rayner, *The Pirate Picture*, Phillimore, London, 1980

Turley, Hans, *Rum, Sodomy, and the Lash*, New York University Press, New York, 1999

Index

INDEX

Index